CW00693788

First published in Great Britain by Open House Press in 2005
6 Ingham Road
West Timperley
Altrincham
Cheshire, WA14 5PX

www.openhousepress.co.uk

Copyright © Tasleem Shakur 2005

The right of the individual contributors to be identified as the
authors of this work has been asserted by them in accordance with
the Copyright, Designs and Patent Act 1988.

All rights reserved. No part of this publication may be reproduced,
stored in a retrieval system, or transmitted in any form or by any
means, without the prior written permission of the copyright owner.

ISBN 0-9544463-1-3

Designed and produced by Open House Press

Cover Design: Andy Butler

Cover Image: Martin Price

Printed by: The Printroom (UK) Ltd, Liverpool

Cities in Transition:
Transforming the Global Built Environment

Edited by Tasleem Shakur

Open House Press

Contents   i

Preface

The last twenty years of the twentieth century experienced a proliferation of exhaustive literature on trendy subjects such as 'Globalisation' and 'Sustainability'. While many branches of the Humanities and Social Sciences have engaged in the stock taking of such phenomena, ironically, literature relating the *'Global Built Environment'* and in particular, the focus on the *'North-South Built Environment'* appears to be minimal.

Under such circumstances, literature on architecture and planning, particularly in the West, does not seem to reflect the overwhelming built environment of the developing world. Neither does it successfully represent the fast changing nature of the inner city built environment, predominantly inhabited by people from non-Western cultures (for example cosmopolitan cities such as Amsterdam, Bradford, Paris, Frankfurt, Oldham or Liverpool).

While the number of Hispanics in the US is predicted to double that of English speakers by 2050, the distinctive characteristics of Latin American and Asian designs now already influencing the built-environment in California or Toronto have yet to attract sufficient attention in many respected Western planning or architecture or Urban environmental literature. On the other hand in the developing world analysis and research into built environments has only recently begun to move away from simple architecture and planning issues into the wider issues of *'development'* and *'environment'*. The scanty literature deriving from the developing world which at times termed as *'grey literature'* has gained neither a sizeable readership nor respect in the Western world.

The international free on-line peer reviewed journal GBER (Global Built Environment Review)* was launched by the International Centre for Development & Environmental Studies (ICDES), based in Edge Hill College, Lancashire at start of the decade. The journal has acquired a large and enthusiastic patronage and support from architecture and planning academics, professionals and students from both the northern and southern hemispheres. Over the last four years in more than ten issues there has been a diverse range of contributions on various aspects of the global built environment, giving rise to many emerging twenty first century concepts moving away from the built environment paradigm.of the 20th century.

This project represents a development of several contributions to GBER focussing on the *built environment* of a wide number of fast changing cosmopolitan cities of the contemporary world.

Like the other two previous volumes, this collection is also conceived with both undergraduate and post-graduate students in mind. The book introduces a host of city case studies for those pursuing studies in Urban Geography, Architecture and Town Planning; post-graduate students and researchers in the fields of Social and Cultural Geography,

Urban Planning and Design (Urban Morphology) should find the concepts intellectually stimulating and challenging.

My thanks go to Open House Press for agreeing to publish this book. This volume would have never come into existence without the contributions of some 15 contributors from all over the world. I am indebted to a number of my colleagues, family members, friends and students who have helped me greatly in shaping this project and keeping my sanity. Special thanks go to Ms Michelle Atherton who originally formatted the text. I would also like to thank Mike Gildersleeves, my second assistant, for his day to day help in keeping me focussed to the job. I am grateful too to Mrs Lesley Warner who painstakingly redrafted and reformatted the manuscript. Sincere thanks also to Dr Clive Grey, our language consultant, Mr Andy Butler, Mr Monjur Mourshed and Mr M. A. Kevin Brice who provided the overall supervision of the layout and production of the book. Dr Peer Smets, Dr Karen Leeming and Ms Karen D'Souza advised me on my initial editorial drafts and tamed my wild expectations of the volume. I acknowledge my gratitude to Edge Hill College and in particular to the Equal Opps Unit, faculty of Humanities, Management, Social and Applied Science and the department of Natural, Geographic and Applied Sciences for their support in the production of this volume. Heartfelt thanks go to the members of GBER international editorial advisors and editors, particularly to Jamie Halsall for his active co-operation. Thanks also to Dr. A.K. Shakoor, MBE and Mr. Imtiaz Patel of Rais Academy for their spontaneous support.

My deep gratitude to my family and particularly to my wife Yasmin who supported me relentlessly despite going through a difficult year. My father in law, the late Janab Abdul Wazid, one time Chief Engineer of Public Works Department, Bangladesh who oversaw the completion of Louis I Kahn's National Assembly Building, provided me with valuable insights into the complexities of North-South Design and Construction interface. Finally my father Janab Abdush Shakur died earlier this year just after I drafted this preface while I was in travelling to meet up with him, and I would like to dedicate this volume to him: the inspiring memories of his lifelong struggle to seek knowledge and to develop his family will always be fondly remembered by all those who knew him.

Tasleem Shakur
30 January 2005

en route to **Dhaka,**
between Manchester and **Doha**

*GBER (2001- 2004)
Global Built Environment Review* www.edgehill.ac.uk/gber, *Free International Journal on Architecture, Planning, Development and Environment, published by the International Centre for Development and Environmental Studies (ICDES), Edge Hill College, Lancashire.*

Introduction:

Emerging trends of the 21st century Cities: Transforming Architecture, Planning and the Global Built Environment

Tasleem Shakur

This volume is developed on the emerging trends in the global built environment in the 21st century based on the research and observations by a group of academics/professionals from the fields of architecture and urban planning/design field. The focus of this study is mainly on cities that are experiencing radical changes.

Attempts were made to develop some emerging thematic chapters based on the contributors' focus and direction of research. To some extent the emergence of the generic themes has been organic as they grew according to the unique subject matter drawn from fifteen different cities across the world. It is therefore expected that the volume will stimulate debate on the development of global architecture, planning, and the built environment both of today and of the future.

CULTURAL IDENTITY IN TRANSITION

The first part of this volume offers three research articles from the Middle East and the Europe where cultural identities appear to be going through a distinct transitional phase. Soumyen Bandyopadhyay (*Problematic Aspects of Synthesis and Interpretation in the Study of Traditional Omani Built Environment)* reports on differing approaches to analysing the traditional Omani built environment. In a way Bandyopadhyay paves the path towards an understanding of holistic methodological tools of a regional built environment focusing on *pan-South Arabian* (Gulf States) culture that is currently undergoing a rapid change. Moving northwest of the Gulf (but still in the Middle East region), Omar Khattab *(Reconstruction of Traditional Architecture: A Design Education Tool)* presents a '*design studio pedagogic knowledge'* digging deep into traditional built environment in Kuwait (close to the current disturbed and volatile zone of Iraq) providing a sound understanding of how to study the neglected vernacular architecture of the region. The final article of Part 1 comes from Noha Nasser *(South Asian Ethnoscapes: The Changing Cultural Landscapes of British Cities)* which examines the changing landscapes of contemporary British society predominantly inhabited by the South Asian diasporic society. Nasser's articulated research article charts the evolution and transitions in the architectural and planning representations conforming to the changing cultural identity and ideologies of both diasporic and host population.

1

Bandyopadhayay's *(University of Liverpool)* opening article attempts to survey the relationship between people, society and material culture through the study of traditional built environments. The article is an outcome of a long-term field research, and argues that such an approach is key to developing a proper historical understanding of the built environment. The author also discusses the problems of undertaking this kind of complex fieldwork, bringing together archaeology and traditional architecture, and researchers in these areas will find it an important contribution to the body of existing literature. The methodological problems of undertaking such fieldwork in the region are documented in detail in this very stimulating article (rigorously substantiated through references from across a range of disciplines), which will be a useful guide for future field research by students and established researchers of traditional Arab architecture. It also examines the *'deterministic and reductive'* processes in interpreting material culture (e.g. economic and environmental determinism as *'temporal and pigeon-holing'* of culture and society) in the Arabian Peninsula. Bandyopadhayay raises serious concerns about the limitations of conventional research approaches for Arab-Islamic built settlement and architecture styles, and argues for a more holistic impact of *'Islamic Culture'*.

The mutual interaction between *culture* and *architecture* is also examined by Omar Khattab *(University of Kuwait)*. In undertaking design exercise for architecture students in Kuwait University, Khattab focuses on some of the most recent examples of *'traditional'* architecture. The author tries to examine how changes in housing style and the function of buildings reflects changing attitudes towards the city of Kuwait among the local population. He urges architects and planners to undertake a proper analysis of the local traditional built-environment. Khattab stresses the importance of the learning process in understanding and interpreting old Kuwaiti houses taking us through the steps that the students undertake to analyse their findings. Khattab's reflections on this pedagogical approach to the *'Design Studio'* give readers an insight into how traditional architecture can be analysed within a rigid theoretical, methodological and socio-cultural framework. The author argues that the reconstruction exercise, skilfully explained through systematic classification, provides students with a tool that enables the process of study and analysis of vernacular architecture. Essentially, what is needed is the adoption of a set of binary relationships between *'theory'* and *'practice'* and *'art'* and *'technology'*, a major theme of much debate in present-day architecture education.

And finally for this part, Noha Nasser *(University of Central England)* examines the intervention mechanisms of the diasporic South Asian in relation to British urban culture. Nasser tends to align more with a social anthropological study through her explanation of *'Biradari'* (extended kinship and village ties) through which the South Asians establish and extend their trans-national network. Her research zooms in on the evolution of architectural representation, which is delineated to have moulded itself around the changing ideologies of the *British pluralist society and planning system*. Here the author seeks to answer some of the pertinent issues generally raised from an ethnographic perspective. The improvisation of the traditional layouts to serve the purpose of South Asian religious houses should be of interest to the contemporary urban designers. This phenomenon is quite similar to my own study of 'the *growing Muslim community, Islamic identity and the development of mosques in a Western setting of Lancashire* (Shakur, T, 1999:133-148). Nasser also stresses the shift of *British multicultural policy* in the 1980s and the '*repoliticisation of South Asian identity'*. This emerging phenomenon is defined as '*the adaptive re-use of the industrial buildings to the creation of the new cultural forms'*. Theoretically, this process could be a comparative study of the '*self help'* housing in the developing world where the housing forms tend to reflect and adjust to either '*hostile'* or '*assimilative'* policies that have changed over time from the 1960s onwards.

Peer Smets and Ton Salman, reporting on a conference on '*Countering Urban Segregation'* (Vrije Universiteit, Amsterdam 14-15 October, 2004) describes a theme concerned the weakening of the *shared imaginary community* within cities.

This is not just about spatial compartmentalisation of the city; it deals with how urban segregation also ultimately affects the identity of urban dwellers in such a way that the formation of socio-cultural enclaves occurs. This is accompanied with socio-psychological effects such as fear, boundary hardening and the erosion of citizenship. The issue triggers the question about governmental responsibility for countering the privatisation of public space (Smets, P and Salman T 2004:76).

Ever since Amos Rapoport (1969) wrote about *culture* and the *built environment* there has been an increasing shift towards a more culturally sensitive architecture, though in practice this has not always been achieved. Under such pretext, the increased research interest in vernacular, traditional and cultural architecture offers a healthy sign of a more appropriate *Built-Environment*.

TRANSFORMING PARTICIPATION AND COMMUNITY

'*Community participation'* had long been the buzzword for the academics, professionals, bureaucrats and the NGOs (non government organisations) in the built-environment, particularly in the housing sector of the capitalist world (both in the developed and in the developing nations). While to date there do exist sufficient literature on the subject, Part 2 offers some more recent and innovative experience on the '*participation scene'* based on case studies from Europe *(Liverpool)*, Central America *(Mexico City)* and North Africa *(Algiers and Cairo)*. Here the three researchers provide some unique examples of how three very distinctly different communities have transformed through persistent but discrete and effective intervention mechanisms both in '*macro urban policy'* and '*micro housing design'* sectors.

Karen Leeming *(Sustainable Urban Development: A Case study in the developed world)* provides what is popularly considered as a successful sustainable urban development model through an innovative housing scheme particularly geared towards the Irish Catholic immigrant community. The interesting aspect of this study is that the target group managed to reverse their problem condition through a unique liaison with the city council bureaucrats and local politicians. Moving far away from Western Europe to Central

America, Pedro Moctezuma-Barragan *(Participatory Planning Under the Mexican Volcanoes)* exemplifies a gratifying experience of a community based participatory planning approach, which the author argues has significant impact on the development of social action research. We are told how participatory and purposeful planning can transform a variety of groups (from school children, teachers, researchers and authorities) who play major roles toward a sustainable future for the local communities. From a historical, the then *quasi socialist* North African cities, Magda Sibley *(Informal Transformations of Formal Housing Estates in Algiers and Cairo)* illustrates the potential of the informal housing sectors participatory initiatives which respond to government built housing to their changing aspirations. In the absence of imaginative design (arising from rigid deterministic approach) in the 1980s the residents of such housing have successfully intervened in improving the overall environment.

Karen Leeming from England *(Edge Hill College, Lancashire)* presents a snapshot of a successful sustainable community based urban development project in the historic city of Liverpool. It is an exemplary case study of a *'best practice'* model of urban development, providing a contextual study of a social, economic, political and historical scenario of a society transformed over twenty years, from virtual stagnation to a viable thriving community. Since the 1990s the importance of stable communities has been reflected in many of the UK's urban policy initiatives and is now identifiable in many local authority urban regeneration initiatives. However, this was not always the case; the industrial restructuring impacted so heavily on the city that it left workers frustrated and cynical and the district became increasingly left wing. One of the strategies that the Development Trust has embraced in the creation of a concept of community-based economic development (or CBED), a non governmental organisation strategy may be compared with OPP in Karachi *(discussed in Arif Hasan's case study in Karachi in part 3)*. *The Eldonians* were a small community founded by Irish Catholic immigrants who worked in the docks and subsequently suffered job losses. It is reported that the social and economic conditions are one of the worst of Western Europe. Today the effort of the Eldonians is considered by many as the *'best practice'* model of successful urban environment, which may be paralleled by communities in New Mexico, Algiers or Cairo as discussed by the other two authors *(discussed below)* in this part of *'transforming participation and community'*. Today many of the *Eldonians* are in either in training or paid employment with community businesses or private sector businesses that have been encouraged to set up in the area.

Pedro Moctezuma Barragan's *(Universidad Autonoma Metropolitina, Mexico City)* research on Mexico City provides a fresh insight into what broad participation from community members and the stakeholders actually means. Participatory planning is often held to be the way forward in the disordered massive settlements of Mexico. As often seen in many developing nations, amid corruption and autocracy there is an unholy liaison

Between the one party state and the irregular urban dwellers in the study area. The Mexican study shows how this notorious phenomenon is being actively challenged by a community-based organisation. Here we also find that the organisation and the University member's involvement have promoted participatory planning on a massive scale. Moctezuma-Barragan also provides us with the current practice of other innovatory planning tools, e.g. the use of GIS (Geographical Information System) and Eco-tourism, apparently to the benefit of the local community.

Shifting focus into North Africa, Magda Sibley's *(University of Liverpool)* research provides a comparative study of informal transformations of formal housing estates in Algiers and Cairo. Unregulated urban housing is now more or less an accepted phenomenon in various parts of the developing world (Shakur, T et al 2001:14-25). However, whilst much data is available from South Asia and Latin America, little is known of practices in North Africa. As such Sibley's case studies should be treated as a significant contribution to the existing literature. What is interesting to note is that in line with the theories of *'self-help school of thoughts of the 1970s* (Turner, J 1972), low income households in Algiers and Cairo are transforming the nature of public housing in line with the socio-economic needs. More importantly, despite the inherent differences in regional politics and economics, there seem to be striking similarities in the transformation processes between the two case studies in Algeria and Cairo.

REDEFINING THE DESIGN INSTITUTION INTERFACE

As a natural progression from *'participatory planning'* the volume embarks into theoretical debates revisiting the traditions and attempting to explain the evolving relationships between the good old *'design process'* and *'the institutional frameworks'*. It may be noted that although in many instances the traditional institutional bases (such as government, county and local councils, financial institutions and Non-Government Agencies) continue to exist, however, with the advent of the *'sustainable development/environment debate'* (since the Rio Summit of 1992) and the phenomenal development of the *'cybernetic approach'* to cope with the 21st century built-environment, the symbiotic interfaces between *'the Design'* and *'the Institution'* have now become far more complex and therefore requires an urgent attention. To address the emerging process three diverse debates are introduced to this part from three different continents of Central America/Caribbean (Cuba), South Asia (India) and Western Europe (England).

In her short article, Dania Gonzalez Couret *(Ecological Design in Cuba-Theory and Practice)* summarises the urban analysis of the Cuban experience and recommends an integrated sustainable approach to planning with a strong emphasis on *'economic sustainability'*. Living in the capitalist world, we still suffer from the paucity of research materials from the communist countries; Couret's research illuminates a new concept to institutional support with increased support from the public sector (something which is on decay in many third world capitalist countries as explained later from the Indian experience). On a more contrasting experience, Peer Smets *(Indian Housing Finance Alliances and the Urban Poor)* stresses the role of the NGOs and the CBOs while advocating the housing finance accessibilities to the teeming millions of the urban poor. Examining the public and private housing finance institutions in India, Smets's (2004) research illustrates the institutional difficulties in addressing the needs of the very poor in the slums of the mega Indian cities like Mumbai. To cap this part on *'Institutions'*, Michael Clark's *(Why not take a Cybernetic Approach to Sustainable Development? Planning and Environmental Management in the North West England during the 1990s)* narrates the cybernetic approach to sustainable planning in somewhat sleepy Lancashire (UK) which developed during the close of the last century. Those involved with Environment Impact Analysis (EIA) and those working in Town Planning, Economic or Development Planning (be it in the first or the third world) would have plenty of lessons to learn from this special case study.

Relevant built-environment literature in English from the non-capitalist world is rare; Dania Gonzalez Couret's *(ISP.JAE, Facultad de Arquitectura de La Habana)* quasi-theoretical article on *'Ecological Design in Cuba'* provides an important contribution in redefining the traditional *'Design Institution Interface'*. Using case studies from many third world capitalist countries, she argues, that politics and social fairness drive sustainable development. However, her article does not necessarily defend all the actions of Cuba's sustainability efforts. It also critically reviews the shortcomings of the country's 1980s adoption of the European styled high technology *prefab* systems. More importantly, the author identifies the failure of the development of renewable energy largely to social resistance to new technologies, and serves us a timely reminder of the situation in many other similar nations in the contemporary world.

On a much bigger scale, Peer Smets *(Vrije Universiteit, Amsterdam)* examines the Indian housing finance alliances and the urban poor. Basing his case study on one of the largest urban slums in the world *(Dharavi in Mumbai/Bombay)*, Smets attempts to resurrect old wisdom suggesting that the non-governmental agencies (NGOs) and the community-based organisations (CBOs) can play an important role in housing the urban poor, especially given the limitations of the development of self-help initiatives. More recently there has been an upsurge of literature on the financing of projects and initiatives targeting the urban poor and Smets's research provide new thoughts into future link programmes between financial institutions and the slum dwellers of the developing world.

Back in Western Europe, Michael Clark *(University of Central Lancashire)* provides an update on a cybernetic approach to sustainable development, based on his *'Planning'* case study in the North West of England during the 1990s. This is undoubtedly a timely research on the much-talked *'Sustainable Development'*

Post-Rio Summit, which faced fierce debate by a host of *developmental environmentalists* around the world at *'Ten years after Rio'* conference in Johannesburg 2002. Clark argues that unlike many other countries the planning and environmental management initiatives in North West England (Lancashire) during the 1990s moved away from rhetoric to a more practical proposals and actions. The aspects of cybernetics and its relationship with the environment and its institutional/political mechanism for sustainable development are clearly explained this article.

CONTESTED SPACE AND THE NEW WORLD ORDER

In the West, especially after the *de-* and *re-territorialisation* of nation states, following the end of the Cold War, we find a number of branches within Humanities and Social Science (possibly not many in built-environment studies) have embarked upon analysing the emerging *'Contested Space'* concept in the emerging new world order.   With the deepening and widening of advanced capitalism (only to be sugar-coated with the magic word *'globalisation'*), and the notion of the so-called *'global village'*, some built-environment studies in the North have widened the research parameters to include *'Post-modern spaces'* (Lefebvre, H 1996: 10-24), *Spaces of Utopia* (Harvey, D 2004: 133-181), and *Cultures of Heteropolis* or try *interrogating global and post-colonial cultures and their impact on the built environment* (King, A 2004: 23-44) as a consequence of which the built environment is characterised by *transience, energy and unplanned vulgarity* (Dear M and Flusty, S 2002: 219). Whereas in the developing world, the current emphasis is on the impact of *'global restructuring* or on *'Culture-Space relationship'* (including analysing the high-tech third generation broadband technologies). In such circumstances, literature on architecture, planning and the environment, particularly in the West, does not seem to reflect the *politicisation* of the increasing built-environment in the developing world (particularly the fast changing nature of the slums, squatter settlements and the shanty towns).

Within such a framework, all three articles of this part come from the developing world with three international authors living either in the *Western /Developing* world or travelling between the both. The first article comes from a Dutch researcher Erik Bähre *(Housing for the Urban Poor in Cape Town: A Post Apartheid Dream or Nightmare?),* questions the delivery of housing and the dwellers' involvement in the *post-apartheid* period of South Africa. While the world media attention is mainly on the devastating impact of HIV and Aids in South Africa, Bähre's painstaking research on the oppressive aspects of development policies, development workers and violent (and at times intriguing) *'community'* raises concerns on the emerging *'negotiated spaces'* and the future and limit of long adored *'self-help'* (Hague, A 1982) *in* the low income built-environment of the developing world. Following such a *politicised space* in South Africa, readers are drawn to another (in the recent past somewhat volatile city) similar, informal setting in the city of Karachi (Pakistan). Distinguished architect/planner, better known as an International urban poor activist, Arif Hasan *(The Changing Nature of the Informal Sector in Karachi due to Global Restructuring and Liberalisation)* brings the current difficult situation with rising inflation, recession and increasing marginalisation of Karachi's peri-urban informal sector poor communities. For the current frustrating situation of the Karachi's urban poor, Hasan points finger to the trade liberalisation of WTO (World Trade Organisation), Structural Adjustments of the World Bank and IMF (International Monetary Fund) policies. The link between the *'New International Order'* and the *'Marginally Negotiated Space* through the middlemen'* (Van der Linden, J 1983) is presented in quasi empirical style but robustly illustrated by Hasan taking cue from the informal settlements of *Sindh Katchi Abadi Authority.* The concluding article for the fourth part comes from the historic/exotic city of Istanbul, a meeting point of the East and West. Hülya Turgut's

(Culture, Space and Squatter Settlements in Istanbul) part theoretical, part case study paper theorises the links between *'Culture, Continuity and Change in the Process of Urbanisation'*. In the second part of the essay the author explores the *'Transitory Spaces of Culture, Space and Spatial Morphology'* through the historic process of squatter housing patterns of the migrant Anatolian villagers who became illegal squatters of Istanbul.

Erik Bähre *(University of Amsterdam and University College Utrecht)* investigates a challenging housing project of post-apartheid South Africa aiming to address the inequalities that existed during the apartheid era. Readers should perhaps be warned that this somewhat recent phenomena, and bold paper may shock even experienced researchers of the housing scene in the poorest urban areas of the third world where political tensions and violence are rife. Very much in the line of the much-respected late Dutch urban poor scholar *Van der Linden's* experience in Pakistan, Bähre investigates the disturbing role of the middlemen, *'dalals'* or brokers (Van der Linden, J op cit) in greater depth in the townships of Cape Town. The research based on the author's relatively long residence in South Africa, was carried out in conjunction with the department of Sociology and Anthropology, University of Western Cape and the University of Amsterdam. The more one investigates it, Bähre argues, the post-apartheid dream for housing has now become a nightmare. As one time researcher of low-income urban settlements in the developing world, I find such phenomena a departure from the myths of the *'Self-help school of thought', which* dominated the literature of urban poor housing for almost three decades (Shakur, T et al, op cit).

Arif Hasan (Orangi Pilot Project, Karachi) provides a comprehensive overview of the urban informal sector of Karachi (Pakistan) post trade-liberalisation. His paper, based on active consultation between the actors in the informal sector, is dedicated to Orangi Pilot Project (OPP), one of the best-known urban poor non-government organisations in South Asia. It may be recalled that the OPP (Orangi Pilot Project) has been awarded the World Habitat Award for 2001. The paper is also an attempt to understand the changes in the informal sector in Karachi with respect to physical/social infrastructure needs of low and lower middle income communities following trade liberalisation. The author charts the negative aspects of the privatisation policies of government institutions.

Hülya Turgut's *(Istanbul Teknik Universitesi)* article examines the relationship between the physical environment of the squatter settlements and the socio-cultural aspect of the family in relation to the recent processes of urbanisation in Turkey. Geographically it is perhaps the furthest point before entering the European boundary that the *'capitalist developing country type squatter settlements'* could be observed. The author reminds us that the effects of the upgrading of squatter settlements have not produced the desired results. Turgut finds that today's squatters of Istanbul are living in unhealthy living conditions in multi-storied buildings and strongly suggests that the decisions regarding equipment, space, unit housing and settlement must be made suitable to the socio-cultural characteristics of the target population. Through case studies the author focuses on how the extended family, following traditional patterns, has been replaced by the more nuclear family. The effects of westernisation in the expectation of preferences for future design solutions seems to have eroded the traditional forms and values of the family life, a common feature of many developing nations.

FROM MULTIPLE TO MULTICULTURAL BUILT ENVIRONMENT

Contributions to the final part deal with one of the upcoming, but to some extent controversial and sensitive themes of the Global Built Environment, including racism, ethnography, diaspora and multiculturalism.

The first two articles discuss the problems that continue to persist in two multicultural European cities, while the concluding article of the volume critically analyses the problems associated with the rapid westernisation of Chinese built environment, probably one of the most remarkable phenomena of this century's built environment.

The twenty-first century experienced a significant deterioration in ethnic relations in Western Europe. In the UK during the latter part of 2001, riots and civil disorders were generated in Belfast (Northern Ireland) over the route Catholic children take home from school as it entails them passing through a Protestant housing estate. For many British cities, rioting is a common theme that has persisted for at least three decades. While ethnic tensions started fuming from the late 1970s in English built environments, serious riots that broke out in Liverpool during 1981 and more recently in the northern English towns of Oldham, Bradford and Burnley. Towns with no real previous history of ethnic tension. Brian Moynahan, reporting on how Islam takes hold in Europe and why the Dutch reputation for tolerance is coming under attack, forecasts that Muslims will soon outnumber Christians in some Dutch cities and that liberal Holland is now erecting barricades (Moynahan, B 2005: 34-43).

Ian Jackson *(Oldham: Separate Development)* reviews the current and the future development plans of the racially divided northern UK town of Oldham, with a reflection on the *'sustainability of such urban centres'*. In Oldham, as in many other European towns and cities, the ethnic population is growing and in some wards it is as high as 75% with a substantial proportion (around 30%) living in critically overcrowded conditions.

However, the market value of these properties is not growing; it is instead experiencing the reverse of the trend found in most of the rest of Britain, and suffering drastic devaluation. Comparisons with some third world slums are obvious here. Jackson *(University of Liverpool)* investigates the tough choices the local council have to make, and which may involve demolition. The role of urban design and planning comes under scrutiny as Jackson illustrates comparison with regeneration schemes in Liverpool. The author discusses the issues related to poor housing, riots and recommendations for the future. Experiencing the existing poor conditions in Oldham, Jackson's article has an air of despair as it outlines the collapse of a one time thriving textile town into poverty. Regaining its sense of identity and dignity could prove a lengthy and painful process. More than two decades ago when a post-graduate student at the Sheffield Town and Regional Planning department, I remember vividly the run down slums of the Scottish city of Glasgow *(the Gorbals)* and the nearby innovative new town of Kilmarnock. I sincerely hope the riot-torn northern towns of Oldham, Burnley and Bradford do not become case studies for future day planners.

In the Netherlands, *Bijlmermeer* (in Amsterdam) is another good example. Here Le Corbusier designed a *'modern functional town'* in the 1960s, now being pulled down, as it has become dysfunctional for the immigrant communities of the *Surinamese* and other ethnic communities who settled there since the 1970s in the neighbourhood. What is more intriguing about Bijlmermeer is that the 21st century design is carried out by Ashok Balotra, an Indian born architect practising in Rotterdam. There are other examples of culturally based design in other parts of the Netherlands, carried out by the architects from Africa where the residents are overwhelmingly African themselves. These are certainly challenging and innovative regeneration programmes yet to be experienced in other UK and European towns and cities. Within the European Union there are a number of different approaches taken when tackling the regeneration of areas with multiple deprivation. Karen Leeming and Tasleem Shakur *(Emerging problems in the multiply deprived area of Bijlmermeer, Amsterdam)* examine some of the effects that the urban restructuring approach used in the Netherlands has had on the residents of a large housing estate on the outskirts of Amsterdam known as *Bijlmermeer or Bijlmer*. Within this area of multiple social and economic disadvantages, black and ethnic groups form the majority of the population. Some of their early findings suggest the transformation of this area from a failed *'Utopian Vision'* into a thriving and successful *'multi-cultural built-environment'* is based on dispersing some of the most socially and economically excluded residents from the area via demolition, renovation and rebuild programmes. This in turn supports the work of other researchers in suggesting that the theory of urban restructuring has been adopted as a policy not to promote *'social cohesion'* but as a policy to prevent *'ethnic resistance'*.

Erica Liu's account of *'The Architectural Fairyland'* in the post-liberalisation period of 1984 and after presents an almost surreal scenario of post-modern architectural extravaganza in the mainland China. Liu highlights the fast developing stylised Western architecture and the mismatch of Mao's institutional practices. The article argues that the *copycat style of architectural practice is leading to a number of pressing problems, including intellectual copyrights, malpractice and lack of institutional development.* After two visits to China in the recent past, I gained the impression that the country was certainly a paradise for *late post-modernist architecture*, dazzling with shiny steel and glass. However, Liu presents us with what could be a potentially serious problem in the near future, particularly in relation to aspects of institutional development. Some may find it contestable when the author debates the *'tradition versus modernism concepts'* in generalising the development of modern Chinese architecture. I am aware that many of us in the West are quick to point out the *'Cultural Revolution'* being a deterrent to modern development in the present day China, I wonder whether such revolution was an asset to

10

embrace economic reforms with similar vigour of the past. The ongoing debate over the *'tradition versus modernism'* is meticulously exemplified by Liu and sprinkled with the views of celebrated western architects like Benjamin Ward and I M Pei. Some fifty years ago modernist architects/planners such as Le Corbusier, Water Gropius or Louis I Kahn had profound influence in post-colonial South Asia (Malik, A 2003: 68-80). Today, however, the Chinese are busy producing architecture, inspired and designed by a host of western architects, it is refreshing to note that (and I say this without being patronising) a few of them do place emphasis on the importance of preserving local traditions. No wonder they are widely praised for their sensitive development of neighbourhood and traditional houses in Shanghai. Commenting on *'Transitional Cities'* Fulung Wu exemplifies *'Space of Globalisation'* through a couple of Chinese cosmopolitan cities

'In Shanghai luxury apartments are reviving historical memories of the division between international settlement and indigenous Chinese quarters. In Beijing the insertion of global modes, such as glittering offices and gated Western-style housing compounds, linked through fast and elevated roads, is skewed towards the northeast of the city. The city can be viewed and experienced quite different vantage points of the expatriate within multinational or the local laid-off worker' (Wu, F 2003:1337).

In conclusion, Liu finds consolation in China's *'emerging multiculturalism in architecture'*. Commenting on *'Materialization of utopias of spatial form'* David Harvey states 'All the great urban planners, engineers, and architects of the twentieth century set about their tasks by combining an intense imaginary of some alternative world (both physical and social) with a practical concern for engineering and re-engineering urban and regional spaces according to radically new designs. While some, such as Ebenezer Howard, Le Corbusier, and Frank Lloyd Wright set up the imaginative context, a host of practitioners set about realizing those dreams in bricks and concrete, highways and tower blocks, cities and suburbs, building versions of the Villes Radieuse or Broadacre City, whole new towns, intimate scale communities, urban villages or whatever. Even when critics of authoritarianism of blandness of these realized utopian dreams attacked them, they usually did so by contrasting their preferred version of spatial play with the spatial orderings that others had achieved (Harvey, D 2002:64).

Some half a century ago, developing cities like Brasilia, Chandigarh or Dhaka have gained the reputation of having both the examples of the finest *modernist designs* (designed or influenced by the Western architects/planners), at the same time they have become typical examples of dysfunctional and unequal cities inappropriate to the overwhelming poor inhabitants (Shakur, T and D'Souza, K 2003:10). On a marginal level (particularly in the overwhelming slums and shanty towns of the developing world), Purewal, based on her research on *'Social Access to Shelter in Urban South Asia'* reopens old wounds of *'Self-help'* by asserting

'I would argue that the theoretical concerns with capitalist development and the role of state in housing provision are still as pertinent as they were over two decades ago. In fact, the luxury of hindsight of the collusion of self-help with capitalist modes of development provides a particularly strong base from which to continue the critique of self-help theory and practice (Purewal, N K 2000:17).

While illustrating the effects and impacts of Urbanisation *of Mega cities*, Kotter (2004) finds that most city situations have no sanitation facilities and rainwater drainage systems are totally inadequate. Only time will tell whether the *post-modernist urban planning, designs and regeneration/restructuring* of Shanghai, Bijlmermeer (Amsterdam) or Oldham (designed by the local architects/planners) would have significant contribution towards creating a more *appropriate, egalitarian and functional 'global built* environment' of the future.

BIBLIOGRAPHY

Dear, M and Flusty, S (2002) Postmodern Urbanism in Dear M J and Flusty S (eds) The Spaces of Postmodernity, Blackwell Publishers, Oxford.

Harvey, D (2002) The Spaces of Utopia, in Spaces of Hope, Edinburgh University Press

Haque, A (1982) The Myth of Self-help Housing: A critical analysis of the conventional depiction of shanty towns, Department of Building and Function Analysis, The Royal Institute of Technology, Stockholm, Williamsons Offsettryck.

King, A, D (2004) Spaces of Global Cultures: Architecture Urbanism Identity, Routledge, London.

Kotter T (2004) Risk and Opportunities of Urbanisation and Megacities, http://www. fig.net/ pub/monthly_articles/_2004/kotter_august_2004.htm. International Federation of Surveyors. Date Accessed: December 6th

Lefebvre, H (1996) Writings on Cities: Henri Lefebvre translated and edited by Eleonaore Kofman and Elizabeth Lebas, Blackwell publishers, Oxford.

Malik, A (2003) 'Post-Colonial Capitals of South Asia: A Critical Analysis of Chandigarh, Dhaka and Islamabad' in Global Built Environment Review (GBER), Vol 3 No 1 published by the International Centre for Development & Environmental Studies (ICDES), EdgeHill, Lancashire, UK.

Moynahan B (2005) Hardline Holland published in The Sunday Times Magazine, Feb 27, 2005.

Purewal, T (2000) Living on the Margins: Social Access to Shelter in Urban South Asia, Ashgate.

Rapoport A (1969) Housing Form and Culture, Pretence Hall Inc.

Shakur, T (1999)'Growing Muslim Community and Islamic Identity in Europe: A Case study of Lancashire, UK' in Abdullah Eben Saleh, M E and Feda Aljojani, A (eds) The Urban Design of Mosques, Volume 3B, pp 133-148, the Proceedings of the

Symposium on Mosque Architecture, King Saud University, Riyadh, Kingdom of Saudi Arabia.

Shakur, T, Dasgupta, N and Treloar, D (2001) Unsustainable Development and the Cities of the Developing World, Hegemon Press, Liverpool.

Shakur, T and D'Souza, K (eds) (2003) Picturing South Asian Culture in English: Textual and Visual Representations, p 10, Open House Press, Liverpool.

Smets, P (2004) Housing Financing and the Urban Poor, Rawat, Jaipur, New Delhi.

Smets, P and Salman T (2004) Countering Urban Segregation-On the Reasons Behind and Struggles Against Current Urban Segregation in Global Built Environment (GBER), Vol 4 No 2 published by the International Centre for Development & Environmental Studies (ICDES), EdgeHill, Lancashire.

Turner, John, F.C (1972) 'Housing as a Verb' in Turner and Fichter (eds) 'Freedom to Build' in Macmillan Company Ltd.

Van der Linden, J. J (1983) 'The Squatter's house as a source of security' in Schoorl, J.W, Van der Linden, J. J and Yap, K, S (eds), Between basti dwellers and bureaucrats: Lessons in squatter settlement upgrading in Karachi, Pergamon Press, Oxford.

Wu, F (2003) 'Transnational cities' published in Environment and Planning, pages 1331-1338, volume 35.

Part One
Cultural Identity in Transition

Problematic aspects of synthesis and interpretation in the study of traditional Omani built environment

Soumyen Bandyopadhyay

Over the last thirty years there has been an enormous burgeoning of field research in Oman Studies. Numerous major excavations have been undertaken either independently or on behalf of the Ministry of National Heritage and Culture (MNHC), by eminent archaeologists and academic institutions, all of which has managed to push back the beginnings of settled life in the peninsula to the 4th millennium BC. We have been able to trace the origin and establish a tentative age of the *falaj* irrigation system, which even today, form the backbone of many isolated oasis communities of the interior. The rest of the world has come to know more about the peculiarities of the Omani tribal system, the cultures and their religious beliefs. MNHC has been successful in collecting invaluable manuscripts from all over the country and preserving them in their excellent facilities in Muscat. Important documentation and preservation work has been carried out on buildings and structures of seminal importance. The *Journal of Oman Studies* (*JOS*) and other important publications of MNHC have contributed immensely towards our understanding of Omani archaeology, the palatial and military architecture and the flora and fauna.[i] This tremendous undertaking of field research has been necessary and important in establishing a basis for further and a mature phase of research.

However, when it comes to the study of traditional built environments and its architecture, we are confronted with a relative paucity of fieldwork and, regrettably, some poor commercially motivated coffee table material parading as academic work. Fieldwork conducted on settlements has at times remained unpublished for various reasons.[i] With rare exceptions,[ii] the academic work, dominated by archaeologists, has remained restricted to high-style (e.g. Costa, 1979; (1985b) or military architecture (e.g. d'Errico, 1983). Nostalgia has played an important part in both, engendering an amorous attraction for the picturesque and for a 'golden age' located in the remote past. The latter has been also instrumental in diverting attention and resources towards studying the palaces and citadels in an artificially 'de-contextualised' manner, by decoupling them from their context and at the expense of the traditional built environment within which it once lay embedded (e.g. Galdieri, 1975).

Thus the much-needed field research on traditional built environment has lagged behind and has remained very much a weaker sibling of archaeology in this respect. Damluji's work, *Architecture of Oman* (Damluji 1998), potentially a perfect vehicle to plug such a shortcoming, unfortunately, has all the indications of why rigorous research into the traditional built environment has remained so few and far between. What she claims to be a 'research into and documentation of the prominent architecture of selected towns and quarters in the Sultanate' is essentially a superficial touristic account from a set of brief visits - more a collection of photographs than a research monograph substantiated by 'broad and deep research' (*Ibid.*: xi).[iii] We can take the example of the now uninhabited town of Manah to illustrate the inaccuracies and inconsistencies of collected and presented information. In listing the constituent settlements of the oasis, she misses out on an important one: Ma'mad (*Ibid.*: 295). The subsequent paragraph describing the Friday Mosque (Masjid al-Jama) effectively paraphrases Biancifiori (Biancifiori 1994), its restorer.[iv]

The space fronting the mosque was never the 'central square' of the settlement - currently a roundabout behind the fort (Husn Manhia), as Damluji claims (*Ibid.*: 295), since the mosque, if one cares to read the settlement plan, falls at the southern end of the beaded string of built fabric.

The focus of the settlement had always been the market (*suq*) square at the northern end of the main settlement (Harat al-Bilad), given its privileged position as an important cattle trading centre in Inner Oman, attracting many nomadic and semi-nomadic groups of the region (Bandyopadhyay 1998: 101). This is why the famous square tower (Burg al-Juss) of the Harat presides over the activities of the *suq* square. Thereafter, she attempts to engage with the description of the Harat, where she presumes Asian expatriate workers inhabiting the settlement (Damluji, 1998: 296). In fact, the settlement has remained completely deserted since the mid-1970's; the mosques and one *sabla* (male meeting hall) continued to be used well into the 1980's and the mosque ablutions as wash/bath rooms into the 1990's.

She seems to be completely oblivious of the fourth mosque within the walled settlement, from which one initially assumes that she only had had the occasion to take a walk down the main street (*Ibid.*: 296). However, two photographs (*Ibid.*: 297 & 298) indicate that she had indeed walked past and failed to recognise the mosque! Incredibly, she gets a number of the mosque photographs wrong; what are captioned as the interior view, the *mihrab* (prayer niche)[v] and the exterior view of Masjid al-'Ayn, respectively (*Ibid.*: 297), are actually those of Masjid al-Sulaymani. In fact, she completely confuses Masjid al-'Ayn with Masjid al-Sulaymani, and, as two other photographs (courtyard and *mihrab*) clearly show (*Ibid.*: 298), the same happens with Masjid al-Shara. Finally, what is described as the town plan of Manah is far from useful information – a scrambled assemblage of meaningless patches of olive green and light purple, presumably depicting the plantation and dwellings, respectively. The author only had to consult the extant aerial photographs at the National Survey Authority[vi] to give it a semblance of truth and reality.

What originally had the potential of a seminal text, in fact turns out to be rather a weak contribution to the study of Omani architecture and built environment. However her collection of photographs and two initial chapters by contributing authors have value and could become useful for future researchers.

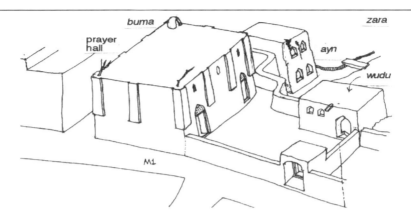

**Figure 01: Masjid al-'Ayn (Bilad Manah): Axonometric showing the components of a
central Omani mosque.**

SYNTHESIS

Very little effort has been directed towards a proper synthesis of the vast amount of
research material that has surfaced over the past three decades. Wilkinson's work in
understanding the tribal dynamics and water exploitation (Wilkinson, 1977), and Potts'
major two-volume work on a synthesis of the Gulf region archaeology (Potts, 1990), stand
out as towering achievements amidst all this.[vii] But these again, by no means, provide any
holistic picture of the material culture of the Omani people. Wilkinson's seminal work, for
example, understandably, given Wilkinson's disciplinary predilections, restricts its
treatment of "tribal settlement" to a macro-geographic level, and thus negates the
possibility of extending the understanding of social forces into the actual physical
settlement patterns (Wilkinson 1977).

Certain more focused pieces of work demand attention, one being an interesting and
rigorous social-historical study by Mershen on rural estates and associated built fabric
(Mershen 2001). Another set of publications, a much earlier study of the Ibra-Mudayrib
area, deals with the relationship between kinship structure and spatial organisation and is
probably the closest attempt to a successful information collection and synthesis and most
relevant to our present discussion. The study is introduced through an overview of the
regional characteristics and a list of tribes and sub-tribes that reside in the settlements
(Bonenfant, *et al*: 1977a: 91-4). The subsequent section investigates the macro-scale
spatial organisation of Ibra, describes its various neighbourhoods, and analyses the specific
nature of the prevalent kinship structure (Grandmaison, *et al* 1977: 95-106 plus plates).

The third and final section is a remarkably detailed study of Mudayrib, which begins with
an attempt to trace the history of the oasis from information collected locally, and through
the reconstruction of genealogical trees of important families resident within the oasis.

This is followed by a detailed description of the *falaj* distribution system. Finally, certain principal structures such as the mosques, *sabla*s, and shaikhly dwellings are described and their constructional and architectural features documented (Bonenfant, *et al* 1977b: 107-36 plus plates). The authors have only provided an 'inventory' of architectural features and except for the East African genealogical connections, no attempt has been made to trace other influences on the extant architecture (*Ibid.* 132-3). The absence of townscape description has left the treatment of some major structures entirely unrelated to the wider settlement fabric. The symbolic quality of this architecture and the decoration has remained unexplored. Dwellings descriptions are generic in nature, which again leaves their relationship with the larger 'sheikhly' dwellings unclear, creating an unbalanced picture of settlement organisation.

INTERPRETATION IN THE MATURE ERA

Interpretation of available data is the key to unlocking knowledge. While significant progress has been made in the field of archaeological data mining, only little exploration of value has been conducted on Omani traditional architecture. It is important to note that, as far as architecture is concerned, research and publications have either been of an environmental (e.g. Cain *et al* 1977; Afsar, *et al* 1998 & others) or of a picturesque (e.g. Damluji 1998) nature with military architecture taking a front seat typologically. Synthesis through comprehensive documentation, detailed inventory formulation, establishment of concordances and so on, are lacking or has been carried out with a dazzling lack of rigour. This evidently leaves the study of traditional architecture in a very disadvantageous position.

The archaeologists, though far better placed in that respect, seem to have found themselves in a time warp. Their unwillingness or inability to engage in interpretation and speculation on the intricate and complex relation between human behaviour, culture and the material remains from the past effectively ignores the entire discourse current within that discipline.[viii] Recent discussions in archaeology have seen the development of two related yet distinct approaches:

'One has been to develop more sophisticated ways of analyzing material culture, clearer and more explicit concepts, models and theories, so that behavioural inferences can be made, including even inferences about cognitive and symbolic behaviours. The second has been to develop ethnoarchaeology, which is ethnographic work done specifically to be applied to archaeology rather than using the more traditional ethnographic analogies - although even those can be useful' (Rapoport 1990: 3).

Following a position commonly termed 'New' or 'Processual' Archaeology developed in the 1960's and the early 1970's, the archaeological research in Oman has been 'primarily descriptive and uninterested in anthropological explanation or in the search for causes' (Preucel & Hodder, 1996: 6) and meanings. The research on traditional architecture, carried out mainly, as already indicated, by archaeologists, bore the same characteristics (e.g. Kervran, *et al*, 1983; Costa, 1985a). Despite the great methodological advances made during this period, as Hodder points out, New Archaeology has failed to understand the often indirect relations that exist between material culture, the mental schema, human behaviour and society (Hodder, 1986: 3 & 6). Material culture 'does not passively reflect society – rather, it creates society through the actions of individuals' (Hodder, 1986: 6). The processual approach creates an additional problem for synthesis, in that, holistic or thematised studies of culture cutting across inventory categories become rather difficult to undertake. The only cultural synthesis possible is one based on chronological phases where the complex nature of cultural exchange is often reduced to its search within such aspects of material culture as the stylistic similarity in pottery (e.g. Whitcomb, 1975).

DETERMINISM AND REDUCTIVISM

The ability to interpret or read material culture and finding the appropriate ways to do so is not however the initial problem; the work crucially depends on an appreciation of the nature and complexity of *what* is being read. If the material to be read is understood to be of a significantly complex nature, it naturally contributes towards a complex methodological demand. Until very recently researchers working on the archaeology and traditional architecture of the Arabian Peninsula have assumed an apparent simplicity in the material they were handling (e.g. certain Islamic epigraphic studies, Zayla'i 2000, Ibrahim 2001). The material culture conditions were, for them, exactly what they *appeared* to be – explicit, autonomous, time-frozen and therefore reducible to a set of mainly environmental or scientific explanations (linguistic, in this case), culminating in an attempt at a precise dating of the artefacts with no underlying or hidden meanings waiting to be discovered. This tendency stems from a mistaken assumption of a direct correlation between subsistence economy and a low level of complexity within the material culture – an example of economic and environmental determinism, as well as, of 'temporal pigeon-holing' of culture and society.

We could take the example of the small cupola atop the mosque prayer halls common in central Oman (Bandyopadhyay 2000) to highlight some of the problems emanating from this reductive instinct. The Ibadhis, in their mosques of central and eastern Oman, seem to have preferred this diminutive form to the towering minaret for the purposes of *adhan* (call to daily prayers), which some scholars have seen as reflecting the inherent simplicity and austerity of their philosophy (Eickelman 1987: 32). However, if that were entirely the case, it would be difficult to explain the presence of elaborate, highly decorative *mihrab*s in many of those mosques. Others have seen the *bumah* as the product of a culture conditioned by subsistence economy. That is, subsistence economy prompted the Omanis to adopt the diminutive cupola, the *bumah*, as a poor man's alternative to the extravagant minaret. This, again, clearly does not explain why it was called a *bumah*, an owl, and was not known by the terms commonly associated in Arabic with the minaret (*manarah/sawma'ah/ mi'danah*). The few archaeologists and Arabists who have cared to comment on the Omani mosques have opined that the name *bumah* was derived from its form being analogous to the owl silhouetted against the sky (Costa 1997: 8; Damluji 1998: 478; Baldissira 1998). However, further problem arises when we come to know that in Arabia the owl has been largely regarded as inauspicious and connected with death, calamity, the spirit or the ghost (Rehatsek 1878: 163-6; Homerin 1985; Stetkevych 1986: 40-42). How, then, did such a profane element become associated with the most sacred of spaces, these commentators fail to address. Surely, there were other underlying factors, considerations and understandings within the Omani mind that contributed towards its peculiar name and form. Thus the *bumah* cannot just be described as an architectural element emerging from the subsistence economy's answer to the liturgical demands within a harsh arid climate. A discourse rather than a description is therefore called for to fathom the complex origins and interwoven connections.

Figure 02: The *bumah* on top of the mosques of central Oman.

Instances of environmental determinism are too common in the study of Arabian traditional architecture to warrant citing specific examples. Two of the very early publications on Oman had produced interesting and sympathetic studies on climactic comfort (Cain, *et al* 1975, reproduced as Afsar *et al* 1998). The fortified settlement, the narrow winding streets, the courtyard, the small windows. And the active nature of the mud-brick walls continue to appear frequently in the inventory of environmental modifiers in the plethora of literature (publications and dissertations) that pours out of the academic institutions each year. While detailed fieldwork on and measurement of microclimatic factors and qualities are necessary, what is worrying, however, is that these factors, coupled with a narrow acceptance of Islamic principles, are often taken as the sole determinants of culture, society and even politics, of the region. These also appear prominently on the menu of the numerous post-graduate environmental engineering and sustainable development courses geared towards students hailing from the Middle East currently on offer in the West. Much of the archaeological explanations have also followed the path of economic and environmental determinism (e.g. Brunswig 1988).

FROZEN IN TIME

In these researchers' minds past cultures never left active traces, they are always dead – they only exist as a legacy of the past, never engaged with the culture of the present. Research on central Oman and especially on the settlement of Manah (Bandyopadhyay 1998) has shown how far removed these researchers were from reality, since many of the earlier cultural traces have remained active ingredients of the more recent culture and society. This is because many of the material culture artefacts and meanings, as I have tried to show through the example of the *bumah*, are produced as a result of unconscious or subconscious cultural engagements (Hodder, 1986: 5). Their origins and conceptions extend far beyond the actual event of their appearance and hence, their precise dating, almost always, is of little consequence. These are products of the existence of very deep-rooted cultural traditions, ingrained in the psyche of the people.

Omani culture displays a build up of a series of cultural influences, of which some of the most important ones came from outside that particular geographic region. If we assume an initial development of a local and purely indigenous form of proto-Arab culture in our area (hunting-gathering in the interior and fishing on the coast), the first strong regional influence would be the appearance of a pan-South Arabian culture. The mosque prayer halls of the recent past demonstrate how a certain form housing sacred functions of that pre-Islamic South Arabian cultural era was adopted, almost unchanged, to house the new sacred function demanded by Islam. The cuboid of the prayer hall, unlike the *liwan*-type mosques found in Saudi Arabia or in the Gulf littoral (King 1978, 1980; Kay & Zandi 1991), appears to be a form prevalent in sacred complexes in South Arabia (Dhofar, Hadhramawt and Yemen) (Bandyopadhyay 1998: 312-31). There followed a long period of influences from further afield, a phase which not necessarily excluded the continued influence of the former. The influence of Mesopotamian culture and ideals, which in all probability, managed to remain unaccompanied by a physical presence or direct control, preceded the more direct but nevertheless intermittent Persian control over the land up till the advent of Islam. These brought in yet another set of influences, which again, can be read in the unique decorative tradition in central Omani mosques. If one looks carefully at the *mihrab*s, one can detect, as part of the roundels of the decorative scheme, the interconnected endless nature of circular motifs (Bandyopadhyay 2001). This band of decoration is in essence a grand "endless knot" motif, a "complex maze-like closed pattern" (Parpola 1994: 56-7) often employed to represent endless or continuous space or time. This motif — found from the Middle East to India, from prehistoric to modern contexts — can be traced back to Mesopotamia of the third millennium BC. Versions of the same motif can also be found on many central Omani doors,[ix] suggesting that having entered *via* Persia bringing with it Zoroastrian concepts of time, it will have taken a deep root within Omani decorative tradition. Undoubtedly, the Persian presence was the strongest of all external influences predating Islam, one which left deep etchings on Omani society and its environment and of which both active artefacts and processes, as well as vestigial remains, provide testimony. The *falaj* system of irrigation, still the backbone of Omani oasis agriculture, one that had had a significant influence on the societal structure and land ownership, is a Persian contribution from *c*.1000 BC (Wilkinson 1977; Potts

1990). The West Semitic Arab tribes arrived over an extended period, mainly between second century BC and second century AD from Yemen and the Najd area of Saudi Arabia and later, at the dawn of Islam, embraced the new religion. However, their socio-political constitution and relationship define and regulate the nature of Omani life and society until today.[x] The control of the caliphate of Baghdad was never strong enough, and they were soon pushed out with the introduction of Ibadhi ideals from Basra. The Ibadhis formed an Imamate in the mid-8th century, which despite major interruptions between the twelfth and the seventeenth centuries, survived until 1959 (Wilkinson 1987). The cosmopolitan maritime attitude of the coastal area *vis à vis* the tribal and theocratic attitude of the interior, divided the country into an Ibadhi-tribal introvert cultural core and an outward looking peripheral sub-culture on the coast around Muscat. However, East African influences penetrated deep into the Omani heartland and left marks on the style of decoration and on Omani architecture (Bonenfant, *et al*, 1977b: 107-36 plus plates; Bandyopadhyay 1998: 195, Fig.-11.34). The expansion of maritime trade in 17th and 18th centuries and the presence of European actors on the scene finally tilted the balance in favour of Muscat and the new Sultanate gradually took shape. Cultural phases introduced even in the remote past, however, remained an active presence in the more recent architecture, built environment and on Omani society.

ORTHODOXY

Superficiality, therefore, has risen from trying to understand traditional architecture from a myopic economic, environmental and time-frozen viewpoint, treating these as if these could be de-coupled from the cultural and social variables with ease. However, a major hindrance has come from the uncritical acceptance of Islam as an absolute and *impervious datum*. No elements predating this membrane are considered to have had an effect on early Islamic environments, let alone accepting their existence within the present architecture (e.g. *JOS*: 3(2); Costa 1997). *Jahiliya*[xi] is now therefore not only the "days of ignorance", but a period entirely ignored and an age about which we wish to remain ignorant.[xii] The influence of Islam on built environment, on the other hand, has been analysed from the perspective of uniform exposure to the doctrine, where analysing complex socio-cultural phenomena have been reduced to a naïve game of matching up with a simple checklist carefully engineered to conform to only the most explicit of liturgical requirements. Mosques, dwellings and settlement patterns have had such a treatment; in the case of the last two, combined with environmental determinism, popular amongst many researchers, guaranteed to produce predictable results. My intention, here, is in no way to criticise the research on Arab built environments from an Islamic perspective; in fact, far from that. My criticism is towards a kind of work that reduces the scope of research on the Arab-Islamic built environment by taking a limited and limiting view of Islam and Islam's manifestation within the settlement and architecture, as well as, a reluctance to understand Islam's presence *vis à vis* the other cultural strands. I am arguing for a deeper, wider and more rigorous understanding of the impact of 'Islamic culture'.

Mosque architecture, especially, has been regarded and for understandable reasons, as a product of Islamic liturgy; a mosque *is a* mosque - the direction of prayer (*qibla*) defining the configuration and organisation of the house of prayer. Few questions have been raised about the peculiarities of organisation, form and nature of decoration and few will realise that many aspects of the mosque, in fact, indicate continuity with the pre-Islamic cultures than a rupture. Why, for example, mosque organisation and form in Oman differs from the Gulf littoral or the Saudi heartland (e.g. Kay & Zandi 1991; King 1978, 1980), we not often ask. If we had, we would have realised that the uniqueness of many central Omani mosques lie in their predominance of a lateral entry in relation to the direction of the *qibla* (Bandyopadhyay 1998, Bandyopadhyay & Sibley 2002) and a cuboid form of the prayer hall. These appear to be a feature of Dhofari (Costa 1979; Oman 1983) and Hadhramawtic mosques and can also be seen in the smaller mosques of San'a'(Serjeant and Lewcock 1983). What is even more fascinating, such form can ultimately be traced back to the pre-Islamic temples of upper Yemen (e.g. Hugga) and to South Arabian temple maquettes excavated that once aided construction and visualisation (Bandyopadhyay 1998, 2002). *Bumah*, the small cupola I cited earlier earlier, has its etymological origin in old Hebrew *bamah* (sacred high place), but connects up with a local derivative *bomah* (prehistoric beehive tombs) and certain Arab tribal notions of sacrifice and vengeance, all dating back to the *Jahiliya* (Bandyopadhyay 2000).

Natural springs (*'ayn*) have remained the centre of spiritual spaces from the very early days of civilisation in that part of the world; at the dawn of Islam, these were transformed into places of Islamic prayer (hence, mosques with such names as Masjid al-'Ayn in Manah). Interpretation of the Quranic *wudu* (ablution) verses resulted in slight variations in the mosque spatial organisation: an insistence on ritual purity of a stranger or traveller resulted in the provision of a direct access into ablution facilities in mosques located next to settlement entrances.

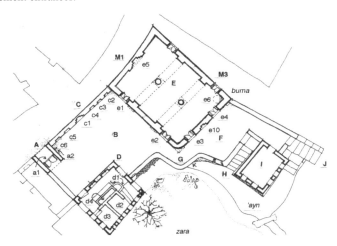

Figure 03: Id al-'Ayn (Bilad Manah): Plan of the mosque. The ablution facilities sit over a natural spring source.

Ritual impurity from the Islamic perspective became laterally linked with a tribal notion of territoriality centred on the settlement, encapsulating the *hadr* (settled population) worldview. Thus spatiality of mosques in desert foreland regions is, in effect, not only a result of Islamic doctrinal requirements, but also a product of the complex processes of sedenterisation amongst Arab tribes (Bandyopadhyay 1998).

Regardless of the nature of introduction and evolution of Islam in a particular region, all built environments in such locations have come to be known as 'Islamic' settlements, severely limiting the scope of intellectual discourse. Phobic attitude towards the *Jahiliya*, the reluctance to accept any digressions from the beaten track and the inability to see beyond the most simplistic of Islamic perspectives, have resulted in only a partial historical understanding of the material culture. Such indications as the infiltration of tribal attitudes and perspectives into Islamic religious practices or the presence of pre-Islamic ideological and architectural components within the built environment beg for a more rigorous and multi-disciplinary approach to the study of traditional environments. An intercourse with 'other' disciplines should not be limited to those of a 'scientific' nature, but should be open to all disciplines dealing with the peoples' relationship with their built environment, which in turn, modifies society and culture. A worrying aspect, in this respect, has been the degree of puritanism held and exercised within certain disciplines - their inability to see/ read and their resistance towards wider possibilities of connection. This is not to argue for the dissolution of disciplinary integrity; rather, it is to encourage exploration and a mature understanding of (what has always been) fuzzy disciplinary boundaries.

CONTEXT – 'WITH TEXT'
It is now generally recognised that the history and archaeology of a built environment "is a way of extending research into the past", both by using data from the past to help understand the present and by using the present to throw light on the past (Rapoport 1990: 191). Through such interplay of the past and the present, patterns are revealed and both benefit (e.g. Hodder, 1986: 180-1). Sadly in the case of Oman, often events and cultures of the past, for which material evidence have been recovered, are treated as hermetically sealed and as I have suggested, time-frozen material entities, seen to be possessing no life of their own, having no influence on or connections or interactions with, the culture of the present. The fact that we do read the past from our position in the present and thereby project ourselves, that is, our present, our spatial constructs, as well as, our ideologies, into the past, needs to be accepted at the outset. Equally, the material culture needs to be evaluated and understood through the analysis of other relationships that may already exist or may have grown recently in their validity. Put simply, there is a clear inability to critically understand the crucial role of contexts in the production of meaning - context of temporal, spatial, environmental, physical, social, cultural, political, behavioural, disciplinary and textual nature – with their differing, often overlapping, scales of operation. To this must be added the critical role of ideological positions or perspectives for such contextual reading. It is also important that in the mature period of research multifaceted meanings are sought, which span from those of an immediate nature to the

ones (often simultaneously) concerned with the human beings' role and place within a wider universe.

A few examples from the Omani situation will, I hope, illustrate my point about this pivotal role of contexts in interpretation. In one of those rare flashes of speculative interpretation found in the study of Omani archaeology and architecture, Friefelt had suggested a possible link between the 3rd millennium BC Umm an-Nar type towers from Bat and the towers employed in the 18th century Omani military architecture (Friefelt 1976: 61; she cites Nizwa as an example).^{xiii} It had remained a wild speculation because, first, she failed to extend her spatial context beyond Oman to substantiate her claim, an example, I would suggest, of uncritical acceptance or myopic definition of domain boundaries.^{xiv} Secondly, she was unable to see the full extent of the connections between her classical/historical context of investigation, and a local and more recent context, i.e., with less obvious but nonetheless common phenomenon in Omani military architecture of lesser prominence. In Yemen, we find a type of tower structure known as *nobah/ nawbah*, where the activities of defence/ surveillance and habitation/ leisure are connected (Serjeant & Lewcock 1983: 464-5, 468, 485-6 illustrations 22.112-3, 488 illustrations 22.114-7; also the fortified tower-houses of Hadhramawt, Doe & Serjeant 1975). Often the *nobah* incorporated a large male entertainment room (*mafraj*) at the top. Interestingly, this is also the case with the observation turrets that partially project beyond the settlement wall in Bilad Manah (Bandyopadhyay 1998: 227-232). There, *sabla*s of certain important tribes, by taking advantage of their fairly continuous occupation, were placed on upper levels pushing into the turrets, doubling up as observation posts complete with loopholes and other defensive openings. Such a discovery has wider implication; it better explains why modern Omanis are keen to incorporate tower-like forms into their dwellings. Costa's comment on the *bumah* (Costa 1997), similarly, fails to explain *why* the miniature minaret is called an owl due to his failure to put it within a wider, but nevertheless valid, evolutionary and historical context. As one begins to search beyond the immediate historical and geo-physical confines, further North into the Nabatean tombs and into pre-Islamic Arab sanctuaries, but also into North Arabian numismatics and early Arabian poetry and mythology, clues emerge thick and fast (Bandyopadhyay 2000). Here, context is not only provided by the spatial extension, contextualisation occurs through the conflation of classical and local traditions with the placement of the available material and 'textual' (i.e. non-material) fragments of evidence, in relation to other relevant material and textual evidence. Again, the accepted wisdom regarding the origin of the *mihrab* in the Greco-Roman arcuated niche for the idol or its equivalent in later Christian worship, appears pathetically incomplete as we learn about the somewhat more secular origin of the word in South Arabian civilisation which continued to have a presence in the Hadhramautic mosques of more recent times (Serjeant, 1959).

Hodder has identified two types of contextual meaning; one refers to the "environmental, technological and behavioural context of action" and the other is to do with the idea of context being "with-text", thus introducing "an analogy between the contextual meanings of material culture traits and the meanings of words in a written language" (Hodder, 1986:

153). Crucially, Hodder emphasises the importance of the notion of 'text' over 'language' (*Ibid.*, 1986: 153), articulating the text's predilection for content over symbol and as an embodiment of content. Such a wider notion of text encourages the researcher to seek contextualization outside those represented in and through the written languages and in disciplines that are not entirely bound by it. Thus alongside written history, oral history, mythology, folklore and such other modes of recording of human thoughts, experiences and events (often summarised by the Greek word *mythos*) become valid information sources, expanding manifolds the real opportunities for the production of meaning. A holistic picture can only be painted when the colours are drawn from a palette of the related disciplines. In Oman and in the study of traditional architecture the entire Arabian Peninsula there often appears to be a distinct reluctance to do this, especially when the drawing of experiences from such 'unscientific' disciplines as mythology or folklore become necessary. The obsession with the 'true scientific historical' method of unravelling the "various strands of history" by removing the embellishment of a "generous dose of legend", (quotes from Wilkinson, 1977:) has resulted in a 'throwing away the baby with the bathwater' syndrome. Speedy economic development has made vital ingredients and clues about how people lived, behaved and built over the last six thousand years disappear rapidly. Certain researchers have explicitly rejected a scientific approach to archaeology (e.g. Hodder, 1986), while others have argued in favour of a much broader definition of science (e.g. Rapoport, 1990: 185-91).

CONCLUSION

If the search for meaning is the objective of knowledge production, one needs to avoid a fatal tendency often detected amongst architectural historians of the Arab-Islamic world: to generalise the specific, the particular and the irreducible aspects of meaning within material culture. This is not to say that generalisation is universally flawed, in fact, generalisation has been the main thrust of scientific theory; research on structure, system or tectonics can produce useful insights through generalisation of their underlying patterns. However, such a method when applied to the arts and the social sciences indiscriminately, has exposed its severe limitations. There, the role of generalisation can often go no further than stating the obvious (e.g. Rapoport's study of traditional street patterns, Rapoport 1990), while for any architectural-historical research, it is critical to oscillate between the generic and the specific. By opening the door towards the so-called non-scientific aspects of material culture study, future research needs to integrate these with the present mainstream 'scientific' avenues of investigation. Also, classical and local traditions often coalesce, shifting the original meaning and altering the original form-content relationship through intricate processes of transformation over time. This we have seen in the case of the *bumah* and the *mihrab*. Assuming an unchanged continuation of the classical, the liturgical, the original or the authentic meaning would only produce stale, predictable regurgitated results.

NOTES
[i] A detailed account of published material on traditional architecture and archaeology appear in Bandyopadhyay 1998: Chapter 4. Few new publications, except Costa's (1997)

and Damluji's (1998), have appeared since. Damluji's work is briefly discussed later in this paper.

ii For example photographic survey by MNHC of the Luwatiyya settlement in Muttrah, Sur al-Luwatiyya, has never been published.

iii *Journal of Oman Studies* (*JOS*), Vol. 3(2) is devoted to a detailed study of the settlement, architecture and social history of the Ibra-Mudayrib area of the Sharqiya region, discussed later.

iv 'Preface' by Prof. Christopher Frayling of the Royal College of Arts, London. Although Damluji adds a couple of disclaimers regarding the non-definitive nature of her work *vis à vis* Omani architecture and that the information was collected over a fairly short period of time (Damluji 1998: xi.)

v Effectively a rebuilding, as Damluji agrees, that has robbed this important structure off most of its original character and materiality, not uncommon in Oman's brief but turbulent history of conservation!

vi The *mihrab* of Masjid al-'Ayn is not white stucco, as she describes (Damluji, 1998: 296) but has for many years remained painted green.

vii This author has managed to locate three aerial photographs dating back to 1968.

viii There have subsequently been a few more attempts at a synthesis of Gulf archaeology: Rice 1994 and Crawford 1998.

ix Current discourse in archaeology has focused on contextual interpretation and a discussion of the material in relation to developments in other disciplines within the Humanities (Preucel & Hodder 1996). Work published in *Journal of Oman Studies*, with a few exceptions already noted, does not bear these characteristics.

x This is the older decorative tradition predating the one introduced from India (either directly from Gujarat or via Zanzibar and East Africa) often regarded as the only decorative tradition found in Oman and in the Gulf littoral.

xi One has to only look at the nature of Omani politics and the constitution of ministries to get an idea of how tribal allegiance and alliances continue to play an important role in today's Omani life. Also, *wasta* (favour through connections) is an important means of getting things accomplished. Here again, tribal/ clan relationships play a vital role.

xii The pre-Islamic era in which the true religion of the earlier prophets were forgotten.

xiii This was not always the case. In the early Islamic period there still remained a significant interest in pre-Islamic beliefs and idols (e.g. al-Kalbi).

xiv Wilkinson's seminal treatment of the Persian origin of the falaj irrigation system (Wilkinson 1977) and Potts' discussion on the eagle sculptures found in the UAE (Potts 1990) are brilliant, yet rare, examples of speculative interpretation.

xv See Rapoport (1990) for a discussion on the importance of establishing domain boundaries. Parpola's work on the Indus script (1994) is an excellent example of why such definition is necessary.

BIBLIOGRAPHY

Afsar, F., Cain, A., & Norton, J. 1998. Indigenous Building in the Third World. In Damluji 1998.

Baldissira E. 1998. Personal communication. *Mihrab* and *bumah* in mosques of Oman.

Bandyopadhyay, S. & Sibley, M. 2002. Spatial Organisation of Mosques in Central Oman: Its ancient Hadramawtic and Yemeni Origin and the Notions of Purity. Paper being presented at the *Seminar for Arabian Studies*, 2002.

Bandyopadhyay, S. 2001. (in press) From Another World! A Possible Buyid Origin of the Decorated *Mihrab* of Central Oman? , During Caspers Memorial Contribution, *British Archaeological Reports* (*BAR*).

Bandyopadhyay, S. 2000. From the Twilight of Cultural Memory: The *Bumah* in the Mosques of Central Oman. *Proceedings of the Seminar for Arabian Studies* (*PSAS*). 30: 13-25.

Bandyopadhyay, S. 1998. *Manah: The Architecture, Archaeology and Social History of a Deserted Omani Settlement*. Unpublished PhD dissertation. Liverpool.

Biancifiori, MA., 1994. Works of Architectural Restoration in Oman. Rome.

Bonenfant, P. & Cour-Grandmaison, C. le-. 1977a. The Ibra and Mudayrib Area. *Journal of Oman Studies* (*JOS*). 3(2): 91-4.

Bonenfant, P. & G., & Harthi, S. al-. 1977b. Architecture and Social History at Mudayrib, *JOS*. 3(2): 107-36 + plates.

Brunswig, R.H. 1988. Cultural History, Environment and Economy as seen from an Umm an-Nar Settlement. *JOS*. 10: 9-50.

Cain, A., Afshar, F., & Norton, J., (1975). Indigenous Building in the Third World. *Architectural Design* (*AD*) 4:207-24.

Costa, PM. 1997. *The Historic Mosques of Inner Oman*. Rome.

Costa, PM. 1985a. The Sur of the Batinah. *JOS*. 8(2):121-94.

Costa, PM. 1985b. Bayt Na'man, a Seventeenth Century Mansion of the Batinah. *JOS*. 8(2): 195-210 plus plates.

Costa, PM. 1979. The Study of the City of Zafar (al-Balid). *JOS*, 5: 111-50.

Crawford, H. 1998. *Dilmun and its Gulf Neighbours*. Cambridge.

Doe, D. B., & Serjeant, R.B. 1975. A Fortified Tower-House in Wadi Jirdan (Wahidi

Sultanate) I & II. *Bulletin of the School of Oriental and African Studies* (*BSOAS*), 38: 1-23 & 276-95.

Damluji, S.S. 1998. *The Architecture of Oman*. Reading.

d'Errico, E. 1983. Introduction to the Omani Military Architecture of the Sixteenth, Seventeenth and Eighteenth Centuries. *JOS*. 6(2): 291-306 + plates.

Galdieri, E., 1975. A Masterpiece of Omani 17th Century Architecture: The Palace of Imam Bilarab bin Sultan al-Yaaraba at Jabrin. *JOS*. 1: 167-79.

Guidieri, R. 1986 (1996 reprint). Illuminations on Some Urban Remains. In Hejduk, John, *et al* (eds.) *Education of an Architect*. New York.

Grandmaison, Le C., Spatial Organisation, Tribal Groupings and Kinship in Ibra. *JOS*. 3(2): 95-106 + plates.

Hodder, I., 1986. *Reading the Past*: *Current Approaches to Interpretation in Archaeology*

. Cambridge.

Homerin, T.E. 1985. Echoes of a Thirsty Owl: Death and Afterlife in Pre-Islamic Arabic Poetry. *Journal of Near Eastern Studies* 44(2): 165-184.

Ibrahim, Moawiyah M. 2001. Tombs and their inscriptions from Nizwa and al-Haymali, Sultanate of Oman. *PSAS*. 31: 97-113.

Kalbi, H. ibn. al- 1952. *Kitab al-Asnam* (*Book of Idols*. N.A. Faris tr.). Princeton.

Kervran, M., Cour-Grandmaison, C. Le-, Soubeyran, M., & Pémille, AV. De-. 1983. Suhari Houses. *JOS* 6(2): 307-16 + plates.

Kay, S. & Zandi, D. 1991. *Architectural Heritage of the Gulf*. Dubai.

King, G.R.D., 1978. Traditional Najdi Mosques. *BSOAS*. 41: 464-98.

King, G.R.D. 1980. Notes on some Mosques in eastern and Western Saudi Arabia. *BSOAS*. 43: 251-76.

Mershen, B., 2001. Observations on the Archaeology and Ethnohistory of Rural Estates of the 17th through early 20th Centuries in Oman. *PSAS*. 31: 145-160.

Oman, G. 1983. Preliminary Epigraphic Survey of Islamic Material in Dhofar. *JOS*, 6(2): 277-90.

Parpola, A. 1994. *Deciphering the Indus Script*. Cambridge.

Potts, D.T. 1990. *Arabian Gulf in Antiquity*. Cambridge.

Preucel, R. & Hodder, I. 1996. Contemporary Archaeology in Theory: A Reader. Oxford

Rehatsek, E. 1878. Some Beliefs and Usages among the Pre-Islamitic Arabs, with Notes on their Polytheism, Judaism, Christianity and the Mythic Period of their History. *Journal of the Bombay Branch of the Royal Asiatic Society* 12: 163-212.

Rapoport, A. 1990.*History and Precedent in Environmental Design*. New York.

Rice, M. 1994. *The Archaeology of the Arabian Gulf, c.5000-323 BC*. London.

Serjeant, R.B., & Lewcock, R. 1983. *San'a': An Arabian Islamic City*. London.

Serjeant, R. B. 1959. Mihrab. *BSOAS*, 22(3), 439-53.

Stetkevych, S.P. 1986. The Ritha' of Ta'abbata Sharran, A Study of Blood-Vengeance in Early Arabic Poetry. *Journal of Semitic Studies* 31: 27-45.

Whitcomb, D. 1975. The Archaeology of Oman: A Preliminary Discussion of the Islamic Periods. *JO S*. 1: 123-58.

Wilkinson, J.C. 1977. *Water and Tribal Settlement in South East Arabia: The Study of the Aflaj of Oman*. Oxford.

Wilkinson, J.C. 1987. *The Imamate Tradition of Oman*. Cambridge.

Zayla'i, AU al-. 1999. Calligraphy and Calligraphers in 'Asm – Saudi Arabia 2nd-5th/8th-11th Centuries. *PSAS*. 30: 243:5.

Reconstruction of Traditional Architecture
A Design Education Tool

Omar Khattab

This paper describes a design studio exercise to reconstruct a traditional house complex. The exercise was conducted at the Department of Architecture, Kuwait University as part of course 'Architecture Design 2' number 'ARCH 205'. Under the main theme of 'Design for Living', students were required to design a house for a Kuwaiti family within the cultural context, so the Reconstruction of a Traditional House exercise represented a logical threshold in the design process. Students were asked to carry out a visual survey of the traditional Behbehani House complex located in al-Watia area, a suburb of al-Qibla area in downtown Kuwait City.

To conduct the visual survey of the Complex, students gathered an array of information about it including survey maps, digital maps, aerial photographs, detailed photographs, measured freehand sketches, and written information available. The goal of the visual survey was to enable students to recreate the house Complex in the form of orthogonal drawings and three-dimensional scale models. The drawings and models of the houses and the Complex formed a solid basis to analyse the cultural and architectural essence behind the formation of the Behbehani Complex.

As (Correa 1994, 13) indicates there are three layers of architecture conscious that architects draw mythic imagery from during the design process. First is the everyday world, second is the compulsive imagery and third is the deep structure. Designers who bounce from the middle layer, with localized images, in a superficial process, only transfer old images and hence imitate the forms of vernacular architecture. While those designers who reach the deep structures in the lowest layer transform images by reinventing architectural expression of their mythic values, or in other words by reinventing tradition.

The reconstruction exercise aims to provide students with a vehicle that could help them to reach the deep structure stratum through analysis of local vernacular architecture. While, as Correa states (Correa 1994, 12), mythic imagery is a basic mechanism in design process, the means to arrive at the mythic imagery are not clearly defined. One of these means could be the deep analysis of the forms of vernacular architectural examples, attempted in this exercise. Students were asked to search for the support structures and subsystems that generated this type of vernacular habitat. As Nay (2001) argues the success of a design studio exercise is in introducing students to the architectural heritage of their region through analysis and design.

THE BEHBEHANI HOUSE COMPLEX

Old Kuwaiti Houses are known for their simplicity. They mainly consist of one floor with a courtyard in the middle surrounded by a number of rooms. Between the courtyard and the rooms there is a colonnaded passage or covered area that is called a Liwan. The Liwan stands halfway between the public domain of the house, which is the courtyard, and the private domain, which are the rooms. The courtyard itself was the centre of the inner world of domesticity, as Nay 2001 denotes. He also argues that the courtyard house is the dominant prototype for almost all architecture of the Muslim world.

The Behbehani House Complex is located in al-Watia area, which means "footmarks" in the local Kuwaiti dialect. The area was given this name because people used to stroll beside the sea shore along the Arabian Gulf bay leaving their footmarks on the muddy sand shore thus giving this area its common name. In the early 1940's Yusuf Shreen Behbehani built this Complex as his first major real estate project. Al-Watia area was a wild and lonely place, where few town people dared to venture. When Yusuf Behbehani bought this piece of land, half of it used to be covered by high tide seawater, so he reclaimed it and made it higher and then started to build, as Al-Rashoud 1995 has noted. This represented one of the first attempts to reclaim parts of the Arabian Gulf bay along the Kuwaiti waterfront, which now became almost common practice in most waterfront development projects.

The Complex was designed by an Iranian architect and built by Iranian workers. The Complex contains one main courtyard-like open space and twenty eight dwelling units each with its own internal courtyard. Half of these units used to be occupied by the Behbehani family and relatives, while the rest of the houses were rented out to foreigners. In the mid 1960's the Behbehani family left the Complex and over time many of the houses fell into a state of disrepair. During the Iraqi invasion of Kuwait, Iraqi forces looted everything and occupied the Complex so that the houses suffered even further. After liberation in 1991, work soon began to restore the Complex and make it habitable again. The original families who used to live in the Complex restored some of the houses, while others were restored by the private sector for commercial purposes.

The houses needed completely repairing, and have needed constant attention subsequently. The renovation involved plumbing, electrical work, work to walls, doors and woodwork, and waterproofing as well as cleaning. In all more than KD 40,000 (approximately $120,000) was spent on returning the houses to a habitable condition. (Topalian 2001).

In more recent times, another form of invasion has occurred, that of restaurants and commercial facilities. Only eight out of twenty eight houses in all are still used as residential units. The rest have changed use and became restaurants, offices, or art galleries. The residential units kept, to a large extent, their original old design, while many changes affected most of the other units. The Complex was for a long time ignored by local authorities. The residents' only hope now is that the National Council for Culture,

Arts and Letters will take over the Complex, which was recently listed as a preserved historical monument.

The importance of Behbehani Complex stems from the fact that it is considered one of the very first two-story residential sites to be developed in Kuwait. One of the houses in the Complex was used as offices of the local radio station before it was moved to Nayef Palace, which is now the Kuwait Government Headquarters. Currently, the Behbehani Complex, as a cluster of dwelling units, is the only remaining intact example of Kuwaiti vernacular architecture. This is reflected in the government decree to preserve the Complex as a listed architectural heritage site (Figure 01).

Behbehani Complex internal street view   **Students on study visit to the Complex**

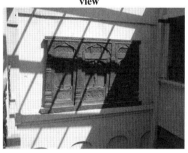 

Wall Mashrabiya inside Behbehani Complex   **Main Façade detail of House # 7**

Renovation of House # 24   First Floor Liwan in House # 7

Parapet details in Behbehani Complex   Parapet details in Behbehani Complex

Figure 01: A Sample of Students' Visual survey of Behbehani House Complex, Kuwait

THE EXERCISE

As part of the main theme of 'Design for Living', the title of the exercise given to second
year students of architecture was 'Reconstruction of an Old Kuwaiti House'. The purpose
of the exercise was to understand the essence behind the formation of the traditional
courtyard house in Kuwait, and to become aware of the social, cultural and behavioural
aspects related to house design. Also, it would enable students to conduct a formal
analysis, or analysis of the form of a simple function building namely the house. The
exercise extended over a period of 4 weeks and consisted entirely of group work.

The Behbehani House Complex at Watia, Kuwait, represents an almost intact living part of
the architectural heritage of Kuwait.   The twenty-eight house Complex represents a type
of traditional Kuwaiti housing, i.e. the coastal type influenced by the Persian domestic
architecture. The first step in designing for living in a certain cultural context should be to
understand and analyse existing types of living. Students were asked to make a visual
survey of the Behbehani House Complex and a reconstruction of it. The focus was the
formal analysis of the individual courtyard houses, as well as the entire Complex as a

whole courtyard entity. Close attention was paid to the masses of the houses and the relation between the solid and void in terms of plan and elevation.

THE PROCEDURE

The class of fifteen students was divided into five equal groups. Each group was assigned a particular task in the visual survey part of the reconstruction exercise. Three groups were given the task of documenting three individual houses from the Complex, houses number 7, 8 and 24. The other two groups were asked to document the entire layout of the Complex. The three individual houses surveyed in detail gave a clear impression of the traditional Kuwaiti type of courtyard house design, while the survey of the entire Complex gave an idea of the groupings of the individual houses into a cluster to form a living quarter, or "Freej" in local dialect.

The three individual houses selected for the sample represented the current uses of the Complex. House number 7 was transformed into a restaurant, and house number 8 was transformed into the offices of a media company, while house number 24, was kept to its original dwelling state by its Canadian tenant Stephanie McGehee. The three houses also represent three different type plans of traditional courtyard houses contained in Behbehani Complex. Houses number 7 and 8 have two complete floors, while House number 24 has one complete ground floor and a partial first floor.

The entire class conducted two extended study visits with course instructor and tutors, where the subject matter was introduced and visual survey techniques were demonstrated in details. A survey of the sample individual houses plus the entire Complex was made during these two study visits. Later on, individual groups went sent back to the site several times to complete their measurements, photos and survey data. They also conducted separate interviews with historians, tenants and architects working or living in the Complex in order to obtain further data about the transformation process of most of the dwellings into other uses. Students also carried out a library search and literature review of all available references on the history and background of the Complex house.

For each house sample, students developed floor plans, sections and elevations based on available data, aerial photographs, measured drawings and photographs. Out of these orthogonal drawings, students made a balsa wood scaled model of each sample.

The, three, sample house plans and sections were quite useful to the groups doing the entire Complex, since they were used to verify data obtained from aerial photographs and digital site layouts and were replicated wherever the same house type existed. A modified and up-to-date site plan and a longitudinal section for the entire Complex was drawn by students, indicating the original design as well as latest additions and alterations made to the dwellings. Students then made a balsa wood scaled site model for the whole Complex.

Students compiled a large number of photos depicting main and secondary features of the Complex, which cannot be seen on either orthogonal drawings or scaled models. These included façade details such as windows and doors types and patterns and woodwork details in balconies, screens and cantilevers. They also included gateway, wall and parapet details, as well as stucco and terrazzo ornamentation and other architectural elements. Photos showed colour, and texture of the houses in the Complex, of the walls, doors, windows, and all other architectural elements. They also showed the current modifications and alterations resulted from the change of use of most houses, such as signs, paving, external furniture and landscape.

THE OUTCOME

The students' final submission included scaled drawings of sample houses and the entire Complex as well as scaled models, forming the basis for the formal analysis of the house types and the Complex. This formal analysis carried out by students was quite informative. As Ching indicates (Ching 1996, 56) architectural form is the point of contact between mass and space and that through the manipulation of forms one can inject a quality or spirit that articulates space. Students embarked on a form analysis of the Behbehani Complex based on principles introduced by Ching 1996, which mainly explains any form in relation to the transformation process of primary shapes or solids.

Based on the plan analysis of the reconstruction of the Behbehani Complex, students found that there were only three main types of courtyard houses repeated throughout the Complex and in some cases with minor variations. They also found that the whole Complex forms, in itself a courtyard arrangement that shares similar proportions of width and depth with the average individual house. Although it was built on stages and grew to its current state incrementally, as the historical search proves, the Complex followed a courtyard model in its growth.

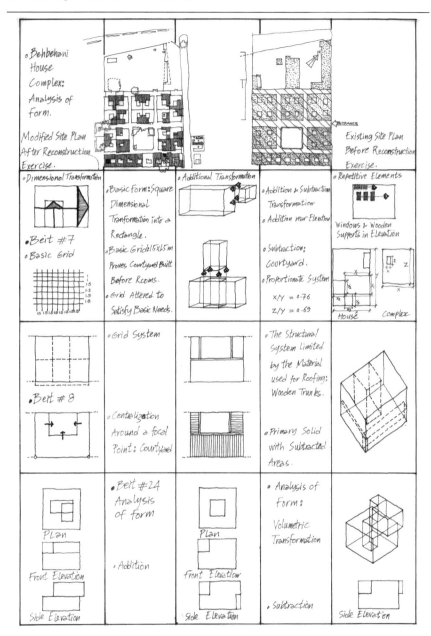

Figure 02: A Sample of Students' Analysis of the Form for the Behbehani Complex, Kuwait.

Variations were found among students who analysed the sample houses. They brought about different attributions to the ways in which similar plan forms had transformed from the primary shapes. These ranged from dimensional transformation of a square into rectangle for both the house and the court, to subtractive transformation of interlocking rectangles from a main rectangle. Students also found that there was an additive transformation in the façades of sample houses as well as repetitive transformation in the form of the wooden cantilevers and the windows. There was similar analysis of room arrangements around the house courtyard and of the housing units' arrangements around the Complex courtyard.

This kind of geometric analysis of underlying structures or the system of settings of the vernacular architecture of Behbehani Complex surprised the students. It also made it possible for them to classify this *type* of vernacular architecture and to compare it, on a geometric basis, with other architectural types. As indicated by (Habraken 1983, 164), this approach may help students to be equipped for a more culturally responsive design approach.

Someday we must be better equipped to chart the mutations and variations of vernacular species throughout the history of human settlements, or at least be able to indicate a way of engaging in such a task and be able to suggest taxonomy of what can be discovered. (Habraken 1983, 164) Based on the previous analysis, students made the connection between the geometric system of settings and the cultural expressions of local inhabitants. They started to *see* the association between the form of space and inhabitants' lifestyle and use patterns studied earlier. In other words, they established a tangible relationship or link between tectonic expressions and cultural expressions. Students also noted that the sample houses, despite having changed use, still maintain the uniqueness and local identity, which proves the ingenuity of local vernacular architecture.

REFLECTIONS ON PEDAGOGICAL APPROACHES TO DESIGN STUDIO

The design studio exercise outlined above attempted to introduce students to local architectural heritage in order to learn some lessons that could be useful in their future designs. In this exercise the design studio instructor proposed not merely a project but a process by which a design solution can be accomplished. Similar experiments were reported in the design studio at the American University in Sharja, UAE. As (Nay 2001, 38) explains:

'A number of approaches to design studio pedagogy for knowledge – content were outlined by (Bar-Eli and Oxman 1998, 314). These are the theoretical, methodological, technological, socio-cultural, pragmatic-integrative, and design as thinking approaches.'

The reconstruction exercise can be classified under several headings: (i) the theoretical, methodological, and socio-cultural pedagogical approaches to design studio, (ii) where students can develop a new formal language on the basis of experimentation and criticism,

(iii) where the methodology and analysis process of design becomes the main knowledge-content of the studio, and (iv) where the main design inquiry aims to establish the relationship between architecture and local community and the region, as well as the relationship to the cultural and social context. These aspects dictate the nature of the design projects and form an integral part of the design process. Students should demonstrate an awareness of cultural and environmental issues affecting architecture and should be able to respond to them in their design. Response to cultural and social issues becomes the main factor in the design process.

The reconstruction exercise aims to provide students with a *tool* that facilitates the process of study and analysis of vernacular architecture. It provides an educational model that enables students to experience the design process of vernacular architecture. An educational model that allows students to put themselves in the place of the initial designers to experience at first hand the rationale behind their designs. Trying new models in design studio pedagogy is encouraged, following Usta et al. 1998 who argue that in architectural education new models and approaches must be tried. Instead of functional problems, approaches that can develop students' creativeness must be tried.

Instead of conventional techniques to create space, which is the basic element of architectural design, expressive techniques performed with three-dimensional models, graphics, and various abstraction techniques could be used. (Usta et al. 1998, 342) The idea is not to imitate successful traditional and vernacular house designs, since this will merely be copying from a nostalgic past. Instead the aim is to learn from these designs in a way that helps students to develop contemporary designs that are loaded with traditional values at essence. Students' designs that address local lifestyle and modern technology, vernacular and contemporary architectural traditions and aspirations, as well as history and the future are encouraged.

In the reconstruction exercise students attempted to find out what makes the Behbehani Complex unique and what makes each of its houses unique. They strive to find out how the local culture of the people and area is reflected in the design, rather than the mere architectural response to climatic and economic conditions. So instead of the common practice of reworking of traditional cultural architectural elements, treatments, motifs, and prototypes in contemporary architecture, they might use the cultural design values, concepts, philosophies, approaches, and cultural specifics that led to the creation of the admired traditional architecture.

The importance of the reconstruction exercise from an educational perspective stems from the fact that it complements in practical terms the theoretical study of the effect of cultural difference in architecture. As Buchanan 1992, explains the opposition between theory and practice, art and technology may be traversed by making the practical exploration of design meaningful and intelligent in the context of production in a technological culture. Therefore, this exercise seeks to outline strategies that preserve the Teaching a design studio that based its design investigations on the analysis of a traditional courtyard house in the United Arab Emirates. Students were led through site visits and documentation of this courtyard house, and then asked to discuss and transfer the lessons they had learned through a contemporary design project. (Nay 2001, 38) Content and methodology of the design studio varies a great deal among schools and instructors although it represents the core of the architectural curriculum. As Bar Eli and Oxman 1998 denote, current research into the pedagogy of design studio indicate the multiplicity of content and methods and a lack of consensus regarding educational objectives and the required profile of knowledge to be conveyed.

CONCLUSION

Traditional vernacular architecture contains a rich source of inspiration for students to draw upon. Through deeper analysis of its components, students can arrive at a better understanding of its design values and outline the underlying structures and system of settings imbedded in its buildings. As Rapoport indicates (Rapoport 1990, 298) walking through vernacular architecture helps in considering the nature of dwellings, the origins of built environments, the meaning of privacy, the equivalence of apparently diverse urban forms, the energy efficiency of settlements, and how meaning is communicated by settings.

Prominent architectural anthropologists like Egenter argue (Egenter 1992, 91) that vernacular architecture can teach us to think about the evolution of architecture right from the very beginning of building. The reconstruction exercise outlined in this paper present an attempt to analyze traditional vernacular architecture. An attempt that uses a geometric analytical approach in formal analysis. As Norberg-Schulz explains (Norberg-Schulz 1984, 13) geometric modes of organization only develop later in life to serve particular purposes, and may in general be understood as a more "precise" definition of the basic topological structures.

Egenter has also suggested (Egenter 1992, 93) that geometry is an expression of primitivity, stressing the importance of the reconstruction of vernacular architecture in understanding its origins. The cumulative result of the reconstruction exercise was an increased awareness of the local architectural heritage and the environmentally and culturally relevant courtyard house prototype. Most design educators do not normally get involved in debates about the formulation of valuable studio models (Bar-Eli and Oxman 1998, 318). The reconstruction exercise presents an attempt of a design educator to get involved in that debate. Since we are likely to find ourselves producing a virtual model or an image of the architectural object rather than the architectural object itself, as (Mazouz 1998, 326) argues, it was a useful educational lesson for students to learn how to reconstruct an architectural object for analysis purposes. The exercise demonstrates a practical way to comprehend the effect of cultural difference in the design process, in the hope that future generations of architects will take this into account and produce culturally responsive buildings of a certain character fusing old and new, local and universal.

BIBLIOGRAPHY

Al-Rashoud, C.F. 1995. *Kuwait Kaleidoscope*. Kuwait: The Kuwait Bookshop Co. Ltd.

Bar-Eli S. and Oxman R. 1998. The Architectural Design Studio: Current Trends and Future Directions. *Forum II: Architectural Education for the 3rd Millennium*. Turkish Republic of Northern Cyprus: Eastern Mediterranean University, Faculty of Architecture: 311–320.

Buchanan, R., 1992. Wicked Problems in Design Thinking. *Design Issues* 8 no. 2: 5-21.

Ching, F.D.K. 1996. *Architecture: Form, Space and Order*. 2nd ed. New York: Van Nostrand Reinhold.

Correa, Charles, 1994. Vistas. *Architecture for Islamic Societies Today*. James Steele (ed.) London: Academy Edition.

Egenter Nold. 1992. *The Present Relevance of the Primitive Architecture*. Architectural Anthropology: Research Series. vol. 1 Switzerland: Structura Mundi Editions.

Habraken, J. 1983. *Transformations of the Site*. Massachusetts: Awater Press.

Lim J., 1998. Abstract: The Designer's Tool Kit. *Forum II: Architectural Education for the 3rd Millennium*. Turkish Republic of Northern Cyprus: Eastern Mediterranean University, Faculty of Architecture: 355–366.

Mazouz, S. and Arrouf, A., 1998. Towards a Project Oriented Teaching of Architecture. *Forum II: Architectural Education for the 3rd Millennium*. Turkish Republic of Northern Cyprus: Eastern Mediterranean University, Faculty of Architecture: 321-328.

Nay, E. M., 2001. A Case Study in Design Education in the Gulf – The Courtyard Prototype. *Open House International* 26 no. 4: 38-45.

Norberg-Schulz, C. 1984. *Genius Loci: Towards a Phenomenology of Architecture*. New York: Rizzoli.

Rapoport, A. 1990. *History and Precedent in Environmental Design*. New York: Plenum. Topalian, Lucia. Resident, Behbehani House Complex. Students interviews. 21 November 2001.

Usta, A., and Usta, G. 1998. Sustainability of tradition in Architectural Education. *Forum II: Architectural Education for the 3rd Millennium*. Turkish Republic of Northern Cyprus: Eastern Mediterranean University, Faculty of Architecture.

South Asian Ethnoscapes: the changing cultural landscapes of British cities

Noha Nasser

INTRODUCTION

All cities have now become part of the global network society, which is dominated by flows of information, images, people, capital, technology and goods. This phenomenon has had major socio-economic and cultural ramifications in which postcolonial cultures are displaced from their territorial fixedness, manifesting themselves in a multiplicity of sites, processes, structures within the urban landscapes of British cities. In this process of de-territorialisation and re-territorialisation, British neighbourhoods are experiencing major changes as a result of these flows of migration or 'ethnoscapes' (Appadurai, 1996:3) emerging from the process of de-colonisation, which has brought a considerable influx of migrants from the Indian subcontinent.

As they have settled, South Asians have adapted, utilized and given new meanings to the built forms of an established British urban tradition. Thus, South Asian culture has undergone a transformation in which everyday practice, social processes, relationships, experiences and understandings have been negotiated in the new context (Massey, 1993; Ashcroft, 2001). These are all part of what Bourdieu (1977) terms *habitus,* as a system of dispositions. The term demonstrates the extent to which 'place' may be seen to be a 'practice' rather than a visual, geographic or topographic location - a process of transformation, by which place is either 'reclaimed' or 're-inscribed' as a network of actions, practices and relationships (Ashcroft, 2001). These various forms of culture practices are further shaped by operations of globalisation (transnationalism) and relations of power in given historical conditions and in particular locales (Wolff, 1997; Gupta and Ferguson, 1999; Smith, 2001).

The engagement of South Asians with British multiculturalism has been a context of inherent contestation of identity. Modelled on Britain's colonial experience, multiculturalism has been established as a recognition of the presence of postcolonial cultures and an attempt to subsume this plurality of cultures within a framework of a national identity. Premised on fixed notions of 'cultural difference' and 'otherness', such imperial constructs have given rise to spatially segregated and radicalized geographies of disadvantage in British cities (Jacobs, 1996). However, the spaces of British cities have also become sites of inter-cultural encounters that destabilise these imperial arrangements, in the process constituting political South Asian identities in resistance to homogenising tendencies. According to Ashcroft (2001:14) 'the most sustained, far-reaching and effective interpretation of resistance has been 'resistance to absorption', the appropriation and transformation of dominant technologies for the purpose of re-inscribing and representing postcolonial cultural identity'. Indeed, the various ways South Asians have adapted and transformed British built forms, as well as created new cultural forms within British cities, and within defined regimes of multiculturalism, offers a fascinating example of 'resistance'. In what follows, a number of examples of the South Asian *habitus* and representation of religious buildings in major British cities are examined, highlighting the emergence of the temple-come-community centre, combining ritual practices with social-based formations.

SOUTH ASIAN COMMUNITIES IN BRITAIN

The heterogeneity of the mélange of South Asians is reflected in the different histories, cultural traditions, social classes and methods of insertions into Britain. Thus, group solidarities are multivalent, constructed around one or more identities such as Bangladeshi, Pakistani, Indian, or ethnic such as Gujarati, Punjabi, Sylheti, or various sects of Islam, Hinduism and Sikhism. These internal divisions however do not necessarily mean that the South Asian community lacks cohesion, but rather that it should be viewed as a political project formed around various solidarities and themes invoked at particular times (Al Sayyad, 2001). This complex geography of identities is activated within particular conditions and circumstances and for particular purposes, as shown in a study by Werbner (2002) on Pakistani Muslims in Manchester, where she describes the 'weaving' together of different types of identity – moral, political and aesthetic (the Muslim, the Pakistani, and the South Asian) - which has created a powerful grass-roots basis for ethnic mobilisation. The various origins of identity, albeit the nation, ethnic origin, faith, sect or even the religious movement has manifested itself in the establishment of places of worship in Britain and the adoption of distinct symbolism and imagery as a display of assertiveness towards the community at large, amongst competing South Asian communities, or amongst competing intra and inter-faith communities. But at the same time, and as a result of a narrow understanding of 'culture' in British multicultural discourse, South Asian communities have sometimes opted for a constructed and recentralised notion of identity as a means of gaining greater control over their new 'home'. This compromise is not necessarily negative, but rather is one way in which the incoming community can articulate a sense of self in new ways, such as providing new arenas for the elaboration of tradition and opening up new economic opportunities (Jacobs, 1996).

CLAIMING A SOUTH ASIAN SPACE IN THE CITY

The first significant settlement of South-Asians was by mainly male workers who had come to Britain for economic betterment but with intent to return (Rex and Moore, 1967; Dahya, 1974). However, the hiatus between the passing of restrictions in immigration laws and their implementation in the mid-1960s saw a sharp rise in numbers of migrants choosing to remain in Britain. As a result, a substantial rise in the sponsorship of village kin and the settlement of migrant families occurred. A third wave of migration took place in the 1970s as African Asians sought refuge from political unrest in Uganda, Kenya and other African countries (Slater, 1996).

At the time of settlement of large numbers of South Asians in Greater London and in the industrial cities of the Midlands, West Yorkshire, and Lancashire, an out-movement of the

British middle-class from the industrial inner and middle-ring neighbourhoods to the outer suburbs was already underway (Whitehand and Carr, 2001). This movement left a significant percentage of the industrial built heritage largely redundant and open to adaptation, conversion and transformation by the new settlers. Simultaneously, the increasing secularisation of British society left many of the picturesque churches available for appropriation. Thus, it was largely the industrial urban heritage that the South Asian communities inherited.

Settlement first took place in spatially defined areas within the major industrial cities corresponding to the late-Victorian and Edwardian (1875-1918) inner and middle-ring neighbourhoods. Racialised housing policies limited choices in the housing market to these localised parts of British cities. Some have argued that a combination of racial politics, discriminatory practices, policies, and labour exploitation were ways of maintaining the spatial segregation of the 'other' (Rex, and Moore, 1967); Peach, 1975; Smith, 1989; Boal, 2000). The highly regular and well-differentiated layout of the industrial urban landscape, characterised by regular streets, long street blocks, standardised plot sizes and repetitive two storey terraces, formed a morphological frame governing urban change (Figure 01). Notwithstanding, these neighbourhoods offered a number of advantages for the early settlers. First, much of the terraced housing stock was vacant; therefore it was both cheap and non-competitive, with the added advantage of being capable of absorbing large numbers of male workers. Second, the High Street, a major thoroughfare of commercial ribbon development connecting the neighbourhoods to the city centre, made these areas readily accessible to the central business, commercial and industrial districts for employment opportunities.

Figure 01: Aerial view of Sparkhill, Birmingham (1950) showing highly regular and well-differentiated layout of the industrial urban landscape (Courtesy Birmingham Central Library Archive Unit).

It was around these established urban nuclei, that South Asian landlords began to establish a strong transnational network through the *biradari,* extended kinship and village ties.

They sponsored fellow villagers and lodged them in their homes shaping a process of chain migration which continued to influence patterns of settlement within specific geographies in British industrial cities. This form of spatialized *biradari*-based social organization had its benefits; it created an environment of social welfare and cohesion in an antagonistic environment; and it fostered the perpetuation of traditional norms, values, and beliefs amongst the new comers (Peach, 2000).

With the arrival of families from the mid-1960s, the village-kin group, as a residential unit, began to ramify into nuclear households of owner-occupied properties in close proximity (Dahya, 1974). Peach (2000) has shown that through social processes of intermarriage and proximity the persistence and stability of the South Asian cultural group has been able to accommodate differences (Shaw, 2000). By the 1980s, however, a combination of natural increase and a new wave of migration marked a sharp rise in the number of South Asians.

This period is characterised by the settlement of the outer suburbs, but nevertheless still maintaining close social ties with local and transnational South Asian *biradari* (Shaw, 2000). Indeed, close proximity to Asian shops, the mosque, good schools and transport has shown to be a primary factor for the stability of the social group in particular areas of the city (Bowes, Dar, and Sim, 2000). Thus within these social geographies and urban morphologies, new relationships were spatialized from the most personal and intimate of relationships – the family group – to those based on religion, commerce, education and politics. This paper focuses on the development of places of worship; the evolution of their architectural representation set against the changing ideologies of British multiculturalism, and subsequently the planning system.

THE HOUSE-TEMPLE

The settlement of families in the mid 1960s created a major impetus for urban transformation. Earlier attempts by mainly male congregations to consecrate space for ritual were relatively few and widely dispersed. In many cases these spaces were informal and temporary making it difficult to trace their origins. Nevertheless, the first mosques are known to have been founded in Liverpool (1887), Woking (1889) and London (1924); the earliest officially listed Sikh gurdwaras were located in Liverpool and Newcastle (1958); and two Hindu Mandirs are believed to have first opened in Birmingham and Coventry (1967) (Naylor and Ryan, forthcoming).

Large-scale conversion of space for religious and cultural use, however, accompanied the settlement of women and children and the sudden increase in size of congregations. The need to establish places in which cultural values and religious practice could be perpetuated became the primary concern. The difficulty in securing financial support from local authorities and Community Relations Councils (CRCs) placed the onus on the communities themselves to raise sufficient funds to purchase property for their use. As a result, the relatively affordable terrace house offered the most readily appropriated vernacular building type. As a space, the building was capable of internal modification and integration of religious and educational functions. Modifications included the demolition of internal walls and additions to the rear.

The adaptability of space for religious worship is demonstrated in the case of one of Bradford's first mosques established by the Bengali Twaquila Islamic Society in 1968. Ethnic divisions during the 1960s had divided the initially cohesive Muslim community into a number of smaller community mosques set up by Deobandi Pathan and Punjabis from Chhachh, Deobandi Gujeratis from Surat, Barelvi Jamiyyat Tabligh ul-Islam, and the Bengalis (McLoughlin, 2003). Therefore, these various factions represented the different Muslim South Asian identities emerging within Bradford's cultural landscape. In the case of the Bengali Twaquila Islamic Society, two adjacent terrace houses had been purchased on Cornwall Road and converted into a house mosque in response to the growing congregation and the need to provide Islamic teaching to children. Barton (1986: 88-9) describes how the layouts of the houses have been adapted:

'The houses are Victorian, with two rooms on the ground floor, two on the first, an attic and a cellar. The wall dividing the two dwellings has been retained, but the partitions within each house have been removed, thus creating two large rooms, with connecting doors, on the ground and first floors of the mosque. The front door of one house is the entrance …The ground floor rooms are used for children's classes and for prayers when there is an overflow from the rooms above…The first-floor rooms are used daily for prayers…The walls are bare apart from one or two calendars, the timetable for daily prayers…In the corner of the inner room stands a purely symbolic carpeted minbar [pulpit], of three steps, which is also the only indication of the qibla, the direction faced in prayer….The cellar has been converted into a kitchen and place for performing wudu, the ablutions, before the prayers. There is a toilet outside, at the back of the building. The attics, comprising two bed-sitting rooms, and a small kitchen, are used as accommodation for the imam [leader in prayer] or others.'

The modifications of the space for religious practices stem from a need to create one space for congregation as well as imbue new meanings to these spaces. In the process of conversion, meanings were inscribed in the space by changing its uses as well as re-using traditional symbolic elements of the mosque, such as the pulpit and prayer niche. Thus by modifying the traditional layout of the terrace house, Muslims were differentiating a space for themselves and their needs. But the conversion of the house mosque did not remain uncontested. On the contrary, many experienced strong opposition by neighbours and local authorities resulting in the wide-spread issuance of enforcement notices on the grounds that these changes constituted 'material change of use' as accorded in Town and Country Planning legislation, as well as presented a 'loss of amenity' to neighbours (Gale, and Naylor, 2002; Barton, 1986). The antagonistic nature of inter-ethnic relations at this time had a direct influence on the outward expression of all appropriated buildings, residential or otherwise. Modifications were restrained to interiors with no extravagant indication of the use of the building nor the application of religious symbols or motifs except the odd banner or sign aimed primarily at signifying a place of worship to the faith community.

The objective was to ensure the building was 'under communicating' its function and blending in with its surroundings.

In the late 1970s, the constraints on South Asian communities to cater for their religious needs were recognized by a number of city councils. In a welcome change of policy, the city councils decided to permit house-temple conversions (Gale and Naylor, 2002). Growing congregations were also placing increasing pressure on the need for extensions. In some cases, planning authorities permitted extensions to the rear of the property, despite the substantial increase in the densification of the plot. More recently, the growing stature of temple communities has prompted new build on adjacent sites. The shift in multicultural policy in the 1980s has been accompanied by an assertiveness in the representation of a South Asian identity. Purpose-built temples are designed with symbols such as a dome, *chhatri, shikhara,* minaret and arches, whereas some of the house-temples have undergone a remodelling of the façade as in the case of the Wimbledon Mosque (Figure 02). Many house-temples today serve as small-scale neighbourhood temples providing religious classes for children and adult training courses (Nasser, forthcoming *a*).

Figure 02: Wimbledon Mosque, London, is a house mosque in which the façade has been remodelled.

ADAPTIVE RE-USE OF THE INDUSTRIAL BUILT HERITAGE

In the late 1960s expanding congregations were outgrowing the existing residential spaces which they had appropriated. In the built environment, this created an impetus for claiming more territory and visibly shaping a South Asian presence in the city. There were a number of initial conceptions to construct purpose-built places of worship, such as the Central Mosque in Birmingham, or the Hindu Shikharbaddha Mandir in northwest London, but varying obstacles of land acquisition, construction costs and planning permission slowed down their realisation. Communities turned to the acquisition of the more commodious buildings of the industrial heritage which had fallen into disuse. In particular, churches, warehouses, schools, community halls, even cinemas and clubs were building types that were converted to cultural use. The most convenient to adapt were those buildings that had a previous religious use resulting in the widespread conversion of churches, synagogues and other building types of religious affiliation by these communities. Any other building type required engagement with the formal processes of planning application. The antagonistic nature of inter-ethnic relations at this time had a direct influence on the outward expression of all appropriated buildings, residential or otherwise. Modifications were restrained to interiors with no extravagant indication of the use of the building nor the application of religious symbols or motifs except the odd banner or sign aimed primarily at signifying a place of worship to the faith community. The objective was to ensure the building was 'undercommunicating' its function and blending in with its surroundings. The most significant aspect of the process of diversification was the emergence of the temple-come-community centre which was specifically intended to provide additional religious, educational and social functions such as a conference hall, library, kitchen and welfare services. For the most part, the rehabilitation of redundant buildings was an important means of tackling the functional and physical obsolescence of the industrial built heritage, imbuing these buildings with new cultural and functional meaning.

One example is the Presbyterian Church of St. Andrew's on Ealing Road, London, which was adapted to a mosque with adjacent facilities for ablution, and a welfare centre. The church architecture of the period c. 1920 uses a combination of a domed bell tower and a gabled roof over the hall. Visually, the dome, although part of the original design, refers to 'Orientalist' imagery. A display of sacred text above the main arched portal further signify the new use. Internally, however, the main space does not conform to the basic prayer requirement to face Mecca (the *qibla* orientation). Thus worshippers align themselves along prayer lines oblique to the walls of the hall. The re-alignment of the *qibla* has been a common method of accommodating constraints posed by the existing built tradition.

The rehabilitation of structures once attributed to British culture and society has been contentious, particularly amongst conservationists seeking to preserve the heritage of a distinctly 'British nation'. The politicisation of heritage as a means of constructing and redefining 'Britishness' and national identity has evoked wide-spread dissent over the re-use of listed buildings by the Other (Eade, 1996; Jacobs, 1996). In Spitalfields, East London, the declaration of an urban conservation area based on its Georgian heritage in 1969 and the listing of most of the Georgian buildings in 1976, led to a 'managed' displacement of the Bengali-based garment manufacturing industry based on a nostalgic return to its historic, white, English roots (Jacobs, 1996). The revival of nationalist sentiment by conservationist opposition was particularly strong at the time the Bengali community needed to construct an additional floor to the Brick Lane Mosque; an appropriated eighteenth century listed Georgian building. The changes were internal modifications, which did not require planning permission, but 'for many non-Muslims the mosque building was a physical expression of both a local English heritage and a gentrified, Georgian present' (Eade, 1996:220). To overcome the threat to Georgian Spitalfields by the Bengali community, the opposition directed its efforts towards spatially regulating and controlling their presence through a discrete and 'genteel gentrification' of the area (Jacobs, 1996).

THE CREATION OF NEW CULTURAL FORMS

As Britain's minorities began to make in-roads into the political arenas of large conurbations, local authorities began to shift in the 1980s to a more pluralistic model of welfare provision which recognised that life opportunities of ethnicised minorities were adversely affected by notions of 'racial disadvantage'. The assertiveness of ethnicised minorities also led to the conclusion that policies of assimilation in which ethnically marked communities were to erase their identities and histories as a price of admission into the white host society were no longer tenable in a world in which notions of white superiority were increasingly difficult to sustain. The effect of municipal multiculturalism was a provision of financial assistance for ethnically marked communities to engage in cultural activities deriving from their ethnicity. The planning profession also underwent a multicultural conversion, a change marked by the publication of the *Planning for a Multi-Racial Britain* report (RTPI/CRE, 1983) which emphasised that Local and Structural Plans should be sensitive to the development needs of different groups. But the absence of national guidelines has meant that there have been wide-ranging regional variations in the report's adoption (Gale and Naylor, 2002). The ability of some South Asian communities to succeed in their struggle for place is attributed to them becoming sufficiently established and well-organised to negotiate with public bodies on their own terms (Vertovec, 1996; Gale and Naylor, 2002).

With respect to the built environment, an assertiveness of South Asian communities has led to the emergence of distinctive forms of architectural expression and co-opting by some local authorities and national development agencies in matters of finance, land acquisition and the granting of planning permission for new cultural forms. Gale and Naylor (2002), for example, have noted that since the late 1970s Leicester City Council have actively demonstrated their 'positive action initiative' by co-opting the construction of sites of worship such as the Conduit Street Mosque through the sale of land to the Leicester Islamic Centre for quarter of the market value, and by making available local and national grants to the *Jain Samaj* for the establishment of the Jain Centre.

Similarly in Birmingham, the city council made available grants for the refurbishment and conversion of Green Lane mosque (1980) (Figure 03), a listed Victorian public library and swimming bath, to serve as a community centre with a library, offices, prayer hall, school and car park. National development agencies had also by the 1990s come to accept that the establishment of ethnic community projects were desirable forms of urban development, such as the financing of the Gujarat Hindu Society Temple in Preston by English Partnerships and the Millennium Commission (Gale and Naylor, 2002).

The conscious act of remodelling elevations with ornamental features and decorative motifs has been a major development in the metamorphosis of the British urban landscape as a means of redefining the presence of the other. Not only localised community centres

**Figure 03: Green Lane Mosque, Birmingham was converted from a run-down Victorian
Public Library and swimming bath**

in the heart of residential neighbourhoods were undergoing this form of transformation, but more prominent sites as well. In Birmingham, for example, the Soho Road Guru Nanak Nishkam Sewark Jatha, located on a major thoroughfare that winds its way through a Sikh-settled area, was converted from a Polish ex-servicemen club to a gurdwara in 1978. Over the ensuing ten years residential property adjacent to the Club was acquired along with land to the rear, allowing the construction of considerable extensions accommodating educational and social functions. In the early 1990s, the Gurdwara committee made a planning application for the remodelling of the exterior to add a grand entrance surmounted by a dome and other ornamental features. According to Gale (forthcoming), there was little objection by the City Council on aspects of style, which, he argues, reflects the council's growing acceptance of such projects as potential landmarks. Today, the Soho Road Gurdwara is an imposing landmark on the urban landscape (Figure 04). It occupies almost an entire street block and is three storeys high. Many of its features have been inspired from the model of the Golden Temple of Amritsar. The extensive use of three different types of coloured marble on the elevation has been used for embellishment and for delineating prominent features such as the grand entrance, fenestrations, and the parapet. The main building is set back from the street accentuating the impressive three storey deorhi, or grand entrance to the sanctum sanctorum. At the third level of the deorhi, a central projecting window, is framed by arches and crowned by a shallow elliptical cornice. Above the three-storey entrance a large ribbed central dome creates a strong visual feature, topped by an inverted lotus symbol and a golden kal. At the base of the central dome are four smaller cupolas, or chhatris, on turrets, one on either corner. The roofline is defined by a heavily decorated parapet of repeated smaller chhatris and turrets. The overall effect is rather elaborate and by no means discrete, on the contrary, it employs a stylistic vocabulary that is inspired from the Indian subcontinent and intended to 'over communicate' a Sikh identity in the area.

Figure 04: Soho Road Guru Nanak Nishkam Sewark Jatha Birmingham, from a distance.

The introduction of a repertoire of exotic forms such as the dome, *chhatris*, *shikhara* (bee hive shaped dome), arch and minaret has created a new cultural urban landscape in Britain. The traditionally rectilinear identity of the British skyline dominated by the pointed church spire towering over the highly regular swathe of low rise brick buildings and pitched roofs are today vying with the new addition of distinctly sinuous forms. But to what extent have these forms been accepted as being part of a new British urban landscape? In Preston for example, Gale and Naylor (2002) have demonstrated how the planning process has been the lens by which the creative stylistic expressions of South Asian communities have been 'domesticated' in order to preserve the 'Britishness' of the urban landscape. They describe how a proposal for constructing the Gujarat Hindu Society Temple in a residential neighbourhood received strong opposition from locals on the grounds that the building was 'alien' to the area and that it would generate large volumes of traffic. Planning permission was granted; however, under the condition that the building had to comply with the character of the area in terms of scale, materials and style of the surrounding terrace houses. Faced with the challenge, the Gujarat Hindu Society were able to creatively combine local forms with elements from Hindu temple architecture as a 'self-conscious gesture of reconciliation'. In the process, a stylistic hybridity between the two traditions

51

created an innovative fusion of brickwork and slate roofing with a *shikhara* and marble entrance supported on four ornately decorated pillars (Figure 05). Examples of architectural hybridity in new cultural forms can be found across many British cities - the result of negotiations between locality and identity that have been part of the struggle of South Asian communities in expressing their sense of belonging in an urban context (Nasser, forthcoming *b*).

**Figure 05: Gujarat Hindu Society Preston Mandir is a creative combination of local forms
with elements from Hindu temple architecture.**

A particularly stunning example is that of the Edinburgh Central Mosque, which represents a meeting of two rather different traditions; Highland castle architecture inscribed with an 'Islamic' sensibility. The massing of the building suggests its strong Scottish architectural language articulated by the location of four stone-clad octagonal towers at either corner of the building. The towers are imposing features contributing to the overall fortified look of the building; clad in a stone finish encircled by large Arabic script inlaid in red brick, small slot windows and lead-covered pinnacles. One tower has been used as a base for the minaret, an octagonal stone-clad shaft and abstracted balcony capped with a lead-clad semi-dome. A central *iwan*-like portal frames the entrance, pierced by a series of recessed pointed arches marking a recognisable feature of the 'Islamic' tradition. The *iwan* is also clad in stone adding to the overall heaviness of the building, separated from the two flanking towers by a narrow strip of glazing. The pointed pinnacles of the towers create a disharmony with the curved forms of the domes, creating a language of confusion, an ambivalent aesthetic.

The ambivalence associated with the interpretation of these new cultural forms opens up the debate between 'tradition' and 'modernity' in architectural expression. On the one hand, the indiscriminate use of historic or extant design features and models by South Asian communities in their cultural buildings reflects an emotional tie with the past and the meanings and value that these architectural conventions ascribe. On the other hand, a more *avant garde* approach attempts to reinterpret various aesthetic themes through exploration based on the setting, form, function, and use of technology, to create a new semblance of architectural identity that does not violate cultural principles. The Shri Swaminarayan Mandir in Neasden is a stunning example of the former approach, a reproduction of a traditional Hindu temple, literally imported from India and designed according to ancient Hindu *Shilpashastras* (texts on architecture). Set in a residential suburb, the mandir and adjoining cultural complex occupy a 3.85 acre site at the heart of a London suburb. According to Naylor and Ryan (forthcoming) the proposal to construct the mandir was marked with conflict and controversy as local residents 'developed new senses of territoriality' to what they considered to be a visual intrusion and invasion of a predominantly white British space. Interestingly, planning permission was granted as the construction of the temple commenced in India. The temple was carved out of limestone and marble by 1,500 sculptors then shipped to London in massive pieces for assembling. Visually, the temple is a stunning example of the grandeur of north Indian religious architecture characterised by a spectacular assemblage of seven *Shikharas* made up of layer upon layer of architectural elements such as *kapotas* and *gavaksas*, and fluted domes, three over the *gopurams* (entrance) and one over the sanctum sanctorum (Figure 06). The temple is raised on a high platform to add to its grandeur. The use of traditional building techniques like the post and beam and corbelled vaulting, pilasters, and brackets, are heavily embellished and intricately ornamented with interlaced forms and carvings of deities. The adjacent cultural centre stands in stylistic contrast using the more domestic Haveli aesthetic. An intricately carved two-storey timber gallery defines the entrance. It is decorated using elaborate traditional wooden craftsmanship. A series of timber posts, beams and ornate brackets support an arched gallery above. The ground floor of the cultural complex is finished in white marble in contrast to the brick-red coloured plaster finish of the top floor. Here, a series of bays are defined by, exposed timber posts, beams and brackets supporting a timber overhanging canopy. Observed within the urban landscape, the idiosyncratic treatment and usage of architectural features, forms, materials and ornamentation in the Shri Swaminarayan Mandir in Neasden bears no relationship to neither time nor context, but evokes a strong visual image to the users and to non-Hindus alike.

A more modernist, *avant-garde* approach, on the other hand, has been adopted in the Glasgow mosque. In this building, first opened in 1984, the architects have made an attempt to move away from a strictly traditional approach by exploring the use of modern technology, materials, and abstraction as a means of reinterpreting various aesthetic themes associated with religious architecture in the Muslim world. The steel frame structure of the building has allowed the external fabric to be articulated freely between brick-clad solids and glazed voids. Light penetrates into the interior through a glazed dome and a series of brick-clad buttresses that lean outwards from the building freeing the sides. The buttresses function to control the intimacy of the building's internal functions whilst still allowing light in. The dome is an outstanding feature of the building, created through the fusion of a traditional architectural element with modern materials. It is raised on a metal drum, angular and onion-shaped in form, with tinted glass panels. The main entrance, however, is a protruding light-frame brick *iwan*-like portal framed by a pointed arch that tapers out as it meets the ground. From the ceiling of the portal hang large symbolic *muqarnas* or stalactite structures that can be seen from the outside. A one-storey arcade of pointed archways adjoins the main building from which springs a minaret. The form of the minaret is both simple and abstract, functioning as a spatial landmark. The Glasgow mosque still communicates its function through the use of abstract reinterpretations of 'Muslim' imagery and symbolism but at the same time it employs local materials and modern technology to arrive to an innovative expression.

Figure 06: Shri Swaminarayan Mandir in Neasden, London

CONCLUSION

This paper has demonstrated that South Asians in Britain have been able to culturally reproduce themselves through the construction of new social relations and everyday practices. Indeed, South Asians have re-territorialised substantial spaces within British cities and neighbourhoods establishing temples as well as homes, commercial areas, and other cultural, political, and social spaces. As part of the place-making process, these new forms of spatialized social relations and practices have been translated into a distinctly South Asian identity constructed in inherently contested contexts. Indeed, South Asian communities have been able to adapt to the local urban tradition and its associated building types in order to attain their social, cultural, economic and physical aspirations. The representation of this identity, manifest in the conversion of built forms and the creation of new cultural forms with strong semiotic meanings, is reflective of a 'resistance' to state-directed projects of assimilation. British assimilationist policies of the 1960s and 1970s had attempted to consume the settler and transform their identities in such a way that they become indistinguishable from the 'host' community. Such policies, however, are belied by the logic of racism which continues to mark the host/immigrant distinction as another variant of the West and the Rest dyad. Notwithstanding, shifts in multicultural policy in the 1980s has been conditioned by shifting positions of power in which South Asian communities have created a dynamic agency of change. This has been influenced by (i) the growth and organisation of South Asian communities from small nationalist groupings to more established diverse sectarian communities with a stronger economic and social position; (ii) the weakening of both Western supremacist discourses and Britain's place within the world. This post-colonial condition makes it more difficult to articulate an unquestioning cultural hierarchy in which white British society is considered to be superior to South Asian settlers; and (iii) the development of British antiracist and multicultural discourses which have influenced the ability of South Asian communities to express themselves in different forms. Within such evolutionary processes of settlement and integration, South Asians will undoubtedly continue to contribute to the changing urban landscapes of British cities. Indeed, these innovative 'ethnoscapes' are common features of the global moment.

BIBLIOGRAPHY

Al Sayyad, N. (2001) 'Prologue. Hybrid Culture/Hybrid urbanism: pandora's Box of the 'Third Place' in N. AlSayyad (ed.) *Hybrid Urbanism. On the identity discourse and the built environment.* Westport, CT: Praeger, pp1-18.

Ashcroft, B. (2001) *Post-Colonial Transformation.* London and New York: Routledge. Barton, S. (1986) *The Bengali Muslims of Bradford.* Monograph series, Community Religions project. University of Leeds, pp. 88-89.

Boal, F. (2000) (ed.) Ethnicity and Housing. Accommodating Differences. Aldershot: Ashgate.

Bourdieu, P. (1977) *Outline of a Theory of Practice.* Trans. Richard Nice. Cambridge: Harvard University Press.

Bowes, A., Dar N., and Sim, D. (2000) 'Housing Preferences and Strategies: an exploration of Pakistani preferences in Glasgow' in F. Boal (ed.) *Ethnicity and Housing. Accommodating Differences.* Aldershot: Ashgate.

Dahya, B. (1974) 'The Nature of Pakistani Ethnicity in Industrial Cities in Britain' in A. Cohen (ed.) *Urban Ethnicity.* London: Tavistock Publications, pp.77-118.

Eade, J. (1996) 'Nationalism, Community, and the Islamisation of Space in London' in B. Metcalf (ed.) *Making Muslim Space in North America and Europe.* Berkeley and Los Angeles: University of California Press, pp. 217-33.

Gale, R.and Naylor, S. (2002) 'Religion, planning and the city. The spatial politics of ethnic minority expression in British cities and towns'. *Ethnicities*, pp. 387-409

Gale, R. (forthcoming) Urban planning and the geography of religion: South Asian faith groups and the planning process in Birmingham, UK. PhD thesis Oxford University.

Gupta A. and Ferguson, J. (1999) "Culture, Power, Place: Ethnography at the End of an Era" in A. Gupta and J. Ferguson (eds) *Culture, Power, Place. Exploration in Critical Anthropology.* Durham and London: Duke University Press, pp. 1-29.

Jacobs, J. (1996) *Edge of Empire. Postcolonialism and the city.* London and New York: Routledge.

Massey, D. (1993) "Power-geometry and a Progressive Sense of Place" in J. Bird, B. Curtis, T. Putnam, G. Robertson, and L. Tickner (eds) *Mapping the Futures: Local Cultures, Global Change.* New York and London: Routledge, pp. 59-69.

McLoughlin, S. (2003) "Muslims and Public Space in Bradford: Conflict, cooperation and Islam as a resource for integration?.

Nasser, N. (forthcoming *a*, 2004) "Borderlands: Br-Asian hybrid urban landscapes" in V. Karla, N. Ali and S. Sayyid (eds) *Postcolonial People.* London: Hurst Books.

Nasser, N. (forthcoming *b*, 2004) 'South Asian Muslims in Britain: expressions of identity in architecture and urbanism' *Journal of Islam and Christian-Muslim Relations.*

Naylor, S. and Ryan, J. (forthcoming 2003) 'Mosques, Temples And Gurdwaras: New Sites Of Religion In Twentieth-Century Britain', in D. Gilbert, D. Matless and B. Short (eds) *Geographies of British Modernity: Space and Society in the Twentieth Century.* Oxford, Blackwell.

Peach, C. (1975) (ed.) *Urban Social Segregation.* London: Longman.

Peach, C. (2000) 'The consequences of segregation' in F. W. Boal (ed.) *Ethnicity and Housing. Accommodating Differences.* Aldershot: Ashgate, pp. 10-23.

Rex J. and Moore R. (1967) *Race, Community and Conflict: A Study of Sparkbrook* London: Oxford University Press.

RTPI/CRE (1983) Planning for a Multi-Racial Britain. London, CRE.

Shaw, A. (2000) *Kinship and Continuity. Pakistani families in Britain.* Amsterdam: Harwood Academic Publishers.

Slater, T. R. (1996) 'Birmingham's Black and South-Asian population' in A. J. Gerrard, and T. R. Slater *Managing a Conurbation: Birmingham and its Region.* Studley: Brewin Books, pp.140-155.

Smith, M. (2001) *Transnational urbanism. Locating Globalization.* Massachusetts and Oxford: Blackwell.

Smith, S. (1989) *The Politics of Race and Residence.* Cambridge: Polity Press,1989.

Vertovec, S. (1996) 'Multiculturalism, Culturalism and Public Incorporation'. *Ethnic and Racial Studies* 19(1), pp. 49-69.

Werbner, P. (2002) *Imagined Diasporas among Manchester Muslims.* Santa Fe, new Mexico: School of American Research Press.

Whitehand, J.W.R and Carr, C. (2001) *Twentieth Century Suburbs: A Morphological Approach.* London: Routledge.

Wolff, J. (1997) "The Global and the Specific: reconciling Conflicting Theories of Culture' in A. King (ed.) *Culture, Globalization and the World-system. Contemporary Conditions for the representation of identity.* Minneapolis: University of Minnesota Press, 161-7, 337-345.

Part Two

Transforming Participation and Community

Sustainable Urban Development: A Case Study of 'The Eldonians' in Liverpool

Karen Leeming

The problems associated with urban development are not just confined to the developing world; in the West cities are seen as a very real problem to local, central and international governments. The increasingly complex patterns of the global economy caused by the fragmentation and geographical relocation of traditional and new industries has led to formerly prosperous regions and cities experiencing accelerated rates of unemployment and population decline. This is creating major stresses within the social fabric of these areas. These stresses are similar to those experienced within Third World cities, namely; poor housing, high crime rates, deteriorated environments, poor health, lack of education and training and few prospects.

In the UK, until the early 1990s, the policies aimed at the regeneration of these de-industrialised areas focused on ideas formulated at the national level concerning the re-training and re-education of the workforce and the enticement of industry back into depressed regions (Allen and Massey, 1988). However, in many de-industrialised regions these policies failed and it was this ineffectuality in dealing with the decline of these areas that has prompted development initiatives that focus on the purely local level (Eisenschitz and Gough, 1993).

During this same period, concern regarding the pollution and degradation of the global environment has come to the fore. World conferences such as the 1992 'Earth Summit' at Rio de Janeiro have highlighted the need for global problems to be tackled at the local level. Globalisation not only has social and economic costs but also environmental costs, and it is through the gradual awareness of these environmental costs that there is "...a growing opinion that we should strive to live our lives more locally, making better use of the human and natural resources that are around us" (Gilchrist, 2000, 149). This need for environmental awareness combined with local development initiatives that tackle economic regeneration in de-industrialising regions has culminated in the - sometimes grudging - acceptance for the need for sustainable urban development. Elliott (1994, 102) considers that successful sustainable urban development has a number of common characteristics that include:

- Housing is also a people's problem;
- The need to build communities;
- The need to organise communities;
- The importance of outsiders;
- The importance of external funding.

(Barton 2000, 52) also emphasises the need to strengthen communities in order to facilitate a number of protective environmental objectives including:

- Reducing the need to travel;
- Reduce car reliance;
- Promotion of local heritage and distinctiveness;
- Reduce fear of violence;
- Accessible jobs for those tied to the locality;
- Facilitate social networks;
- Increase user/citizen control;
- Management of decentralised systems.

Since the beginning of the 1990s, the importance of stable local communities has been reflected in many of the UK's urban policy initiatives and is now a readily identifiable goal of many local authority urban regeneration initiatives, however, this was not always the case as the following case study exemplifies.

HISTORICAL CONTEXT

The hub of Merseyside is the city and port of Liverpool, and the inner city problems that have been identified by so many authors (see, for example, Cox, 1973; Harloe, 1977; Harvey, 1973; Herbert and Smith, 1989) have been with this city for at least a century. The idiosyncratic culture of working-class Merseyside and its particular social problems rest on the fact that the whole economy of Liverpool has been based on and around the port.

Although to non-residents of the UK, Liverpool is probably best known for producing the Beatles pop group in the 1960s its history began a long time before that and until the turn of the twentieth century it was the '...western gateway to the World' (Lane, 1997, 1) with an economy and infrastructure that was based almost completely on the movement and storage of goods. The port had developed rapidly because of its geographical position - it was in the ideal position for the industries of Lancashire and Cheshire to export their manufactured goods from and, for the importation of raw materials from the New World and the Colonies (Meegan, 1995; Middleton, 1991). Liverpool was also a primary port for those embarking on emigration to the New World, which encouraged massive migration into the city and its environs from the rest of the country and from Europe - Ireland in particular (Lane, 1997; Meegan, 1995; Prestwich and Taylor, 1990). This meant that not only did the port expand rapidly, but so did the population - from 4,240 in 1700 to 222,954 by 1841 (Simey, 1992). The sheer pressure of these numbers ensured that the majority of the populace lived in appalling conditions as the whole social infrastructure was placed under intolerable stress. Additionally, as many of the immigrants were used to extreme poverty and were willing to work for a pittance this ensured they remained in poverty whilst the merchants became richer, further inflaming antagonism towards both new immigrants and the employers (Smithers, 1825). High birth rates amongst the immigrants plus potential emigrants to the Americas ensured that the population grew at a rate of over 20 per cent per decade (Lawton, 1986).

The problems associated with a large, economically poor population became compounded after the First World War due to the global restructuring of trade. The war had led to a scarcity of manufactures for export, which led to the importing countries initiating indigenous industries to replace the lack. After the war, these indigenous industries flourished and the need for imported manufactures radically decreased which led to less trade for the Port of Liverpool, massive recession and severe unemployment throughout the 1920s (although there was an improvement in the last few years of the decade) and catastrophic unemployment in the 1930s which lasted longer than elsewhere in the country (Poole, 1960).

The port's economy rallied during the Second World War as trade focused on the Atlantic in attempts to break the shipping embargoes in the Channel. However, this renaissance attracted the attention of Germany's bombers whose raids caused massive infrastructural damage around the docks, compounding the already severe housing shortages. For example, during 'May Week' in 1941, the city was bombed continuously for seven nights in succession destroying over 6,000 houses and damaging another 125,000 (Middleton, 1991). This led to the 1944 Merseyside Plan which was devised in an attempt to revitalise the area by moving both population and industry away from the city centre core - building on an exodus that had started several decades before (Lawton, 1982). This was achieved by slum clearance and then decanting large sectors of the population into poorly planned and poorly built municipal housing estates in the suburbs. This may have partly solved the housing problems, but it just meant that the existing social and economic problems of these people were removed from the city, and then exacerbated by physical and social isolation created by poor transport and the rupturing of family ties - problems that are prevalent in many of these estates today.

After the Second World War, the port continued its decline. The focus on port-based activities had meant that, the provision of employment was dominated by large firms who generally employed casual, semi- and unskilled workers (Cornfoot, 1982; Lane, 1997). This meant that the region had not historically built up a base of skilled manufacturing workers who could readily switch into other areas of growth. In addition, those working outside port-based activities tended to be employed in distributive and food processing trades, which were attractive to national and multinational companies looking to expand their holdings. Once absorbed, these industries became particularly vulnerable to rationalisation and centralisation, which led to closures, and many job losses (Parkinson, 1990). This 'branch plant' economy extended also to the small manufacturing base of the region and was exacerbated by the growth of the car industry during the 1960s. This growth initially helped to ease the immediate problems but reinforced the dependence on external employers who were not accountable to local economic conditions, but to national and international markets (Lloyd, 1979). One of the major 'problems' with Merseyside, and Liverpool in particular, is that, the manufacturing sector is dominated by non-locally controlled employers; for example, by the 1980s only one of the 20 largest employers in the region was locally controlled (Parkinson, 1985). These companies are subject to strategies that are formulated with international and national trends in mind, strategies that have no local affiliations or accountability, and it leaves these plants extremely vulnerable to rationalisation measures, which can disproportionately affect their suppliers. These are usually small locally based firms dependent on the larger companies for the majority of their business. For example, from 1979 to 1984, Liverpool lost 40,000 manufacturing jobs, almost half of those in the sector, in this manner (Parkinson, 1985).

THE ELDONIANS

One area that felt the full brunt of all of these problems and changes within the city is Vauxhall. Vauxhall is in the north of the city and the community is well over one hundred and fifty years old. It was founded by Irish Catholic immigrants and the majority of the male population worked either on the nearby docks or in dock related industries which meant that the closure and continual rationalisation of factories in the area as well as the changes in cargo handling and the resultant job losses impacted heavily in the area. The high unemployment levels in the area were also matched by shoddy housing, which consisted of generally poor quality, high-density tenements that, in many cases, were in a bad state of repair. The social and economic conditions of the area were so poor that, until recently, the area had one of the highest infant mortality rates in Western Europe.

THE POLITICAL CONTEXT

Politics in Liverpool are important and they are key to the case study area. Unlike the majority of large UK cities, the Labour party did not take power in Liverpool until the mid 1950s, and even then they had to share control of the city with the Conservative party until the mid 1970s (Parkinson, 1985). Historically, this was due to there being large numbers of unskilled and semi-skilled workers, an absence of unions for skilled craft workers and religious tensions between the working class Protestants and Irish Catholics. These divisions combined with a tradition of electing right-wing Members of Parliament whilst the local constituencies were more left-wing meant that there was constant ideological conflict within the Labour party (Parkinson, 1985, 1990), which meant that its hold on the city was slight. This hold was broken, in the 1973 elections, by the Liberal party, who emerged unexpectedly by taking seats from Labour and the Conservatives. They managed to do this because Labour councillors were seen as being too old and out of touch with their constituents as well as presiding over the inner city clearance that had broken up communities and sent the population into high rise flats in peripheral estates (Parkinson, 1985, 1990). The Liberals made housing their platform in order to retain votes and the 1974 Housing Act gave them the funds to start on their programme. This was to prove to be an important development for the Vauxhall area.

From the middle of the 1960s Vauxhall had been subjected to continual upheaval because of the building of the Kingsway road tunnel and the Liverpool ring road and by 1979 the Liverpool City Council, which was still Liberal, had solidified this upheaval into a planned programme of tenement demolition. The decline of the docks, dock related activities and population meant that there was no need for high density housing in the inner city and so the plan was to demolish the tenements and move the people into peripheral municipal estates. However, although the council was uprooting long-standing communities, it made no attempt to retain those communities on the new estates. People were moved piecemeal, very often many miles away from family, friends and neighbours, which led to the collapse of many supportive social networks.

One group of Vauxhall residents who were centred around the *Our Lady of Eldon Street* church did not want to see the destruction of their community and also wanted to remain in the same area. This initially proved to be a problem as the City Council found it difficult to believe that people would rather stay in the tenement blocks than move to a three bedroomed house with a garden and so demanded proof that this was a community decision rather than the wishes of a few residents. In order to demonstrate this 'proof' a group of residents formed an action team that organised a survey of their 'church' community of Portland Gardens, Eldon Street, Burlington Street and Lime Kiln Lane and they found that approximately 80% of the residents wanted to stay. Armed with this they persuaded the city council to allow them to take control of their own lives by forming a housing co-operative with the council agreeing to provide land, support and to seek funding for them.

The group identified the worst housing as being in Portland Gardens and came up with a plan whereby those residents that wanted to leave would be re-housed by the council elsewhere and then those residents in Portland Gardens would move into the vacant properties. Portland Gardens would then be demolished and replaced by new build housing that would be paid for by the council. When the houses were built they would then be bought from the council and managed by the Portland Gardens Housing Co-operative and the original residents would be moved back in. This rather complex financial process was decided upon because in doing it this way they would saving 15% of the cost of rebuilding as Value Added Tax was not levied on council housing. When the original residents moved back into Portland Gardens this would once again create vacancies, and people in the next identified area for renewal could move in to these and the same process would then start over on their old properties. This was planned as a rolling programme that would take many years until all the housing was eventually renewed and managed by the Housing Co-operative.

Around this time, the economic situation of the area worsened when Tate and Lyle closed their sugar refinery with the loss of 1,700 jobs. Many of those made redundant came from the Vauxhall area and they felt that the city council had not made a strong enough effort to keep the jobs. In addition to the economic problems, the political situation in Liverpool had also worsened. The first reason was that the Liberal Party had engineered artificially low public spending by spending the City Council's reserves rather than raise local taxes.

This had an unexpected cost when the Conservative Party took over Central Government in 1979 and reformed the grant system. The new system allocated money on the basis of historical spending patterns - and Liverpool's were apparently low. This meant that the grant to Liverpool was cut, and continued to be cut each year. The unfairness of the grant system was compounded because Liverpool was also penalised for overspending Central Government's assessment of need figure. This was based on population figures and Liverpool's population had fallen dramatically and so the Government's assessment was that it would need to spend less and so reduced its grant accordingly. However, the

Authority argued that the remaining population was socially vulnerable and so more expensive to provide for and additional to that, historical social commitments made for a large population cannot be suddenly terminated (Parkinson, 1985). What all of this meant was that by the time the Labour Party took over the city in May 1983 the city had lost £270 million pounds in grant aid (Parkinson, 1985) which had exacerbated already entrenched problems.

The second reason for the worsening political situation was that during the latter half of the 1970s and early 1980s the Labour Party in the city became increasingly left-wing. This was because the industrial restructuring that had impacted so heavily on the city had left workers frustrated and cynical (Meegan, 1989a) and more open to 'confrontational politics or at least to those that 'put the interests of Merseyside and Merseysiders first'' (Meegan, 1989b, 93). This enabled the extreme left-wing, the so-called Militant Tendency, to come to the forefront of local politics. Although as a group it remained a minority within the council, it wielded enormous power as it not only had the broad support of the rest of the Labour party but also a large number of the council's employees including the Direct Labour Organisation who made repairs to the city's municipal housing (Parkinson, 1985, 1990).

When Labour came to power in the city in 1983 one of their first political statements was that they would build 1,000 municipal houses within 12 months. They fulfilled this goal within three months. In part, this was achieved by retaining houses, being built for co-operatives across the city, including the Portland Gardens scheme. Although many of the communities who were losing their co-operative housing through this tactic opposed the City Council's plans they had little impact on events. Additionally, the community based around the *Our Lady of Eldon Street* church - now known as the Eldonians - were told that the rolling programme was ending, the tenements were to be demolished and their occupants dispersed.

The Eldonian community leaders refused to accept this proposal and they went to the ward Labour Party - the local representatives - to register their disapproval of the policy. They expected the ward Labour Party to be willing to present their views to the City Council. Instead they were allegedly intimidated and ignored in meetings by a ward Labour Party that was dominated by a number of activists who lived outside the area and who were dictating local policy. Their reaction was to rally the local community into deposing their local representatives and one night 120 members of the community went and joined the ward Labour party. At the next meeting these members were allowed to vote and they voted for the existing committee of activists to be disbanded and for a new committee that truly represented the community drawn from its members. This new committee then informed the City Council that the current housing policy was not supported in their ward and so should be reversed. The City Council retaliated by then refusing to acknowledge that they had a case until they had taken over the constituency that is a number of wards. Reluctantly the Eldonians agreed, however, they also started compiling a dossier on the activities of deputy leader and the policy leader of the City Council.

The City Council allegedly continued to use obstructionist tactics on the Eldonians in order to try and disband the co-operative. For example, in 1985, when the Eldonians, with the backing of English Estates, applied for planning permission to have the Tate and Lyle site changed from industrial usage to residential usage in order to build 70 homes, it was refused on the grounds that there were noxious smells from the nearby offal works. However, the Council's own plans for the site called for the building of 125 municipal dwellings. The eventual public enquiry found in the Eldonians favour.

Throughout this period, the city was attempting to gain extra funding from Central Government to replace the lost grant revenue and initially there was some sympathy within Whitehall to the city's plight. However, this was soon lost when Militants used the state of the city's finances to manipulate a series of confrontations with Central Government by setting an illegal budget and making housing a central issue.

The effect of all of this was that Central Government was predisposed to be very sympathetic to the Eldonians when they approached it. It saw a way of taking the housing war back to the Council by making grants available to the Eldonians, backing their redevelopment plan for the area, extending the boundary of the Merseyside Development Corporation - initiated to reclaim derelict industrial and dock land on both sides of the River Mersey - to include the community and so by-pass the need to apply to the council for planning permission for the redevelopment, and by allowing the resurrection of their housing association - which now manages around 500 properties.

The relationship between the Eldonians and Liverpool City Council is very different today to what it was in the late 1970s and early 1980s. This is because the Militant Tendency became an outlawed organisation within the national Labour party as it was causing immense damage to the national electoral chances of the Labour party. In 1986 the national Labour leadership suspended the Liverpool Labour party and then expelled those who were the leading lights of the Militant Tendency for their membership of the organisation. 1987 hammered another nail into the Militant Tendency's coffin when the House of Lords finally confirmed the view of the district auditor that the Labour councillors had not protected the fiscal interests of the city and disqualified 47 of them from office. The 47 councillors were replaced by other more moderate Labour councillors who attempted to maintain the Militant Tendency's policies whilst repairing relationships with the local citizens, the private and voluntary sectors and Central Government (Crick, 1986; Parkinson, 1990). Since then Liverpool has seen every conceivable hue of Labour administration - however, control never fell back into the hands of the extreme left-wing faction - and more recently (1998) a switch to the Liberal Democrats that has been sustained to date (2005). The one thing that all of these varying councils acknowledged was that divisive and confrontational politics were not the way forward. Instead, partnership between the public, private and voluntary sectors and the local communities has been held as the key to local social and economic regeneration, from the surrounding environs.

WHERE IS THE SUSTAINABLE URBAN DEVELOPMENT?

As well, the tempering process that the Eldonian residents had gone through in their battles with the City Council and their success in the redevelopment of their housing meant that they strongly identified with their community. This community is now called the Eldonian Village with strongly demarcated boundaries that separate it the community has long advocated the need to view housing, jobs and social welfare as 'part of the same package', they have extended beyond their initial brief to save their housing by forming the Community Based Housing Association into employment, training, project development and fund-raising activities through the formation of the Development Trust and social welfare, community events and activity groups via the formation of the Community Trust.

COMMUNITY BASED ECONOMIC DEVELOPMENT

One of the strategies that the Development Trust has embraced is the concept of community based economic development or CBED.   CBED is a non-government organisational (NGO) strategy that was originally adopted by local Labour authorities as an alternative to the free market policies advocated during the 1980s (Parkinson, 1989; and Nevin and Shiner, 1995a, 1995b). CBED usually takes the form of community businesses, which Hayton (1996, 4) defined as meaning a trading organisation with certain characteristics:

- it creates jobs for residents of a particular area usually having high levels of unemployment and social deprivation. The area of benefit is defined in the articles and memorandum of association of the business;
- these jobs are eventually to be self-financing (or sustainable) in so far as costs are covered by trading income;
- ownership and control of the business is vested in those living within the area of benefit; and
- trading profits are to be either reinvested or used in ways which benefit local residents.

The first Eldonian community business was the Eldonian Garden Market Centre. Unfortunately, although the capital was available to initiate the project and to take it through its first year, business acumen was lacking and no thought had been given to future revenue. The people involved had assumed that if the community owned the business they would retain all of the profits to be used for the community's benefit. What they had failed to realise was that they also would have to accept all of the risks and the losses. Enthusiasm took the place of experience and within a very short space of time the business was in trouble. Fortuitously, a businessman who was looking for an outlet in Liverpool became interested and took over 75% of the business and retained the existing employees who were local. The Eldonians learned their lesson from this and since then every other business has been in partnership with other organisations in order to both spread the risks and to bring in outside experience in areas where they have little or none.

Their next scheme was a purpose built residential care home with 30 bed spaces for frail elderly people in the area that required some degree of nursing. This was undertaken in partnership with a larger association with experience in this field who also supplied a skilled manager. The home was planned in order to enable the residents to stay in the area close to family and friends. Although this scheme was established by and is run by the Community Trust this is a community business in the fullest sense. It was established for the benefit of local people, between 40 to 50 local people are employed by the home as auxiliary staff and it is also used as a training centre for local people who want to enter this form of employment.

Another scheme is the Eldon Woods Day Nursery, which was built in conjunction with the Littlewoods Pools Organisation, and the building is jointly owned. The Eldonians manage the building and provide all of the staff other than the manager. The nursery also offers training in childcare. Of the 50 childcare places, 20 are taken by employees of the Littlewoods Pools Organisation, 20 are taken by civil service staff and 10 are taken by local residents at a subsidised rate. Apparently the demand for childcare places is so high that plans are being considered to either extend the existing nursery or to build a second.

The only business that is completely owned by the community is the Village Hall, which acts as a focal point for the social activities of the Eldonian Village and is also run as a conference centre. This is proving to be a popular venue because it is very near to the canal and the Eldonians have capitalised on their heritage by ensuring that this particular canal reach is very attractive in the hope that it encourages people who are holidaying on barges to moor and use the local facilities.

In addition to the community businesses and the paid administrative employees, the Community Based Housing Association has other employees. These include two gardeners, who ensure that the Village flora is kept under control, and four security staff that monitor the condition of elderly residents, keep ebullient teenagers in check and who report suspicious incidents to the police. This has ensured that the Village has one of the lowest crime rates in the area. The Eldonians are continually looking for new opportunities to enhance their community and this combined with their proven track record makes it relatively easy for them to both raise funding and to find private sector partners - avenues that are not necessarily open to other communities.

CONCLUSION

The Eldonians are now considered by many - including Liverpool City Council - to be a 'best practice' model of successful sustainable urban development. They made their housing a 'people's problem' and used this as a springboard to foster the development of community businesses and social networks that exemplify the protective environmental objectives of Barton (2000).

Many of the Eldonian community are in paid employment or in training with one of the many community businesses or private enterprises that have been encouraged to set up in the area. This minimises both the need for travel and for private transportation as jobs are available locally and public transport into the city centre is reasonably frequent. Their development of the local environment has attempted to promote the distinctiveness of the local heritage and the security force has reduced the fear of violence within the community, especially the elderly residents – although this, and the many Housing Association rules has led to some observers likening the Village to a 'mini-police state', albeit one approved of by the residents. Nevertheless, regardless of this aspect it cannot be denied that the Eldonians' control of their housing and businesses has increased the user and citizen control over key areas of their lives and this has in turn facilitated many social networks within the community   However, as Elliott (1994) noted in her assessment of successful sustainable urban development in Third World countries, this building and organisation of their community from one on the brink of destruction into one that is vibrant, forward looking and confident was not completely reliant on the talents of the residents - although their tenacity and their vision were the driving force. Not only did outsiders in the shape of the local council and Central Government and external funding have a significant role to play in this transformation, but this process was also a fairly lengthy one that included many setbacks as well as the triumphs. Within urban policy initiatives this time factor is often grossly underestimated as it is assumed that the 'community' already exists when in many cases it patently does not and it may, in fact, need careful nurturing over what can be a period of years to strengthen it to the point where it can not only manage its own affairs but also accept that if an initiative is not an immediate success it does not have to derail the whole process of sustainable urban development. After all, Rome, and the Eldonian Village, were not built in a day.

BIBLIOGRAPHY

Allen, J and Massey, D. (eds.) (1988) The Economy in Question, London, Sage Publications Ltd.

Barton, II. (2000) "Do Neighbourhoods Matter?", In: Barton, H. (ed.) Sustainable Communities: The Potential for Eco-Neighbourhoods, London, Earthscan Publications Ltd, 49-65.

Cornfoot, T. (1982) "The Economy of Merseyside, 1945-1982: Quickening Decline or Post-Industrial Change?" In: Gould, W.T.S. and Hodgkiss, A. (eds.) The Resources of Merseyside, Liverpool, Liverpool University Press, 14-26.

Cox, K.R. (1973) Conflict, Power and Politics in the City: A Geographical View, New York, McGraw-Hill Book Company.

Crick, M. (1986) The March of Militant, London, Faber and Faber.

Darville, G, and Munday, B. (eds.) (1984) Volunteers in the Personal Social Services, Tavistock.

Eisenschitz, A. and Gough, J. (1993) The Politics of Local Economic Policy. The Problems and Possibilities of Local Initiative, Basingstoke, The Macmillan Press Ltd.

Elliott, J.A. (1994) An Introduction to Sustainable Development: The Developing World, London, Routledge.

Gilchrist, A. (2000) "Design for Living: The Challenge of Sustainable Communities", In: Barton, H. (ed.) Sustainable Communities: The Potential for Eco-Neighbourhoods, London, Earthscan Publications Ltd, 147-159.

Harloe, M. (ed.) (1977) Captive Cities. Studies in the Political Economy of Cities and Regions, London, John Wiley and Sons.

Harvey, D. (1973) Social Justice and the City, London, Edward Arnold.

Hayton, K. (1996) "A critical examination of the role of community business in urban regeneration", Town Planning Review, 67, (1), 1-20.

Herbert, D.T. and Smith D.M. (1989) Social Problems and the City, Oxford, Oxford University Press.

Lane, T. (1997) Liverpool City of the Sea, 2nd revised ed. of (1987) Liverpool, Gateway of Empire, Liverpool, Liverpool University Press.

Lawton, R. (1982) "From the Port of Liverpool to the Conurbation of Merseyside", In: Gould, W.T.S. and Hodgkiss, A.G. (eds.) The Resources of Merseyside, Liverpool, Liverpool University Press, 1-13.

Lawton, R. (1986) "Population", In: Langton J. and Morris, R.J. Atlas of Industrializing Britain 1780-1914, London, Methuen, 10-29.

Lloyd, P. (1979) "The components of industrial change for Merseyside inner area: 1966-75, Urban Studies, 16 (1), 45-60.

Meegan, R. (1989a) "Paradise postponed: the growth and decline of Merseyside's outer estates", In: Cooke, P.N. (ed.) Localities, London, Unwin Hyman, 198-234.

Meegan, R. (1989b) "Merseyside in crisis and in conflict", In: Harlow, M., Pickvance, C. and Urry J. (eds.) Place, Policy and Politics: Do Localities Matter?, London, Unwin Hyman, 87-107.

Meegan, R. (1995) "Local Worlds" In: Allen, J. and Massey, D. (eds.) Geographical Worlds. 1 The Shape of the World, Oxford, Oxford University Press, 53-104.

Middleton, M. (1991) Cities in Transition: The Regeneration of Britain's Inner Cities, London, Michael Joseph.

Nevin, B. and Shiner, P. (1995a) "Community regeneration and empowerment: a new approach to partnership", Local Economy, (9(4), 308-322.

Nevin, B. and Shiner, P. (1995b) "The left, urban policy and community empowerment: the first steps towards a new framework for urban regeneration", Local Economy, 10, 3, 204-217.

Parkinson, M. (1985) Liverpool on the Brink, Hermitage, Policy Journals.

Parkinson, M. (1989) "The Thatcher Government's urban policy, 1979-1989", Town Planning Review, 60, (4), 421-440.

Parkinson, M. (1990) "Leadership and Regeneration in Liverpool: Confusion, Confrontation or Coalition?", In: Judd, D. and Parkinson, M. (eds.) Leadership and Urban Regeneration. Cities in North America and Europe, vol.37, Urban Affairs Annual Reviews, London, Sage Publications, 241-257.

Poole, H.R. (1960) The Liverpool Council of Social Service 1909-1959, Liverpool, The Liverpool Council of Social Service (Inc.).

Prestwich, R. and Taylor, P. (1990) Introduction to Regional and Urban Policy in the United Kingdom, Longman, London.

Simey, M. (1992) Charity Rediscovered: A Study of Philanthropic Effort in Nineteenth-Century Liverpool, Liverpool, Liverpool University Press.

Smithers, H. (1825) Liverpool its Commerce, Statistics and Institutions, Thomas Kaye.

Participatory Planning Under the Mexican Volcanoes

Pedro Moctezuma-Barragan

INTRODUCTION: IN THE EDGE OF AN UNSUSTAINABLE MEGA-CITY

Mexico City lies in a Valley inside the Central Mexican Basin at 6,800 feet above sea level and enclosed by mountains. The staggering problems the eighteen million inhabitants of the Mexico City Metropolitan Area (MCMA) face are related to its unsustainable growth trends, suffering from chronic water undersupply and air, soil and water pollution[i]. Due to high altitude, Mexico Valley´s is subject to thermal inversions that trap emissions and waste causing important health and economic impacts (Pezzoli, 1998).

The housing deficit in MCMA is vast. 70 percent of the population are reported to seek access to land to build human settlements through self-help on long periods of time. However, since 1975, real wages have lost 66 percent of its value and the purchasing power is much lower now than 25 years ago while the price of land has tripled (Valenzuela 1999). The strongest pressures to occupy land are observed on the Southeastern area of the City (in the neighbouring areas to *Sierra Nevada*) were mostly illegal developers propagate the urban slums at record annual growth rates that go from 7 to 14.5%. Since 1950 the chaotic urbanisation sprawl started in the Iztapalapa area and continued during 1970's towards Los Reyes La Paz. In the 1980's the urban tide proceeded to the east in Chalco which had 68.813 inhabitants in 1980 and grew to hold a population of 282,940 only ten years later. In the decade 1980-1990 the dynamic swirled farther east to Ixtapaluca, which had 137,357 inhabitants at the start of the decade and ended with 327,690 by year 2000 (Burns, 2000).

Urban sprawl advance in Southeastern Mexico City 1950-2000

Circle	Decade in which growth showed higher increases	Example	Population at the beginning of the decade of highest growth	Population ten years later
First circle	1950	Iztapalapa	76,621	254,355
Second circle	1970	Los Reyes La Paz	32,258	87,284
Third circle	1980	Chalco	68,813	282,940

Fourth circle	1990	Ixtapaluca	137,357	327,690
Fifth circle	2000	Tlalmanalco	38,766	?
	2000	Amecameca	45,354	?

The new communitarian and environmental problems we face today in a fast growing, unbalanced world using unsustainable development means, open a broad new field for planning practices.   In the case of Sierra Nevada experience, the survey-plan-implementation process includes the members of the community-based organisation, in a "participatory planning" approach. The development of social research carried out by a team encompasses professional action researcher and members of an organisation or a community seeking to understand the process (Moctezuma, Crespy and Reyes 1989).

Further on, the team promotes broad participation in the research process and supports actions leading to a more just or satisfying situation for the community members and stakeholders. Together, the professional team of researchers and the local participants define the problems to be examined, to generate relevant knowledge about them, learn and execute social research techniques, take actions, evaluate and interpret the results of actions based on what they have learned.

There have been a variety of previous experiences linked to action research and participatory planning in the interface area of confluence of disordered massive popular settlements in Mexico. Two of the most interesting experiences belong urban popular movements, in different areas of the South eastern periphery of Iztapalapa, Mexico city: San Miguel Teotongo in the Santa Catarina Sierra and Cananea in El Molino have developed pioneering experiences (Cheetam, 1984; Dávila, 1990; Garza, 1996). There, after many years struggling against illegal developers the *Union de Colonos de San Miguel Teotongo* started a participatory dynamic towards Neighbourhood Development Program approved in November 6, 1992 and an Environmental Program for the Sierra de Santa Catarina Zone (Sáez de Nanclares 1997). Parallel to that, having designed and built an alternative neighbourhood harbouring 1087 families, *Cananea*'s community-based organisation proposed a Development Program for El Molino, that was approved years later on September 15, 1993 (Meffert 1993; Connolly, 1993). The approval of these Programmes validated 18 years of community struggle in Iztapalapa in a time where planning was becoming suitable and community based organisations emerged playing a role in purposeful planning and sketching a future (Moctezuma 1999).

Corruption and autocracy engrained in the alliance between the traditional *Partido Revolucionario Institucional* (PRI) head of the one-party state, and the irregular urban developers (Moctezuma and Navarro 1984) were challenged by a rank of community based organisations. Nevertheless in the overall dynamic, the process found enormous barriers. The appearance of new forms of activity among a previously quiescent group invoked a response from the power holders, who wanted to re-establish their control. The leaders of squatters were PRI loyals. The government offered its followers tolerance to their illegal activities and even promoted new irregular settlements in exchange for votes for the official party. During the 1980's, the urban tide overflowed the municipality of Chalco, creating a vast and precarious new city almost overnight (Hiernaux, 1991). In the 1990's, the urban popular movement became incapable of contributing to influence the reorientation of urban growth.

THE NEW FRONTIER: WESTERN SIERRA NEVADA

With the turn of the century, the circles of growth of large-scale informal and unplanned popular settlements in the periphery of South Eastern Mexico City advanced towards the rural areas of the periphery of the Metropolitan Area dwelled by forest and agricultural traditional communities overlooked by the Popocatepetl and Iztaccíhuatl volcanoes, two of the three largest Mexican volcanoes.(Tortolero 1993), in an area of rich cultural and architectural patrimony (Noyola, 1999, López ,1999) .

The Western Sierra Nevada micro region has 216, 499 inhabitants living in 11 municipalities. The territory is divided in three micro basins: The *Rio de la Compañia* micro basin to the north, The *Río Amecameca* micro basin located in the midpoint of the micro region and the *Arroyo Nexpayantla*[ii] micro-basin placed to the south. The first two micro basins are linked to the Iztaccíhuatl volcano topographic system and the last one is connected to the Popocatepel volcano. The Project for the Zoning of the Metropolitan area of the Valley of Mexico[iii] identifies Western Sierra Nevada as an area of irrigation and groundwater replenishment, endowed with strategic forest resources, but suffering from extensive and uncontrolled urban growth. Tlalmanalco and Amecameca are the two largest municipalities in the micro region and both face urban growth problems.

México is unusual in that it is a country that has tested a mixture of private individual and community-based property rights within a modern capitalist environment for over 70 years[iv] (Alcorn and Toledo, 2000). But formal communal ownership achieved during the Mexican revolution does not mean real control over the resources managed on the name of the people. The traditional associative communal land modes in Mexico (*ejidos* and *bienes comunales*) have been unable to contain threats for forest and agricultural lands, and the *ejidos* have not made any significant contribution for the social well-being of the community since the 1960s. The majority of the stakeholders are too unaware of basic facts to be a real part of the decision making process. This procedure also alienates women and children of *ejidatarios* and *comuneros* (it is mostly male adults that have rights to common lands). The *ejido* was an open institution in the early decades of the XX century that provided access to resources for the population to work with, but it came to be controlled by minority groups, the decisions being manipulated by a hermetic bureaucracy and the benefits from natural resource management have been distributed exclusively among few organisation members. Many presidents of the *ejidatarios* and *bienes comunales* are suspected to be involved in illegal squatting activities and clandestine logging contributing to the ecological deterioration of their common lands.

73

Frequently, local government officials are also affected by corruption and favour irregular urban development as a source of wealth and political support from the new settlers. The links between government officials and illegal urban developers are frequently strong enough to paralyse any top-down planning process.

However, the decay of traditional associative modes in Mexico has led to new forms of organisation that were formed by migrants, women, young people and the unemployed or underemployed. The local movements have their origins in small and diverse groups, with different socio-cultural, ethnical, class and age-group backgrounds, different gender roles and different levels of formal and informal instruction. They have also included different orientations in regard to external collaborators. The soul of the initiatives resided in popular groups that joined forces with students and middle class professionals to promote collaborative efforts calling for environmental protection and local community development. They also shared their experiences and wisdom with multidisciplinary researchers to generate alternative models of development in both rural and urban settings (Moctezuma 2001).

Since the 1993 reforms on the General Law of Human Settlements were sanctioned, enforcing citizens' participation on local plans and programmes. Community based organisation and University members have promoted participatory planning seeking to consolidate community organisations and, at the same time, expand the scale of community promoted participatory plans, which in the past experiences were not ample enough to make a difference in the overall process.

Purposeful prospective planning has a major role for community based organisations in sketching a future that promotes self-reliance and sustainable development, taking into account their social, economical and political context and the official planning framework. Territorial organisations may have great influence in environmental regulations, urban development plans and programmes, and zoning, as well as in local development plans.

The *Sierra Nevada* University-Community Project (*Proyecto UAM Comunidad Sierra Nevada*) emerged in the past five years in a socio-spatial frame of chaotic expansion due to informal settlements rapid growth in the border of Mexico City's built up area. The 1996-2001 period corresponds to an era of intense institutional and political changes. The triumph of President Vicente Fox, displaced the traditional PRI dominance in the national level, but not in the state government, and in the other hand, other political actors were elected to head local governments. The planning process has been brought up within the cultural shifts and the recent democratic transition in Mexico and had to face the Popocatepetl volcanic eruption.

A key to alternative proposals development in *Sierra Nevada*, has been participatory research, and participatory planning which involves people in the analysis of their own situation and the formulation of strategies. The planning experiences included urban development, cultural heritage preservation, risk prevention and ecological issues.

PARTICIPATORY PLANNING IN TLALMANALCO

One of the first processes to develop in *Sierra Nevada* took place in the municipality of Tlalmanalco on the northern side of Sierra Nevada. Inhabited by 38 thousand people, this municipality is located under the Iztaccíhuatl volcano[v]. The town has a rich cultural and architectonic heritage dating back to 1275. The community's "water commissions" had managed their water since 1906 and the local *"ejido"* owns 12,000 hectares of land, a good part of it being forest. This community is well located to attract tourism.

Participatory Planning in Tlalmanalco promoted the community participation in the diagnosis, the strategic proposals and their implementation from a methodological perspective. The process started during 1996, when various local community members were active searching for solutions to their problems: the Cultural Commission of Tlalmanalco was actively seeking to rescue downtown historical sites and to combat the strong pressures for informal urban settlements on ecological area: the *Calpulli Cihuatl* women group had been organising nutrition and health workshops and promoting productive projects; some *ejidatarios* were also seeking for agricultural alternatives for their lands, and for more democratic decision making processes in their assembly. The integration of members from *Universidad Autónoma Metropolitana (UAM)* to the community, allowed the promotion of ecological workshops with children, an evaluation of the natural resources of the Iztaccihuatl Popocatepetl National Park and a Community self diagnosis undertaken form February until October. The overall dynamic brought together people with different backgrounds to address local social and ecological problems

The Community diagnosis was followed by a workshop on Municipal Planning and a purposeful planning exercise outlining the vision of a common future built through self-reliance and sustainable development. Meanwhile, the local branch of the official party (PRI) was weakened, and in November of 1996 an opposition party *Partido de la Revolucion democratica* (PRD) won the election for the municipal government of Tlalmanalco. Promoted and supervised by both University members and community organisers, a participatory planning process at the municipal level was launched.

In February 1997, the newly elected local government signed an agreement with the Dean of the UAM to carry out the 1997-2000 Municipal Development Plan (MDP). In each locality, the plan was discussed through participatory methods (mandated by the Organic Law of the State of México, although rarely respected) and the promoters organised open forums to discuss different issues: water, forest, health, tourism, wastes, culture and urban development. The participatory process involved intensive work from January until April 1997, in a series of dynamics of self-diagnosis, strategic planning and implementation proposals based in public forums and meetings, in three stages: the community self diagnosis, the strategic planning and the diffusion and formalisation. The Municipal Development Plan developed by the people of Tlalmanalco was approved in the town council on April 20, 1997.

Alongside this, in the midst of the participatory dynamic the university members established *Project UAM Comunidad Sierra Nevada (PUCSN)* in March 1997. This is an interdisciplinary project in applied research and social service, drawing on students and teachers from the Universities three campuses. Its objective is to encourage research projects linked with planning and sustaining the area's abundant and vital natural resources that were under threat from the metropolitan area's growth. This relatively small-scale bridging organisation has supported micro regional social and economic development based on the sustainable use of natural resources and has been a greenhouse for local projects related to cultural, social, economic and ecological activities.

Some of the objectives of the MDP were:
  a)   to regain a downtown area that had been lost to an irregular open market that was destroying the area;
  b)   to stop the urban sprawl
  c)   to mount a recycling communal enterprise,
  d)   to build a Health Centre focused in alternative medicine;
  e)   to rescue 64 hectares of forest in El Faro, San Rafael and use it as an environmental education area called *Bosque Escuela* (forest school),
  f)   to consolidate and modernise the community water management,
  g)   to open the council meetings to the population,
  h)   to name and to give their proper role to the Commission for the Municipal Planning part of the legal dispositions of the Organic Law of the State of México

Unfortunately after the Municipal Development Plan was approved, the municipal authorities turned out to be reluctant to implement it and not only failed to meet the commitments they had made, but even secretly changed some aspects of the document and elaborated a new version. Furthermore, they refused to publish the MDP and did not prepare a budget to ensure the Plan was implemented, deviating the resources to other means. The reason was that they were not ready to be accountable for actions and had looked at participation in the plan as window dressing for their administration.

However, many community members did not stop promoting the MDP and began to look for alternative resources to implement it. Members of the community appealed to the inhabitants of Tlalmanalco to contribute with local resources, green T-shirts with the picture of the snowy volcano with the shape of a sleeping woman appeared everywhere reading: *Tlalmanalco: Green Municipality.* As a result of the cohesive a proactive approach developed by civic actors, in June 1997 all the different groups that had participated in the Tlalmanalco plan founded a local community based association: *Consejo Social Iztaccíhuat(CSI),* interested in community welfare and in the conservation of the local cultural and natural heritage and started a careful search the support of state and federal agencies (Mendez Lavielle, 1999).

In January 1998, the Tlalmanalco downtown historic square was recovered for public use, in the first and only action that the local authorities took that was in accord with the Municipal Development Plan. When the merchant squatters threatened to take over the area again, a social mobilisation was convoked and hundreds of inhabitants gathered in the square. During a cultural revival, between May and August, 1998 many families that had guarded precious archaeological pieces for generations donated these to be kept, classified and exhibited at a community museum with the support of the National History and Anthropology Institute. The *Museo Comunitario Nonhualca* was founded in August 1998 while the cultural house, *Casa de Cultura Xochipilli* was remodelled. All of this was promoted by the *Consejo de Cultura* through volunteer work with no support from local authorities.

In May 2000, a collective movement rose against the promotion of new settlements in ecologically sensitive areas of the municipality. Hundreds of people moved to press the municipal president Ruben Vargas Rebollo from doing business with irregular developers, and forced him to sign an agreement, later validated in the town council, not to authorise any more urban settlements in the outskirts of Tlalmanalco.

To accomplish one of the objectives of the Municipal Development Plan, the women's group in Tlalmanalco adopted the name *Ixchel de los Volcanes* and promoted the construction of an alternative health centre, using homeopathy, massage, and an indigenous sauna called *temazcal,* (Farfan, 1999). Starting in 1997, the women group had support from the local authorities only to legalise the land donation obtained from the *Tezopilo* neighbourhood, the place in which the Centre was to be built. However, the women were able to rely on public donations and support first, and then to build an agreement with the federal Ministry of Social Development to gather the resources required to build the Health Centre. It was finally inaugurated four years later, in July 2001. Almost one year after the 1997-2000 Municipal Plan's period and the administration of Ruben Vargas had concluded, but they did so with the local community, *PUCSN* and *CSI* support.

PARTICIPATORY PLANNING IN AMECAMECA

Amecameca is located under the Popocateptl volcano in the south of Sierra Nevada. The volcano -whose name means "Smoky Mountain" in Aztec language- has cyclic eruptions which could affect the surrounding communities, although so far there have only been two preventive evacuations during periods of high activity in 1994 and 2000. The 45 thousand inhabitants' municipality is the most important in the micro region.

To elaborate the Municipal development Plan for Amecameca 2000-2003, in August 2000 the new local authorities asked the *PUCSN*, to promote a participatory dynamic. However, unlike Tlalmanalco there were no community based groups ready to participate in the planning process.

A first Municipal Assembly was appointed on September 20, where the *PUCSN* and the new authorities convoked the population to think and discuss about their vision for the future of their town, and started a top-down process. The first step was to name a Commission for the Planning of Municipal Development (COPLADEMUN) in charge of the MDP.

The planning process was promoted among the dwellers of the different villages, traditional *barrios* (old neighbourhood units), high school students and their parents, and citizen commissions integrated according to different themes or areas of interest. The participatory process involved intensive work from September until December 2000, in a series of dynamics of community self-diagnosis, strategic planning and implementation proposals based in the schools and in public meetings, it had three stages: the community self diagnosis, the GIS participatory research, geo positioning and mapping and the rapid technical assessments.

The most active and aware citizens met weekly with the COPLADEMUN in an open reunion to conduct the plan elaboration, the facilitation was provided by *PUCSN* and The Social Development Direction of the Municipality. It was also asked to the new Municipal president Federico Del Valle to be present in as many meetings as possible.

This dynamic meant the possibility to go a step further to brake the traditional way to run local affairs by small groups of interest, being the population passive and in a dependant and demanding attitude towards the providers of services (Gaventa and Cornwall, 2001). The authorities normally made decisions and budgeted according to the economic wealth or political power of the people demanding solutions. The new attitude invited local communities to be pro-active and participate in the design and planning of new development strategies that also respected the environment.

The presentation of diagnosis and proposals from local communities and High schools was accomplished on November 9th, 2000, during a Second Municipal Meeting in an auditorium filled with of peasants, students, local officials, teachers, university researchers bringing their charts, proposals and maps. Those diagnosis were followed by their strategic proposals; the Third Municipal Assembly was held in the downtown square on November 25, to present the MDP proposal and officially appoint the members of the new Municipal Commission for Planning and Development (COPLADEMUN), 11 persons including people from different villages, age range, gender and occupation were designated for the task, out of the most distinguished participants of the 4 months process.

Some of the objectives of the MDP were:
  a)   to regain a downtown area that had been lost to an irregular open market that was destroying the area;
  b)   to stop the urban sprawl
  c)   to mount a recycling communal enterprise,
  d)   to build a Health Centre focused in alternative medicine;
  e)   to rescue 64 hectares of forest in El Faro, San Rafael and use it as an environmental education area called *Bosque Escuela* (forest school),

f) to consolidate and modernise the community water management,

g) to open the council meetings to the population,

h) to name and to give their proper role to the Commission for the Municipal Planning part of the legal dispositions of the Organic Law of the State of México

Instrument, Scope& Initiative	Underlying Rationale	Methodological Tools
MDP **Tlalmanalco 1997-2000** **Bottom-up**	Participatory building of a common vision. Participatory diagnosis and planning.	Group discussions Territorial and Sectorial Community Diagnosis Sanctioned by Formal Public Assembly
MDP **Amecameca 2000-2003** **Top down**	Institutional means of articulation of relevant actors Participatory diagnosis and planning.	Group discussions Territorial and Sectorial Community Diagnosis Participatory GIS High School Diagnosis Municipal Assemblies
M R D P I **West *Sierra Nevada*** **Bottom-up**	Participatory diagnosis and planning. Transformative collaboration	Urban Municipal Planning Micro basin Diagnosis Participatory GIS High School Monitoring

Three common principles of community participation, sustainable development based in natural and cultural resources and self-determined management of natural resources, where present in both plans, and in both cases, the initiative guiding principle of an urbanisation process controlled by community was not accomplished, even if some progress was made to slow the dynamic, and to have formal commitments from the local authorities not to promote irregular growth.

The constraints of both experiences were the high level of efforts, the lack of collaboration from interest groups within the local government, and the lack of budget to implement the plans with municipal financial support.

Regarding the institutionalisation of public accountability, in the case of Tlalmanalco the COPLADEMUN was never appointed, as it was in Amecameca, but it will be necessary to examine the future practical development of this Commission. The interest groups within the local government continue to seek personal benefits from contracts or gifts linked to the public work assignment to private enterprises

The benefit of the process in the case of Tlalmanalco was the strong influence from community participants in the approach to development, and the fact that the MDP catalyzed community self-organisation to promote implementation of its tasks.

THE *WEST SIERRA NEVADA* MICRO REGIONAL DEVELOPMENT INITIATIVE (MRDPI)

However, it became clear that to be effective in dealing with a sustainable development project, there was a need to aim for a higher and wider reach. Plus it was needed a deeper social involvement shifting form municipal level projects to a broader network, within which to promote awareness-raising and changes in cultural behaviours as a first step to the start a bottom up process able to use a extensive set of planning instruments, and to influence policy and local governance. The five stages of new planning initiative have covered: Inception, definition and diagnosis, planning, implementation and Supervision

THE INCEPTION

Since 1997, Participatory planning accompanied by the development of sustainable local projects has been a key alternative in the inception period. To do so, popular groups joined forces with students and professionals. They sought to demonstrate new models of urban and peri-urban development that met their needs, while avoiding the chaotic informal processes by which most low-income settlements develop. They also sought to ensure good natural resource management and the protection of their rich and diverse cultural heritage. Since its foundation the *PUCSN* consistently scaled the scope from the municipal level to the micro regional level. Opened the scale first to six to municipalities in 1999, two years later, the planning process involved participatory dynamics in all the eleven municipalities that comprehend the micro region.

A coherent effort was made to do participatory diagnosis and wide diffusion about the key elements of micro regional natural resources, the urban development problematic and the volcanic risk factor; a monitoring network was launched and community productive projects were promoted.

The dynamism of group formation within Sierra Nevada associated with local community groups, started a networking effort coordinated through regional meetings: the Regional Encounters for Sustainable Development (*Encuentros*) were the hard core activities for prospective planning and network promotion.

Since the first meeting in Tlalmanalco in 1997, the *Encuentros* have been held in different towns of the Sierra Nevada, the meetings were held in Tepetlixpa in 1998, Ozumba 1998,

Amecameca 1999 and Atlautla in 2001. Each meeting has meant a step forward in the regionalisation of the networking efforts following the communities' internal rhythms and considering the micro region's specific spatial connotations in the different places.

The *Encuentros* allow the exchange of successful experiences in the micro region and in neighbouring states as well thematic meetings on issues like Planning, Health; Agro-ecology; Recycling; Television, radio and community museums; Eco technologies; Eco tourism; Environmental Education and Youth. There are also analyses of the social, economical and political context in which each group developed its initiatives and the institutional framework they operate under.

To meet its internal duties, *PCUSN* has been working not only with university professors and students, but mainly with committed local community members of different backgrounds and young UAM graduates living in the micro region. In June 2001, the 6 core members of the project formed a social organisation, a co-operative named *Sierra Nevada* to take on some of the work tasks, and to fully integrate the team to the micro region as a social organisation.

DEFINITION AND DIAGNOSIS

The general objective of the micro regional development effort agreed by the community-based network is to convert the micro region into a green belt of sustainable development that will control unplanned urban sprawl and halt its destructive activities and offer environmental services to the Valley of Mexico. It aims at the transformation of social relations and practices in natural resource management [vi] and community development.

This is done through supporting local groups' initiatives in sustainable management and convoking policy changes to allow a new form of local governance. Conceived to provide the community with "geographic literacy", the PUCSN began in 1999 with a diagnosis of the natural resources in six municipality of Western Sierra Nevada, undertaken by members of the community, schools, *ejidos* and communal organisations (Burns, 2000). With support from the University, community participants learned to diagnose the situation of water, forest and soil within their local communities and in wider micro region.

The project took hold of new technologies and put them in the hands and at the service of the communities The use of a participatory a Geographical Information System (GIS) in Sierra Nevada showed that young people, promoters and school teachers were able to manage this technology, after being trained in their use, and given open access to equipment and data. Using the GIS, they walked with maps locating the boundaries, forests, and sources of water, river pollution and volcanic hazards. These locations were geo-positioned and integrated into a Regional Geographical Information System. Through the GIS the communities were eager to produce, systematize, locate and map information to be used for participatory planning as well as in community implementation, monitoring and evaluation processes.

The main objective of the Atlases has been to provide key sectors of the population with the information needed to make them responsible for a better management of their resources. The Atlases contain: a) maps and texts based in the analysis of the municipal natural resources, b) indicators of sustainability for the local monitoring of natural resources, and c) the identification of options for the funding of micro-productive projects to improve the management of the resources. The Municipal Atlas of Tlalmanalco, Ecatzingo, Amecameca, Tepetlixpa, Atlautla and Ozumba were released between December 2000 and October 2001.

A first micro regional planning workshop was effectuated in January 13th, 2001. The *PUCSN* along with *CSI,* and representatives of *ejidos*, *bienes comunales*, schools, producers, cultural promoters and other community members coming from 10 out of eleven municipalities in the micro region met to start an assesment. After a first introduction, the meeting was divided into groups belonging to different municipalities and different themes of concern. Each group was provided with the participatory GIS diagnosis and a set of initial proposals generated by *PUCSN*. The aim of these meetings was to identify the global problematic and the linkages between different problems to have further understanding of the main areas of concern, and the possibilities of community initiatives in the face of promoting urban development plans, ecological ordinances and promote an organisation of producers.

It was agreed that every municipality would meet afterwards to deepen the diagnosis and to consensus building along with other stakeholders and the local authorities. The main problems are identified and discussed by themes:

      a) Sustainable urban development

      b) Environmental protection

      c|) Waste recycling

      d) Water management

      e) Agro ecological diversification

      f) Cultural and Eco tourist initiatives and networking

      g) Building wide consensus among stakeholders and an institutional framework for a micro regional Council.

PLANNING

Complementary to the bottom up dynamic, and taking advantage of all the possible window of opportunities, the *PUCSN* had been doing a broad set of contacts to build a permanent micro regional development initiative for West *Sierra Nevada*. The advocacy aimed at transform the collaboration efforts with the institutional framework, and to build partnerships for research and for projects implementation.

Agreements were signed with two federal Ministries: Social Development Ministry (*SEDESOL*) and Environment and Natural Resources (*SEMARNAT*), with the state governments, ministries of Ecology and Urban Development, with the United Nations

Development Program and with a private Fund, *Fondo Mexicano de Conservacion de la Naturaleza.*

CSI and *PUCSN* went one step further fulfilling three objectives: a) to do comprehensive micro regional urban, rural and natural resources participatory assessments; b) to promote the implementation of strategic detonation initiatives and at the same time to make the communities ready to meet the challenge of partnership trough a greenhouse for productive enterprises. c) to promote participatory monitoring and evaluations.

A micro regional initiative for alternative development planning and implementation was promoted. To build mechanisms capable of reorienting urban growth, it was necessary to make a broad coalition, promoting urban and environmental development programs with a common vision, that would help to transform in some degree the space profiles and the social situation of the areas where the slum chaotic expansion needs to be limited and reverted.

Throughout the last *Encuentro Regional*, held on July 2001 at the Technical High School of Atlautla on the hills of the Popocatepetl elevation, the participants joined efforts to promote local organising in the three West Sierra Nevada micro basins: *Rio Amecameca*, *Rio Tlalmanalco* and *Arroyo Nexpayantla*, to create micro basin Councils. The urban development plans are the only instrument able to put legal barriers at the urban sprawl, through the definition of land uses, and the design of implementation tools. The meeting also agreed in participating the urban planning process to be completed by January 2002 in eleven Municipalities in the micro region. An agreement with the State of Mexico's Ministry of Urban Development allowed *Sierra Nevada* co-operative to start working on the five of the Plans and to be part of a joint co-ordinate of the eleven plans since September 2001.

IMPLEMENTATION

Chaotic urbanisation on *ejido* lands displaces agricultural uses. The idea of elaborating medium and long term plans based on the rational use of land and water, that include diversification, forestry, eco tourism and accept the participation of the community's women and young people is key for the reorganisation of the *ejido*. To further develop organic agriculture is an important goal, along with a trade network for natural products including marmalades, honey and herbs.

The Programme aims to foster the local economy and reorient the inadequate current management through encouraging productive projects of sustainable management, highly visible and easily replicable, so as to create the basis for a model for sustainable development. The *PUCSN* is creating a "greenhouse" of micro-productive projects to link and support strategic projects and build networks to be more competitive. This is done in partnership with the micro regional community based movement, it includes training and the encouragement of cooperation between local micro-projects. Projects, such as the *Bosque Escuela* Ecological Park, *TV3 Tezcaltepetl* communitary television, *Tlachaloni* eco touristic communal enterprise and the women community-based organic marmalades enterprise *Madre Tierra*, represent concrete achievements in this process.

Eco tourism helps local communities and visitors to be aware of and take care of the cultural and natural heritage and does not require large investments in hotels and restaurants. The only thing needed is training and organisation to help the local population form their own enterprises as guides that are in contact with the ecosystem and their history, and promoting out door activities like horse riding, bicycle, camping and rappel. During 2000, five community groups took part in a training process to create their enterprises, Atlautla, Tecomaxusco and Ecatzingo, are the outstanding projects.

PARTICIPATORY MONITORING: GUARDIANES DE LOS VOLCANES

The training of local groups – especially through interventions in high schools – in environmental monitoring is another initiative. Once a vision for the region's future was developed, key members of the communities across the region have to be able to monitor the impact and report regularly on the State of the Region. In doing so, the *PUCSN* not only hopes to measure the efficacy of its interventions but also to supply communities with scientific tools to allow a more conscious and effective management of its natural resources. During 2001, under the name of *Guardianes de los Volcanes,* 140 teachers were taught to promote participatory planning through training sessions conducted in 33 high schools. It is a type of public participation in which young people in the micro region belonging to diverse stakeholder families are included in the monitoring process: choosing the issue and collecting and analysing data. This research links experts and non-experts: schoolchildren and young people, teachers, researchers and authorities. These groups are developing a partnership for effective and socially inclusive monitoring, contributing to change cultural habits and promoting connections to the policy making process.

The innovative goal of this effort is to broaden the urban focus with a deeper territorial approach that strongly emphasises in the environmental impacts of urbanisation and takes into account the *Popocatepetl*'s eruption risk factor. Ten out of eleven municipalities in Sierra Nevada are within the volcanic hazard-area while the eleventh is the door out in case of evacuation. Along with strengthening the ecological calling of the region and the preventing rapid urban growth from happening in the West Sierra Nevada areas, the *PUCSN* proposes a community information system and the promotion of rail transportation

Participatory purposeful planning plays a major role in sketching a sustainable future for local communities. With their influence situated in the local level, territorial organisations are able to diagnose their reality and build influence in zoning, or urban development plans and programmes in the local arena. The communities have as well a privileged location to promote, participate and enjoy benefits from the implementation of plans that take into account the human and environmental needs of the region.

NOTES

[i] Located within the central region of the Méxican Republic, With 18 million inhabitants the Metropolitan Area of Mexico City (MAMC). The capital city is the nucleus of an urban system composed by six other cities in Central Mexico: Cuernavaca, Puebla, Tlaxcala, Pachuca, Queretaro and Toluca that add to 30 million people.

[ii] . The *Arroyo Nexpayantla* micro basin includes the municipalities of: Tepetlixpa, Ecatzingo, Atlautla, Ozumba. The *Rio Amecameca* micro basin includes the municipalities of Juchitepec, Tenango del Aire, Ayapango and Amecameca: the *Rio Tlalmanalco,* also known as *Rio de la Compania* micro basin includes the municipalities of Temamatla, Cocotitlán and Tlalmanalco.

[iii] *Proyecto de Programa de Ordenación de la Zona Metropolitana del Valle de México(1997).*México: D.D.F., Edomex, SEDESOL

[iv] México has seen many mixtures of private individual and community-based property rights within a modern capitalist environment for over 70 years. The Mexican mix includes: corporate community-based land-holdings (66.3 % of the production units and covering 59% of the land area of Mexico); private individual holdings (comprised of 30.8% of the production units and covering 40.9% of the land area); and mixed systems (including 2.9% of the production units and covering 0.1% of the land area) (National Census, 1990). See Alcorn Janis and Toledo Victor (2000) "Resilient resource management in México's forest ecosystems" in Berkes , Fikret and Folke, Carl (2000) *Linking Social and Ecological Systems.* Cambridge: Cambridge University Press.

[v] The Iztaccíhuatl is a snowy mountain shaped like a young woman lying down, from her long haired head to her toes. The Aztec name for the volcanoe means "White Woman". The volcanoes' ancient legend is a monumental Mexican "Romeo and Juliet" episode referring to Iztaccíhuatl is a feminine volcano and Popocateptl a masculine one. Both volcanoes are very important for Mexico´s identity, as mother and father region of *Anáhuac* as the indigenous confederation was known before the Spanish invasion.

[vi] Raufflet, Emmanuel "Collaborations and collaborating in Tlalmanalco:one forest, five organizations and seven collaborations". Unpublished.

BIBLIOGRAPHY

Alcorn Janis and Toledo Victor (2000) "Resilient resource management in México's forest ecosystems" in Berkes , Fikret and Folke, Carl (2000) *Linking Social and Ecological Systems.* Cambridge: Cambridge University Press.

Burns, Elena.(ed) (2000) Atlas Municipal de Recursos Naturales. Tlalmanalco: *PUCSN.*

Connolly, Priscilla; Huarte, Concepción and Cruz, Marisol (1991) "Sociología Urbana en la UAM Azcapozalco" *Sociológica 15* .

Pezzoli, Keith (1998) *Human Settlements and Planning for Ecological Sustainability.* Cambridge :MIT Press.

Plan de Desarrollo Municipal de Amecameca 2000-2003. Amecameca: Ed H. Ayuntamiento.

Tortolero, Alejandro (coord) (1993) *Entre Lagos* Connolly, Priscilla.(1993) "The go-between": CENVI, a habitat NGO in México City. *Environment and Urbanization*, 5 (1), April. 80-81.

Cheetam, Rosemond (1984) "Estado del Conocimiento Sobre el Fenómeno Metropolitano". *Revista A* V(11).

Cornwall, Andrea and Gaventa, John (2001) "From Users and Choosers to makers and Shapers: Repositioning Participation in Social Policy". Working Paper 127. Sussex: IDS.

Dávila, Julio (1990) "Mexico's urban popular movements: a conversation with Pedro Moctezuma. *Environment and Urbanization* 2 (1).

Farfan, Liliana del Rayo (1999) *Ixchel de Los Volcanes.* Mexico: CSI-DEMOS

Mendez Lavielle, Guadalupe (1999) *El Consejo Social Iztaccihuatl.* Mexico: CSI-DEMOS

Garza , Gustavo (1996) *Cincuenta Años de Investigación Urbana y Regional, 1940-1991.* México: El Colegio de México.

Hiernaux, Daniel (1991). "Servicios Urbanos, Grupos Populares y Medio Ambiente en Chalco, Mexico" In"*Servicios Urbanos, Gestion Local y Medio Ambiente*" Schteingart, M. and d,Andrea L. (281-304), Mexico D.F. Colegio de Mexico.

López, Alejandro (1999) Monografía Municipal de Amecameca. Toluca: Instituto Mexiquense de Cultura

Meffert, Karin. (1993) "Co-operative Self-Help Housing: The Case of El Molino in México City" in *Beyond Self Help Housing*, edited by Kosta Mathéy. London-New York: Mansell

Moctezuma P. And Navarro B. (1984a) "Los Fraccionadores Clandestinos en San Miguel Teotongo", *Revista "A",* Universidad Autonoma Metropolitana-Azcapozalco.II (11):149-168.

Moctezuma,P. Crespy, Ch and Reyes T.(1989) "Antecedentes de UCISV Libertad AC." México: Fundacion Federich Naumann-Universidad Autonoma de Chapingo.

Moctezuma P. (1999) *Despertares. Comunidad y organización urbano popular en México 1970-1994.*México: UAM-UIA.

Moctezuma, P. (2001) "Community-Based Organisation and Participatory Planning in Southeast Mexico City".*Environment and Urbanization.*October. 117-133.

Noyola, Jaime (1999) Monografía Municipal de Tlalmanlaco. Toluca: Instituto Mexiquense de Cultura *y Volcanes.* Zinacantepec: El Colegio Mexiquense.

Valenzuela, J (1999). Estado y Políticas Sociales en el Neoliberalismo. México: F.. Ebert.

Oclayo Chàvez Cortes, J.M. and Nuri Trigo Boix (coord.) (1996), Programa de Manejo para el Parque Nacional Itzlaccihuatl-Popocatépetl, collecion Ecologia y Planeacion, UAM, Xochimilco, México, Mex.

Ley General del Equilibrio Ecológico y la Protección al Ambiente (1996) Semarnat: México D.F. pp 46-47.

INE (2000) Protegiendo al Ambiente. Políticas y getion institucional. Logros y retos para el desarrollo sustentable 1995-2000, INE: Mexico D.F. p 91.

Raufflet, Emmanuel (2001) "Managing natural resources - lessons from the history (1947-1995) " mimeo.

Simonian, L. (1995), Defending the land of the jaguar, a History of Conservation in Mexico, University of Texas Press, Austin.

Vargas, F. (1998), Iztaccihuatl- Popocatépetl, un parque nacional, SEMARNAP, DF, Mexico

Informal Transformations of Formal Housing Estates in Algiers and Cairo

Magda Silbey-Behloul

In the last four decades, the combination of high population increase rate, acute shortages of housing and governments' attempts to respond quickly to a crisis situation has resulted in the wide-spread of mass housing estates the suburbs of North African cities. Four to five storey walk-up apartment bocks have become a familiar urban landscape in cities such as Algiers and Cairo.

It is widely acknowledged today that the design and spatial organisation of the dwelling units in most of these estates have been far from adequate in responding to the needs of their occupants in terms of family size and lifestyles. Lack of space within the dwelling units triggered various adaptive alterations carried out by the residents' themselves in order to make their housing units more habitable. As the housing shortages have been worsening in most North African countries due to political and economic problems and a continuously rapidly increasing population, the vast majority of the residents in these estates have no possibility for moving out to larger units as their family circumstances change over time. This has caused further pressure on the already limited space in the dwelling units, particularly with the return of the extended family scenario. Newly wed sons are forced to share their parents' dwelling unit as the acquisition of an affordable flat for most newly wed couples is almost impossible.

It is evident that Governments' initiatives and resources to house a continuously growing population are, on their own, far from being sufficient. Research has revealed that residents' transformation of government built dwellings and households' own initiatives to house themselves provide a number of lessons that cannot be ignored.

This paper sheds some light on how lower middle class and low-income households in Algiers and Cairo take initiatives to adapt Government built housing to their changing needs and circumstances. It also highlights the striking similarities in housing processes, built forms and space use patterns within the four to five walk-up dwelling blocks, in spite of regional political and economical differences.

HISTORICAL BACKGROUND

During the 1970s and early 1980s the political systems in Egypt and Algeria were of a socialist tendency. National economic plans were prepared on a four to five year periods and included, amongst other priorities, the urgency of addressing the problem of the rapidly increasing housing needs of the population. Thousands of housing units were to be built on a yearly basis. Because the desert constitutes a very high proportion of the overall national territory in both countries, the objectives of food sufficiency programmes meant developing a strategy for safeguarding agricultural land. This led to a great increase in the population density at the inhabited areas in Egypt, namely the Nile Valley and its Deltas, which placed Egypt amongst the most populated countries in the world. Because of the clear disparities between the living standard of urban and rural areas, migration to urban areas increased. This has led to an increase in the urban population growth. A policy was therefore prepared by the state for re-distributing the population by encroaching upon desert lands and establishing new urban communities. These would assimilate population increase in order to reduce the population densities and the cramped conditions in the existing urban areas. The law No 59 for the year 1979 of new urban communities was issued, encouraging the development of societies in the desert lands and redistributing the population through planning and preparing new areas of attraction outside the agricultural area. One of the prior objectives was the provision of low cost housing for the unprivileged and under paid who represent the vast majority of those in great need of housing in Egypt. These initiatives have led to the construction of 12 new towns. A target to build 300 000 housing units per year was set and this resulted in the proliferation of five storey walk-up dwellings.

In Algeria the annual rate of population increase between 1977 and 1987, was among the highest in the world, being estimated at 3.08 per cent. During that decade, the Algerian population virtually doubled, from 12 millions to 23 millions with 57 per cent of the population under the age of 20 by the later date (El Moudjahid, 1988). Targets of building 100,000 dwellings yearly (INERBA, 1980) meant that criteria of cheapness of construction, mass production and the reduction of the housing unit floor area in order to build a greater number of units per project were given a high priority. This has led to the spread of five storey walk up dwellings (similar to those in Egypt) in the suburbs of most Algerian cities and towns.

In both Algeria and Egypt, it was assumed, by the decision makers in the 1970s that households were evolving towards a 'modern way of life' which would be appropriately catered for in prefabricated mass housing dwellings. It was also assumed that households would quickly adapt themselves to the dwellings they were provided with. Such a deterministic approach, combined with the urgency to meet the housing needs resulted in the wide spread use of almost the same version of five-storey walk-up dwellings in various geographical areas without any consideration neither to different climatic conditions nor to households' different social background and lifestyle. An 'average' size of dwelling has been decided upon for an 'average' size of household. The 'average' household size being estimated at 6 to 7 people. Another common factor is the high level of unemployment and the strong family ties which provide, to a certain degree, a safety net for the young unemployed population who depends on parents and relatives for food and shelter

The dwelling units are usually organised along a corridor serving on each side the living room, bedroom(s), bathroom and kitchen. As for private external spaces, the kitchen is

provided with a loggia to 'compensate' for the traditional courtyard and a balcony is
sometimes available with the living room (see fig1).

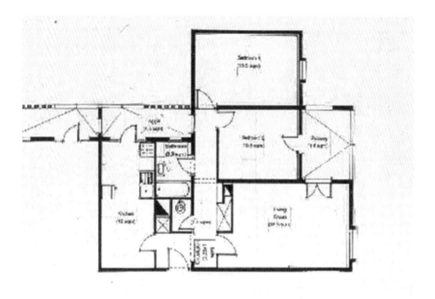

Figure 01: Typical plan of the 1980's mass housing estate in Algiers

(the Garidi estate)

INFORMAL EXTENSIONS IN CAIRO

The changing conditions of the residents over a period of time and the impossibility of
housing mobility results in major alterations and illegal extensions of Government built
Four to five story dwelling blocks. Extreme cases of extensions have been studied and
documented 1980's and 1990's by Steinberg (1984), Tipple et al (1985) and Salama
(1994).

The case of 'Ain El Sira', a housing estate of 5000 dwellings built in the late 1950s in
Cairo illustrates clearly how the distress brought about by overcrowded conditions has
provoked uncontrolled extensions and construction activities by the inhabitants. These
have been witnessed, by the author, in 1993 during a study visit to that housing estate took
place (see Figure 02).

Figure 02: Uncontrolled extensions in the Ain Al Sira estate, Cairo

In his survey of 208 flats in this estate, Salama found that almost half the sample had built extensions (Salama, 1994). The total average area gained depended on the flat location. Larger extensions were observed in the ground floor flats which gained an average of 67 sqm compared to an average of 30 sqm for flats on other floors. However, there was also evidence that some parts of the estate remained unchanged. One of the important findings in Salama's study was that 96 per cent of the three-roomed units had extensions compared to only 38% of all one-roomed units. This suggests that extensions and alterations are not always a direct consequence of shortage of space but are mediated by other factors such as the financial circumstances of the households. The socio-economic homogeneity of the households living in the same block of flats was another factor found to influence the occurrence and type of transformations. This was particularly important in the case of vertical stack extension where households are expected to co-operate and contribute financially to the building of the initial structure.

In the case of the Workers City (Helwan), which was built in the early 1960s, resident's initiatives resulted in major changes to the initial five storey walk-up blocks. These changes started with the closing off of balconies and ended with the building of five storey extensions. Extensions have been carried out in two roomed blocks and commercial stores have been added to the flank of the walls particularly along the main internal roads (Tipple et al, 1985). Open spaces have also been taken over and used as private vegetable gardens.

Residents of top floors have taken over the roof spaces for keeping animals and/or for building further rooms. It is evident from these two examples that the informal sector is capable of building and financing multi-storey extensions.

INFORMAL ADAPTATIONS IN ALGIERS
Less major informal extensions in public housing estates are also found in Algiers as recorded by the author in the late 1980's in a survey of 128 dwelling units in four mass housing estates in Algiers (Behloul, 1991). The largest proportion of the dwellings in the surveyed estates consists of three-roomed apartments (one living room and two bedrooms) designed for an 'average household' of seven people. A systematic record was made for each of the surveyed 128 units of the way the dwellings were furnished and altered by their occupants.

HOUSING DESIGN AND LIFESTYLE
The need for extra space was evident amongst households of different types and sizes. The residents took various initiatives in order to cope with the lack of space. These included the closing off of balconies and verandas to gain additional floor area (see fig 3) as witnessed in the Cairo cases. Furthermore, the kitchen was found to become an additional bedroom and the closed off loggia took the role of a very small kitchen. The examination of the way the dwellings were occupied by households of different sizes revealed interesting facts in relation to how the space within the dwellings was managed.

Figure 03: Closed-off balconies in the Garidi estate, Algiers

THE 'AVERAGE' HOUSEHOLD AND THE THREE-BEDROOM DWELLING

Most households of seven people reported using the living room as a sleeping space during nighttime, as the need for separating daughters and sons meant that the living room had to accommodate a bedroom function. It was found that the parents occupy the master bedroom, the daughters the second bedroom and the sons the living room. This has of course a number of consequences on the furnishing and the use of the living room. In these cases, a traditional flexible furnishing is used, which consists of traditional bunks used for sitting during the day and sleeping during the night. Such furnishing sometimes co-existed with 'modern' types of living room furnishing.

SMALL NUCLEAR HOUSEHOLDS (LESS THAN SEVEN PEOPLE)

For this type of household considered as 'modern', where both parents are educated and work outside the home, the two bedrooms flat seems to be a satisfactory size at the stage where children are still at a young age. However, the aspiration of some respondents for a larger flat was justified by the need to separate a son and a daughter once they reached teenage years. It is interesting to note that in the exceptional cases of three bedroom flats occupied by small households, the living room space was used exclusively as a guests' reception room, furnished with a lounge suite and a dining table and was mostly under used. One of the bedrooms took the dual function of a family living room and bedroom and was therefore traditionally furnished with bunks and cushions. The traditional furnishing arrangement consists of bunks arranged around the perimeter of the room and a large tray put on a stand and placed in the middle of the room. Such an arrangement allowed for a flexible use of the space as a sleeping space during the night and a living space during the day where the family gathers to watch the television and sometimes have meals.

LARGE NUCLEAR HOUSEHOLDS (OVER SEVEN PEOPLE)

When recording the furnishing layout in some of the large households' dwellings, it was clear that there was a strong tendency to furnish the living room with the 'modern' type of furniture, usually a wall unit, a suite and a dining table which was rarely used for family meals. Those who could not afford such furnishing, made it clear in the interviews that they were planning to acquire it in the future. The need to display a 'modern' way of living was found to be even stronger amongst families that have moved from rural areas or from the over-crowded courtyard houses in the Casbah of Algiers. The association of 'modern furnishing' with social promotion meant that modern standard furniture was acquired and used at the expense of the family's own comfort within the already cramped dwelling unit. In some blocks of flats, major disagreements between neighbours from different social background was causing tension and reducing the likelihood of joint initiatives between neighbours.

LARGE EXTENDED HOUSEHOLDS

The fixed targets in the 1970s for housing production in Algeria have never been reached because of the sudden fluctuations in the oil market in the beginning of the 1980s and the worsening economic conditions of the country. This has had serious implications on access to housing for new households resulting in the return of the extended family and severe overcrowding conditions in the mass housing dwellings. The national average occupancy rate per dwelling reached 7.55 in 1988 (O.N.S, 1988, 79).

Because of the acute shortage of housing, it is usually the case that children will live with their parents until they get married. The custom is that the husband will provide accommodation for the new household and therefore daughters are expected to leave their parents' flat when they get married. However, the impossibility of the marrying sons finding a flat results in their co-habitation with their parents, adding more pressure on space in the already crowded dwelling unit. Conversions of spaces such as the conversion of the kitchen space into another bedroom and the transfer of the kitchen to the loggia have been frequently triggered by such circumstances.

Extreme cases of occupancy of seven people, adults and children in one bedroom have been found. In this case the furnishing of the bedroom consists of a large number of mattresses piled up in one of the room corners during the day and spread on the floor at sleeping time.

COPING MECHANISM AND ADAPTIVE ALTERATIONS

One of the patterns that emerges from the analysis of furnishing and space occupancy of the dwelling units is that, unless limited by their financial means and/or by a very high occupancy rate per room, there was no compromise on the part of the vast majority of the interviewed households to reduce the number of furniture items in their living room. As mentioned previously, the traditional furnishing was perceived as more comfortable and more flexible. However, the importance of receiving guests in a modern living room meant that the 'modern' type of furnishing was used as a symbol of social promotion. This illustrates the conflict between the tendency to conform with modernity and the persistence of traditional space use patterns and traditional forms of furnishing, which are clearly more responsive to the needs of large households. Receiving guests and relatives remains an important activity in the social life of most North African households. The usual concern about an eventual visit of guest's results in the living room being under-used during the day and even closed when space is available to watch television in another room. As mentioned previously, cases were observed where a clear separation has been made between the living room and the guests' reception room.

Because of overcrowded conditions within the dwelling units, children and male adults tend to spend most of their time outdoors. One of the striking features observed during visits to the housing estates was that some of the spaces adjacent to the blocks of flats have been illegally fenced off and landscaped by the residents (see Figure 04). Such initiatives provided shaded and pleasant spaces for men to meet outside their dwellings and compensated to some extent for the small size of the flats (see Behloul, 1993). The appropriation of such public spaces was not necessarily done by households living on the ground floor apartments but also by the residents of the upper floors. Such initiatives presented several advantages. Not only did they reduce the scale of the public spaces, which are rarely landscaped and maintained, they also created important privacy buffers between the ground floor flats and the public spaces. The cumulative effect of residents' different initiatives led in some cases to a naturally occurring complexity and variety in the external environment and improved the overall appearance of the estates.

Figure 04: Private Gardens in the Ain Nadja estate, Algiers

THE ROLE OF THE INFORMAL SECTOR

The increased occupancy of the dwelling units in the widely spread mass housing estates in Algiers could lead to the Cairo scenario where the whole block structure is extended. The current housing conditions within these estates built in the 1970's and the 1980's could lead to a very rapid degradation of a huge housing stock. Such a situation will significantly worsen the already exacerbated housing needs. This could be avoided if the informal sector is channelled to play an important role in sustaining acceptable living conditions in theses estates and possibly provide the support for adaptive extensions.

According to estimates for Tunis, the informal sector building accounted for 40 per cent of housing construction in the late 1970s and early 1980s and this was provided at 40 per cent of the cost of legally constructed residential areas. Estimates for Cairo suggest that, for the same period, informal housing construction accounted for 82 per cent of new houses (El Kadi, 1987). Vigier (1987) has described a typical example of the development of an informal settlement on the outskirts of Tunis. A plot of land is sold by a landowner to an individual family, or a small developer who will divide the plot. Each plot will be taken by a family, who will build a single room and fence off their area. The house is gradually extended when the family has accumulated enough savings. The construction of the extension is carried out either by the family members or the informal sector labour. As the family grows in size so extra rooms are added on a second floor. One of the characteristics of this process is its incremental nature and its reliance on social and community network. The urban and spatial characteristics of the informal housing settlements present a number of qualities. Unlike public housing estates they are organised along streets and follow the topography of the site. They present a better urban response to the local climatic conditions than most of the public housing estates. The settlements are generally of high density and are under constant transformation. Their development over time results in a mixed-use settlement with integrated shops, workshops and community facilities such as mosques, schools and cafes. Social relations develop over time and result in a strong sense of community and neighbourhood.

One could argue that a feasibility study into the involvement of the informal sector in improving a large formal mass housing stock is a potential that is worth considering in order to provide a basis for a positive transformation of the 1970's and the 1980's mass housing estates in North African cities.

CONCLUSION

Because of the limited degree of housing mobility, adaptations and extensions should be conceived as part of the long-term future of mass housing dwellings in order to respond to the changing needs of the residents. Extensions could be planned through either the closing off of available private external spaces or through actual extensions of the building structure. The rapid deterioration of the mass housing dwellings in North African cities, due to over crowding conditions is likely to result in a huge housing stock that needs urgent attention, exacerbating the already critical housing situation. Enabling, facilitating and channelling the potential of the informal sector might be an answer to such a problem.

BIBLIOGRAPHY

Behloul, M (1991) Post Occupancy evaluation of mass housing estates in Algeria: The case of four mass housing estates in Algiers. PhD thesis Sheffield University

Behloul, M (1993) " The Environment Outside Dwellings, Residents' Reaction in Four Housing Estates in Algiers". In Open House International 1993. Vol. 18 No.4 27-34.

Behloul, M (1993) "Housewives Satisfaction in Four Mass Housing Estates in Algeria" A Paper Presented to the International Conference on Urban Environment in Developing Countries, Futures, Ideas, and Directions. June (16-18) 1993. Eindhoven – The Netherlands.

Behloul, M (1994) " Housewives' Perception of Mass Housing Dwellings in Algeria" A Conference Paper Presented to "Ideal Homes? Towards a Sociology of Domestic Architecture and Interior Design". September 6-8th 1994. School of Human Studies. University of Teeside.

Behloul, M (1994) " Space Use Patterns and Coping Mechanisms of Algerian Households in Mass Housing Dwellings"A Paper Presented to the International Symposium on People,

Place & Development. Centre for Architectural Research and Development Overseas (CARDO). University of Newcastle. December (1-2) 1994.

El Kadi, G. (1987) "L'Urbanisation Spontanee au Caire" Urbama Fascicules de Recherche 10.

El Moudjahid (1988) Daily Newspaper, Monday 18th of April issue, Supplément social,. VII. Algiers.

MUCH (1979) Ministry of Urban Planning Construction and Housing. Prescriptions Fonctionnelles et Techniques, Normes, Recommandations et Instructions Relatives au Logement Social Urbain, Algiers.

O.N.S. (1988) "Statistiques, Armature Urbaine, 1987", Les Collections des Statistiques 4, Office National des Statistiques (ONS), Algiers.

INERBA (1980) Institut National d'Etudes et de Recherches du Batiment, (1980) Procédés de construction : Etudes générales de développement du secteur du batiment, Algiers: Ministère de l'Urbanisme, de la Construction et de l'Habitat.

Kardash, H & Wilkinson, N., (1991) "Development within development: User extensions of four- walk-ups housing in Cairo- the case of Helwan" Open House International 16, 1, 9-17.

Salama, R (1994) " The phenomenon of User Transformation of Public Housing in Egypt". in Awotona Editor. Proceedings of an International Symposium on People, Place & Development. CARDO (centre for Architectural Research and Development Overseas) University of Newcastle. UK.

Steinberg, F., (1984) " Ain el Sira in Cairo: the Architecture of Poverty" Open House International, 9, 2, 35-42.

Tipple, A.G., (1991) "Self Help Transformations of low cost housing: an introductory study" Urban International Press. Newcastle Upon Tyne.

Tipple, A.G., Wilkinson and M'Nour (1985) "The Transformation of Workers City, Helwan: Multi-storey extensions observed"Open House International, 10, 3, 25-38 Vigier, F. (1987) " Housing in Tunis". Cambridge, MA:Harvard University Press.

Part Three
Redefining the Design Institution Interface

Ecological Design in Cuba - Theory and Practice

Dania González Couret

During the last ten years or so the word 'sustainable development' has developed from the original narrow meaning into a wider concept, which includes not only the ecological, but also the economic and the social dimensions. Despite the fact that there is a consensus about the necessity to reconcile economic development with the environmental concern and the demand for social equity, the economic model imposed by globalisation gives economic growth prominence before integrity and equity. The priority given to each of the three dimensions depends on the professional discipline and the political perspective of the observer. Nevertheless - according to the widest and most complete approach - sustainable development should mean environmental safety, economical viability and social fairness. That is why ecological design is only a part of sustainable development.

SUSTAINABILITY IN DEVELOPED AND DEVELOPING COUNTRIES

The expansion of cities of great economic and political power was achieved by the appropriation of resources from neighbouring regions and other countries. That is the case during colonialism, neo-colonialism and, more recently, the post-industrial neo-liberal globalisation (Coyula, 1997). Hence the developed countries are the ones that bear the largest responsibility for today's environmental crisis. It was they, who imposed the model of development, which dominated during the last three centuries, a model, which has also been a major aspiration for developing countries. On the other hand, the developing countries have been victims. They need to develop, but they do not get access to the advanced and environment-friendly technologies (González, 1995).

There are different approaches to sustainable development. The developed countries - which have solved their essential problems - approach sustainable development as a 'cult', a way in which ecology is a worry. In the developing countries, on the other hand, basic problems such as housing, food, health and education are imperative. Therefore sustainable development is a way to survive. It is a completely different thing to adopt certain lifestyles (for example, to eat only vegetables or to go by bike) as an alternative to other possible options in order to protect the environment, compared to the situation where you have to adopt a solution as the only possible one, an option that is imposed by external forces.

This situation is provocative to Third World countries. The same is true for Cuba. Solutions for sustainability could be perceived by people as 'a necessary evil', as a sign of backwardness and as a temporary solution until a 'true development' can be achieved (according to the Western model).

SUSTAINABLE HUMAN SETTLEMENTS

The built environment plays an important role for achieving sustainability. This is particularly true for urban settlements, because their scale and concentration of population make them a burden for their hinterland. The irreversible character of the urbanization process has been recognized as desirable because of its advantages for people (despite the 'urbanization of poverty'). That is why developing 'more sustainable settlements in an urbanizing world' is a major goal in the Habitat Agenda (UNCHS, 1996).

Cities are huge processors of food, fuel and other goods. These processes constitute very complex metabolisms. They are artificial because they are concentrated to a small area. They consume water and materials in amounts much bigger than nature can supply and, consequently, they generate huge amounts of garbage and wastewater. Nature cannot provide resources necessary to make urban life sustainable. Neither can nature dispose of the residues produced.

There is not one single sustainable urban model. According to the bio-ecological approach, the city is an ecosystem, which should improve its own organization, and reduce its dependence on fossil fuel (instead of the sun) as a source of energy. A sustainable city must be strongly resilient and not vulnerable.

Applying the principles of natural recycling to the urban environment one may say that a sustainable city implies a circular metabolism (Yunén, 1997). This means that every output could be reused or recycled, affecting only a smaller area. Using local recycling as much as possible for water, garbage, energy and food is a way to achieve more sustainable cities and thus, a more sustainable world. It means a better use of existent abundant human resources, of the precious natural resources and of the scarce financial resources (at least in the Third World).

Another important point to take into account is the scale of the settlement. A large and differentiated city generates a great environmental burden that affects other regions. To divide cities into smaller units is a good way to divide big problems into smaller ones and thereby solve them more easily. Some innovations - such as bicycles, urban agriculture, local economies based on small and medium enterprises, and using technologies responsive to the environment - contribute to reduce the environmental burden (González, 1998; 1999). But sustainability should not only be a model to survive. It should not only be a question of stopping or go backwards.

Some basic needs will continue to worry citizens of the world in the coming century: attractive jobs, healthy food, clean water, appropriate disposition of solid and liquid wastes, saving and reusing resources, education, health care, culture, sport, recreation, alternative sources of energy, efficient public transport, affordable and appropriate housing, attractive urban and rural environments, productive enough to feed the population and good enough to prevent migration to the cities (Coyula, 1997).

CUBAN EXPERIENCES OF SUSTAINABLE DEVELOPMENT

Since 1959 - almost 30 years before the concept 'sustainable development' was coined - several processes and solutions for sustainability have been developed in Cuba. Created in 1960 - the Committees for the Defence of the Revolution (CDR), organizations that gather people in the neighbourhood - had as one of their main tasks to collect recoverable materials (glass, paper, carton, metal) in order to recycle and thereby save money. Without precedent the CDRs have served as social mechanisms for the collection and recycling of inorganic wastes. This was done despite the fact that its motivation was economical and not ecological. In practice it has not gone beyond its educational objective to be a useful economical tool.

Actions to stop the unbalanced growth of the capital city, and to address the differences between city and countryside that started in the early 60s, are today internationally recognized as basic principles for sustainable development. Regional and urban planning activities were started, including a national system of human settlements and the creation of basic rural settlements directly related to agricultural production. A mistake made was the reproduction in these rural settlements of urban models that were neither sustainable, nor appropriate. Conceptions were applied that have impeded the natural evolution of these settlements.

Unsuccessful attempts to bring food production near the urban areas also started in the 60s. Another example is the idea of the 'Havana Green Belt', which was initiated to supply agricultural products to the urban population who worked on it. This experience failed because the goals were mainly educational and not economical (Barony, 1993).

During the 60s, before the Cuban building industry became occupied with heavy prefab systems, a lot of research and experiments were carried out to develop appropriate materials and technologies for mass housing based on the real possibilities and resources of the country. In this period many constructive ideas were developed, based on open, flexible and small-scale systems. Unfortunately, these studies were abandoned in the 70s, when preference was given to European high tech prefab systems. The purpose was to satisfy in a short time the massive housing demands, but the lack of sustainability became evident in the 90s, when Cuba had to continue building housing based on its own resources.

Research related to the use of renewable sources of energy had a boom in the late 70s and the early 80s, probably as an answer to the energy crisis of 1973. Since then a lot of research projects and experimental production of equipments have been developed. Many practical applications have also been carried out. One important application of renewable energy is the electrification of many isolated rural communities, mainly in the mountain regions. Here small hydropower plants, i.e. solar water heater systems, were installed in social buildings as hospitals and nurseries. Units for biogas production were installed in many stables for light production. The latter experiment was not successful, however, because skilled workers were not engaged.

Otherwise the development of renewable energies constitutes one of the most successful steps to Cuban sustainable development, despite the fact that there have been some failures due to remaining social resistance to these new technologies. On the other hand, these applications are not generally introduced in wider projects with an integral sustainable conception, which limits its scope (González, 1997).

THE TURQUINO PLAN

The first application of a coherent and integral sustainable development concept was implemented in the 'Turquino Plan' from 1987. Then the idea of 'sustainable development' had not yet been officially established. The 'Turquino Plan' intended to promote social and economical development of the mountain regions in as self-sufficient ways as possible, in order to stop migrations to the lowlands. It was considered necessary to repopulate these areas because of the economic importance of some agricultural products grown there (coffee, cocoa, wood). It was also motivated by the concern for survival in case of attacks by foreign forces. Therefore the population needed their own resources and production (González, 1989).

This Plan for the integral development of the mountain regions had, among its basic principles:
- To take advantage of renewable energies and all resources locally available;
- To safeguard a local production of the major possible amount of required resources. For this purpose, not only crops and cattle areas were developed, but also industries to produce conserved food, offering new job opportunities, mainly for women;
- To recycle residues and to create feeding chains, using permaculture techniques to grow food in an intensive way;
- Alternative solutions for transportation, where animal traction played the main role as a renewable resource;
- Alternative solutions for services and facilities.
- In the 90s, when the Turquino Plan should be reoriented in construction and social policy, it became evident that it had failed. The idea of 'high quality' meant that the local context was disregarded. Houses were, for instance, not always locally produced. From 1990 Cuba entered a deep economic crisis as a consequence of losing its main commercial partners (East European countries).
- This brought about important economical and social changes that affected the whole country. Survival was to be achieved by relying on the country's own scarce material resources. Thus, instead of being an explicit goal, alternative and sustainable solutions were imposed during the so-called 'special period'. Among the main achievements during this period were:
- The increased use of renewable energies. Almost 100% of the energy consumed in the sugar industry have been of its own produce (sugar cane biomass.)
- At least certain types of food production were incorporated to the daily urban life. Urban agriculture is today part of the urban landscape. It constitutes an important factor for community participation in the economy.

- Alternative solutions for urban transportation were assimilated, mainly at the scale of the neighbourhood. Small towns introduced a massive use of bikes and animal traction vehicles.
- Heavy prefab systems and similar projects were abandoned and substituted by lower energy building solutions based on specific projects built with locally available materials.

The economy of the country is today in a process of recovery. Therefore some of these sustainable practices run a risk of getting lost or substituted by solutions from the Western development model. The survival practices applied up to now were not the only possible alternatives, but for the sustainable experiences to survive they have to be seen as appropriate alternatives also in situations without economic crisis. For that to happen popular education is very important. Sustainable practices should be the result of conscious choices.

CUBA SOLAR

Cuba Solar is a non-government organization (NGO) for the promotion of renewable energies in the country, combined with social, economical and other environmental goals. It was created in 1994. Despite its short life it has made important achievements. One of the important ones is the electrification of 'doctor houses', communities and schools in isolated, mainly mountainous, regions. The electrification is based on renewable energies such as hydro-power and photovoltaic systems. The electrification of 'doctor houses' includes a communication system between the doctors and hospital with better diagnosis and treatment facilities. The social impact of these projects is much more important than their economic and environmental ones.

Other projects of Cuba Solar intend to improve people's living conditions, mainly in isolated regions. In these areas alternative and more efficient technologies are provided, such as buildings for water pumping and cooking. We also work hard in environmental education, mainly with young people and children. For that purpose, experimental 'labs' have been developed in rural schools. Several publications have been issued, including a popular magazine and a textbook for secondary schools.

Attempts at sustainable practices have not always been achieved as initially conceived. That is the case with the 'ecological settlements system' related to sugar cane production. Here practical applications reduced their true 'ecological' character. Important efforts have also been made to introduce more ecological approaches in new tourist developments, mainly in the 'protected areas'. Unsustainable concepts still predominate among investors and public employees. There is no a proper market study to orient Cuban tourist product towards a true eco-tourism. The 'Environmental Impact Law' has recently been approved and it establishes the necessity to carry out environmental impact studies as a prerequisite for approving an investment.

RESTRICTION TO REAL SUSTAINABLE DESIGN

There are not many Third World countries, which can show similar actions for sustainable solutions, taking into account that they do not constitute isolated experiences. Nevertheless, in the Cuban experience some insufficiencies subsist, which limit the real sustainability of some of these attempts:

- Sometimes, top-down approaches are predominant and they limit active participation of involved actors from the very beginning. Such participation is essential for success

- True sustainable solutions and processes should be specific, because they develop from inside to outside and bottom-up. However, the centralized conduction of some processes sometimes limits their success. Attempts to generalize good experiences may prevent their application.

- Decisions are sometimes based on partial analysis, without taking into account consequences that could be considered in a more integral analysis. For example, life cycle analysis is not considered in building decisions. Partial analysis could also lead to pragmatic approaches.

- The role of architectural and urban design for sustainability, energy consumption, comfort and quality of life has not been sufficiently considered (González, 1986, 1997).

Resistance to changes is a proven fact. This resistance comes not only from the users, but also from the old institutions in charge of promoting new solutions.

Summarizing, the analysis of the Cuban experience confirms the importance of the integral sustainable approach, including its three dimensions. Neither social sustainability alone, nor ecological sustainability, is enough. If an experience is not economically sustainable, it can not survive.

BIBLIOGRAPHY

Baroni, Sergio, 1993, personal interview, Havana.

Coyula, Mario (1997): 'Ambiente, población y desarrollo en un mundo en urbanización', *Quiénes hacen ciudad?,* Ediciones SIAP, Cuenca.

González Couret, Dania (1986): 'La Arquitectura Solar en Cuba', *Arquitectura y Urbanismo*, No 3, p 14-20, ISPJAE, Havana.

González Couret, Dania (1989): 'La vivienda en la Montaña, un nuevo enfoque', *Arquitectura y Urbaismo*, No 2, p 8-15, ISPJAE, Havana.

González Couret, Dania (1995): 'Bioecological Architecture in a Developing Country'. *REBUILD*, Corfu.

González Couret, Dania (1997): 'Asentamientos sustentables en Cuba. Experiencias y perspec-tivas', Conference *Ciudades Confortables para todos*, ARC-PEACE Peru, Lima.

González Couret, Dania, et al (1998): 'From a Scholar City to a Solar City', Renewable Energy, *Energy Efficiency, Policy and the Environment*, World Renewable Energy Congress, Florence, Italy, Part I.

González Couret, Dania (1999): 'Sustainable Solutions for La Lisa Municipality in Havana', *REBUILD*, Barcelona.

UNHCS (1996): *Habitat Agenda* Istanbul. Yunen, Rafael E. (1997): 'Medio ambiente urbano: marco conceptual', *Quiénes hacen ciudad?*, Ediciones SIAP, Cuenc.

Indian Housing Finance Alliances and the Urban Poor

Peer Smets

Apart from the public and private interventions in the housing finance market, it is thought that non-governmental organizations (NGOs) and community-based organizations (CBOs) can play an important role. One of the NGOs dealing with housing finance is the Society for the Promotion of Area Resource Centers (SPARC), which has experience in this area in especially the Indian city of Mumbai. The focus will shift to the activities of the alliance between the NGO SPARC, the National Slum Dwellers Federation and the Mahila Milan (a federation of CBOs). Following this, the potential roles of NGOs and CBOs in an alliance with public and/or private institutions will be discussed in a model-like approach developed by Igel and Srinivas for the city of Bangalore. This will be followed by the discussion of the Dharavi scheme in Mumbai. Finally, the potential for serving the urban poor on a large scale through alliances will be reconsidered. Here, it will be shown that those controlling the flow of large sums determine the policies to a large extent, neglecting needs and desires of local dwellers.

HOUSING FINANCE NGOS AND CBOs
Public and private housing finance institutions in India face problems in adequately serving the poor with housing finance (Smets 1995; 1997). They face difficulties in adjusting to the needs of the poor, or what Seibel (1997: 9) calls an institutional adjustment strategy of downgrading. Such an action of downgrading formal housing finance institutions is rather problematic, due to the predominant idea that housing finance should be characterized by large amounts, generally a mix of savings and credit. Moreover, the loans involved are generally long term in nature. This conflicts with the short to medium-term livelihood strategies of the urban poor (e.g. Smets 1999). To improve access of the poor to formal housing, NGOs and federations of CBOs can be seen as an alternative channel to serve them. Here, solutions are found in alliances with NGOs and/or CBOs.

One of the Indian NGOs being involved in alliances is SPARC, which is mainly known for the creation and strengthening of CBOs, such as financial help organizations among slum and pavement dwellers in Mumbai. For this purpose, SPARC works together with the National Slum Dwellers Federation (NSDF), in which slum leaders are organized, and the Mahila Milan (MM), which is a federation of women collectives. The alliance SPARC/NSDF/MM has not only established ties with other Indian cities such as Bangalore and Kanpur, but also with other communities in countries such as South Africa, Namibia and Cambodia.

Through financial self-help organisations that were established by the alliance, savings are pooled and a fund for crisis loans has been established. For a period of approximately three months, new female participants are expected to undertake a training process to learn how such a financial self-help organisation works. Once operational, additional external finance enables the provision of loans for income generation activities and for construction. However, before housing loans can be provided, other activities have to take place such as a survey of the slum concerned, conscious building, and training in communication skills resulting in a pilot project. If such a pilot project deals with housing, attention has also to be paid to construction skills, the costs of materials, production of building materials and the provision of basic facilities (e.g. Bolnick & Mitlin 1999; Patel 1999; Patel, Bolnick and Mitlin 2000).

In order to bring the shelter dreams of the urban poor alive, dwellers can display life-size house models made of a wooden frame covered with cloth at a housing *mela* or exhibition. Such a housing *mela* enables dwellers to communicate with bureaucrats and officials of the local and state government about issues of security of tenure, lending rates of housing loans, the establishment of infrastructure and basic facilities in the settlement and the norms and values associated with the construction process. This offers the possibility of discovering out how state-provided subsidies and subsidised housing loans in combination with other financial sources, and construction materials and techniques promoted by the building centres can be used to improve the habitat of slum dweller communities (SPARC 1999).

A MODEL FOR BANGALORE

To close the gap between demand and supply of housing finance to low-income households, Igel and Srinivas (1996) have developed a credit delivery model for squatter housing in Bangalore, India. The idea is that formal credit is channeled to low-income households through a tentative model involving four groups of agents; representatives of public sector agencies, private sector financial institutions, NGOs and CBOs. The community-based credit committee, as a CBO, is supposed to bring the 'most' attractive characteristics of the operations of the 'informal' financial market together; 'timely credit, obligation to save, flexibility and reciprocity to tap household savings and provide the means to channel formal finance to low-income borrowers.' (Igel & Srinivas 1996: 294-295).

The credit committee at the core of the model was supposed to be formed from within the slum by leaders and members of CBOs. Each member must save a predetermined and specified amount with the credit committee on a daily, weekly or monthly basis. Loans of a maximum of twice the savings of a specific member will be provided. Apart from individual savings, Rotating Savings and Credit Associations (ROSCAs) can be set up, from which a round of contribution collection has to be handed over to the committee to establish a reserve and emergency fund. The savings can be used partly as collateral for future loans from commercial banks or housing finance corporations. The credit committee is constituted from within the settlement, which enables a good representation of the low-income borrower's view and interests. This would minimize power manipulations driven by greed and profit maximization (Igel & Srinivas 1996: 295-298).

The structure and activities of the credit committee may change overtime. When the economic conditions of the participating slum dwellers improve, four stages can be distinguished. Firstly, the credit committee only deals directly with the slum dwellers and collects savings from individual slum dwellers. Moreover, several ROSCAs can be organised. A ROSCA is a financial self-help organisation in which participants pool regular contributions, which will be given, in whole or part, to each participant in turn. In the second stage, the credit committee also extends its operations to formal financial institutions. The collected savings can be deposited with a bank, where loans for individuals or groups can be arranged. To enable a direct link between the financial institution and the slum dwellers in the third stage, external commission agents are appointed by the banks to pay out loans and collect repayments. Such agents can help to establish mutual understanding between the dwellers and the financial institution, and to facilitate drawing up of contracts between the two parties involved. The agents are a step towards stage four in which slum dwellers, based on self-regulation and control, are expected to have direct links and financial contracts with the formal financial institutions. In this period, the credit committee employs a role of support and co-ordination by securing the loan by, for example, providing collateral or guarantees (Igel & Srinivas 1996: 300-303).

DHARAVI SCHEME MUMBAI

Sanyal and Mukhija (2000) analysed the Dharavi scheme, Mumbai, which aims at redeveloping the area by providing new infrastructure and housing, and establishing housing co-operatives for the local dwellers. In various stages of the preparation and implementation of the Dharavi scheme, conflicts arose between the stakeholders involved; housing finance agencies, public sector organisations (the Municipal Corporation of Greater Mumbai, the Maharashtra Housing and Area Development Authority, and the Prime Minister's Grant Project), private contractors, SPARC, NSDF, and dwellers participating in a housing co-operative.

Conflicts arose at different stages of the scheme. At the planning stage, the original government project was challenged by SPARC, who surveyed the project area and discovered that more dwellers had to be involved in the scheme than the government had originally estimated. Moreover, a plan was created by members of the housing co-operative, which rejected the planned five-story buildings and proposed two-three stories that would lead to declining construction costs.

Source	Share of housing costs
Subsidy Prime Minister's Grant Project	10%
Interest free loan	20%
(also subsidised by Prime Minister's Grant Project)	
Housing finance agencies	35%
Beneficiaries own contributions	35%

Table 1:`Financial sources for housing in the Dharavi habitat improvement scheme (Sanyal and Mukhija, 2000: 8)

To cover the housing costs, the Prime Minister's Grant Programme –set up to enable the Prime Minister to influence the allocation of some funds - proposed a share of the costs as laid down in Table 1. In 1989, it appeared that the Prime Minister's Grant Project had insufficient finance to complete the Dharavi scheme. The Prime Minister's Grant Project was only willing to provide the direct costs subsidy and withdrew from the provision of interest-free loans and a guarantee for external loans.

In the meantime, the housing co-operative and SPARC started constructing houses, using a downpayment from the co-operative members to hire a private contractor. To obtain housing finance, SPARC approached the public sector housing finance agency HUDCO (Housing and Urban Development Organisation) on behalf of the co-operative. HUDCO was willing to provide the credit, but demanded conventional collateral. They suggested a guarantee of a state government housing authority, a land mortgage or a bank guarantee against a fixed deposit. However, the Prime Minister's Grant Project, as being the project's promoter, refused to advise that the state government housing authority should lease the land to the co-operative. Later on, SPARC managed to motivate the Municipal Corporation of Greater Mumbai to lease the land to the housing co-operation, so that it could be mortgaged for the HUDCO loan. Due to the delays in the release of housing finance, the private contractor ceased construction activities. Nevertheless, SPARC attempted find a way out and guaranteed the HUDCO loans from its own funds. HUDCO released 75% of the first loan installment to the housing co-operative that was responsible for its repayment, withholding 25% for the interest payments. A new contractor was employed, who was a relative of a co-operative member. Finally, SPARC succeeded in arranging an interim bank guarantee for additional loans until the land lease was executed.
Later on, new financial problems arose and SPARC was not eager to increase the downpayments with the contractor and consequently the debt burden. Again, a new contractor stepped into the project and was willing to invest substantially in the scheme without further HUDCO loans. The new contractor was even eager to repay the HUDCO loans, reimburse SPARC for the bridge loans, and to return the subsidy granted. In return, he/she was allowed to sell 70% of the housing units on the free market. Only 30% had to be provided free to the residents. The co-operative members were pleased with the contractor's initiative and did not protest against the construction of additional floors. In practice, the dwellers had to pay an average of Rs. 35,000 for these 'free' houses. SPARC suggested that the co-operative members had been bribed to accept this offer.

As has been sketched above, different conflicts arose between the co-managing institutions during the preparation and implementation of the scheme. The conflicts between private entrepreneurs and SPARC led to the development of a more market-oriented attitude of SPARC. Moreover, the frictions between the public agencies and SPARC stimulated SPARC to gain control over a part of the public sector. These experiences led to the centralisation of SPARC's internal organisation. Furthermore, the way that SPARC dealt with the communities transformed 'from an open-ended, all inclusive and participatory way to a relatively selective style where it worked with a few trustworthy individuals.' Instead of advocacy only, the original mission of SPARC became one of social investment in profitable enterprises. Finally, it should be noted that the Mumbai case is unique; it took place against a background of rapidly increasing real estate prices and new private-sector-friendly governmental policies for low-income housing areas in the 1990s (Sanyal & Mukhija 2000: 4-5, 28). I quote:

'The public policy changes instituted to attract private developers included an increase in Floor Area Ratios (the ratio of the floor area of the built-project to the area of the site), larger allowance for free-sale of housing for cross-subsidizing the cost of housing construction and the introduction of Transfer of Development Rights (TDR – unbundles the development potential of a land parcel from a site specific context and allows property-owners to transfer the development potential from an 'origin-site' to a 'receiving site').' (ibid.: 5).

This study of the Dharavi scheme not only reveals that institutional pluralism may be accompanied by conflict, but that such conflict does not necessarily have to have a negative impact on the institutions and the target group. Moreover, a possibility of institutional conflict require its acknowledgement, clear-cut devises and unambiguous rules about the division of labour when implementing habitat improvement schemes, and the creation of a centralised institution that may mediate disputes among the various parties involved in slum rehabilitation (Sanyal & Mukhija 2000: 27).

DOWN MARKETING, HOUSING FINANCE THROUGH SCALING UP RECONSIDERED

The down marketing of housing finance in India is facilitated by financial injections of e.g. the Asian Development Bank. In 1997, the Bank released a loan of $ 300 million (Rs. 12.9 billion), which was intended for the provision of housing finance to the National Housing Bank (a subsidiary of the Central Bank of India), the HUDCO and the private sector institution HDFC (Housing Development and Finance Corporation). The purpose of this loan was to strengthen linkages between housing finance corporations and CBOs. This was done with the aim of supporting low-income housing and slum improvement, but also the refinancing facilities of the National Housing Bank. For this purpose, greater insight is required into the operation and maintenance of the informal housing finance market and the willingness for alliances to channel 'affordable' credit to the urban and rural poor. In the same year, $ 600,000 was approved by the Asian Development Bank to ameliorate the institutional constraints of housing finance institutions. Another additional amount of $ 500,000 was approved to support the shift of the government's role as provider of houses towards a facilitator's role (ADB 1999: 3; Vora 1999: 10-11).

The financial injection from the Asian Development Bank was expected to help in down marketing housing finance. However, NGOs generally face a shortage of funds for providing credit. As a consequence, external sources of finance had to be mobilised in addition to the pooled savings from the associated CBOs. For this purpose, the NGOs should be trusted by the financier, who tends to ask for conditions such as a complete

building plan including targets before the credit will be released. The NGO SPARC (1996: 6) describes it as follows:
'Every agency which had lent us money behave with the alliance as though we need to be hundred percent definite about all aspects of the construction. Almost as though they are doing us a enormous favour to lend us money.'

A development of the institutions in line with the demands of providers of housing finance creates the possibility of co-operation between public and/or private institutions. The housing finance corporations in India spend a lot of money on hiring consultants to design systems. The same sums could be used to start pilot projects, which will create better knowledge on policy and procedures (SPARC 1996: 7). The alliance SPARC/NSDF/MM 'is working to secure land tenure, standardize house construction and design costs and negotiate with housing finance institutions to convince them of the need to lend directly to low-income households' (Patel 1999: 165).

The model of the alliance SPARC/NSDF/MM is seen as vulnerable by Patel (1999) in four respects. Firstly, the complete process is dependent on trust; all individual members have to trust that all parties will behave and act in accordance with the collective's interests. Secondly, a growth of the decentralised development process may obstruct innovation and adaptation. Thirdly, it is of crucial importance to maintain a more or less balanced working relationship with the government. Especially when the alliance depends on public sector initiatives, there is a danger of encapsulation by the government or conflict between the stakeholders involved. Only when some distance from the government can be established is the alliance able to develop new alternatives for housing and finance. Fourthly, the model is not financially sustainable and dependent on external finance (ibid.: 167-168).

Public or private sector agencies tend to demand the institutionalisation and legalisation of the NGOs and CBOs they are dealing with. However, institutionalisation and legalisation often leads to more bureaucratic procedures for the NGOs and CBOs, which are required

to upgrade activities such as financial extension services, training personnel in book-keeping and financial management, promoting innovative savings schemes, internal resource mobilisation through debt instruments, in mediating contacts with banks or donors, collecting and safekeeping savings, checking the creditworthiness of clients, negotiating bank loans, as well as in practices of lending, collecting instalments, bearing the credit risk, and repaying bank loans (Seibel 1997: 15-16).

The financial terms and conditions for housing loans, including interest payments and the means of institutionalisation and legalisation, are often to a large extent determined by the lender. The housing loans provided by the housing finance corporations and the HUDCO are generally intended for complete housing units. Nevertheless, the loans are too small for the construction of a housing unit and a contribution from the beneficiary and/or the NGO is required. Still the housing loans are large and require a long term of repayment. Alliances between NGOs and formal housing institutions are backward due to the long term of housing loans and the short-term perspective of many NGOs, which are forced to work on a-project-to-project basis due to a shortage of internal resources (Garilao 1987: 117). Furthermore, many NGO projects tend to remain small scale and cover only small tracts of land in the target area (Bowden 1990: 146), while there is an enormous need for improvement of the habitat conditions of the increasing number of the poorer sections of the fast growing Third World Cities.

One alternative financial condition, which is more or less accepted by the HUDCO, the National Housing Bank and the housing finance corporations, is the social control mechanism, such as peer pressure, as substitute for conventional collateral. Moreover, creditworthiness is accepted on the basis of proved savings behaviour. For such groups, community building may be required to enable the participation of the beneficiaries in a sustainable way. Bowden (1990), however, considers community building not be very sustainable due to 'natural' tension between group members, which can affect each group, high turn-over of field workers, too much direct assistance given, lack of consensus about methods that enforce cohesion and sustainability, big role of charismatic leaders, problems in generating self-help decision-making capability (ibid.: 145-146). In addition, community-level action encourages external agents to refrain from lending their assistance, placing the burden of habitat improvement on the slum dwellers themselves (Douglas 1995: 25). The most encouraging community level action is characterised by 'households capable of pooling resources and dividing labor into complementary tasks; strong inter-household support networks; security of tenure; leadership arising from within that is also recognized by the state; the presence of NGOs that seek to empower rather than undermine community organizations; democratic regimes; and community-oriented support from international assistance agencies. While this exact profile is difficult to find in Asia, many of the elements exist or are appearing.' (Douglas 1995: 27).

In addition to the social control systems, relatively small loans require larger overhead costs, which may cause frictions with financiers. In this respect, an employee of the National Housing Bank complained that the overhead charges of the NGOs (8-10%) are very high compared with 3% of the housing finance corporations. The National Housing Bank aims at bringing down these overhead costs. In the meantime, the NGOs are held responsible for the repayment of loans.

To make housing loans affordable for the poor, housing loans may be subsidised. The HUDCO subsidises the housing loans for the poor, while the National Housing Bank and the private housing finance corporations subsidise the relatively small loans for the poor and non-poor. Grants and subsidies for housing finance programmes can improve access to housing finance by the target group, but it reduces the potential of replicability of the scheme unless the grants or subsidies continue. Credit, provided it is repaid, is preferable to grants, because a revolving fund can cover more people in the long run. Furthermore, obtaining and repaying a loan requires a more active and self-reliant involvement of the beneficiaries (Copestake 1996: 24). Such involvement can be established through small savings and credit groups.

If a housing finance scheme becomes dependent on finance from donors in the West, the danger arises of what Garilao (1987: 118) calls 'the trap of dependency'. To avoid the trap of dependency, the NGOs have to mobilise local resources. The Federation of Thrift and Credit Associations even refused to accept external sources of finance. When it concerns finance from an Indian public institution, there is a danger that debts will be written off. There is a tendency that borrowers will anticipate this and thus not repay the credit. In general, it can be said that it is 'the surest way to kill a movement is to smother it with money.' (Korten in Hulme 1994: 268).

In order to defend the interests of the poor and their own interests, NGOs can organise themselves in an NGO centre to strengthen their operation and maintenance by exchanging experiences (Steinberg 1994: 8). Baken and Smets (1999) suggests that an incremental building process, instead of aiming at the construction of complete dwelling units, is beneficial to the poor. Such incremental building activities to extend the size or improve the quality of the shelter, taking place over years and even decades, are dependent on the individual household priorities, the means available and change according to the family cycle, or changes in the life of migrants in the city. Therefore, housing should be considered a process. Housing should not be judged according to its physical appearance, but its users' value has to be the main point of evaluation. In other words, 'what it means' for its users instead of 'what it materially is'. There is a continually changing variety of individual and/or household needs, priorities and possibilities, which helps spread the costs of the construction activities over time. The components required for the construction process should be left up to the individual users, or to de-centralised local and small-scale institutions. Large organisations tend to provide standard products and cannot adequately deal with the enormous variety of changing housing needs (e.g. Turner 1976).

In practice, it appears that incremental building is increasingly seen as a good policy alternative. However, incremental financing is not commonly accepted. For example, the Indian Grameen Bank replica SHARE, working in rural areas of the state Andhra Pradesh, decided to provide housing loans with a term of four years after consultation with its beneficiaries. Such a term fits the livelihood strategies of the poor who have a short or medium term planning horizon. An additional result is that the friction between long-term financing and the relatively short to medium-term planning horizon of the NGO can be reconciled. A NGO's planning horizon is largely determined by funding agencies, which finance activities for a short to medium term only.

CONCLUSION

The role of NGOs and CBOs in the Indian housing finance market is very limited, but there are possibilities of expansion within certain limits. NGO's role in the delivery of housing finance is not only restricted in scope due to a lack of financial means available and the long-term bias of housing finance, but also due to an inadequate ability to cope with the provision of financial services. In addition, pre-existing financial services are difficult to expand due to institutional and contextual constraints. The financial terms and conditions are to a large extent determined by the formal housing finance institutions, which encompass mortgage lending, subsidised interest rates, mainly long-term and repayment in equated monthly installments. In general, these loans are provided for buying a dwelling unit or for building one. In general, the beneficiaries have to take out a big loan amount. By subsidising the interest rate and enlarging the term the size of the monthly installments can be reduced to an 'affordable' level.

For community-based housing finance an empowerment orientation is required. Here, savings and credit associations can play an important role by evoking trust and self-respect among the beneficiaries. Such a strategy must be proved successful in establishing CBOs. However, enlarging the scale of delivering housing finance is rather limited due to the finance available with the CBOs and the NGOs. In order to increase the funds, alliances can be sought not only among other CBOs and NGOs, but also with institutions in the private and public sector. If an NGO acts as a guarantor or borrows from a housing finance corporation, it obtains credit, but also has to deal with the housing finance corporations' norms and values. Their norms and values conflict with the short-term planning horizon of NGOs, and the norms and values of the poor, who build their dwellings in an incremental way. A better means of serving the poor with housing finance is to adjust the financial terms and conditions to the incremental building process of the poor. In other words, downmarketing housing finance through NGOs is limited unless the poor are given the opportunity to build in an incremental way. Therefore, the slum dwellers must be empowered, possibly with the help of an NGO, to be able to obtain such housing finance schemes to improve their living conditions over a long period. Furthermore, forming alliances among CBOs and NGOs can strengthen their negotiation capacity and position with other stakeholders in the housing finance market, where those having access to large sums of finance tend to dominate the terms and conditions of habitat improvement schemes. Here, is the challenge to overcoming periods of institutional conflict and conflicting norms and values to obtain improvements of the urban habitat in a synergetic fashion.

BIBLIOGRAPHY

Baken, R.-J. & P. Smets (1999). Better a 'hut' on the ground than a castle in the air: public and informal housing finance for the urban poor in Andhra Pradesh, India. In: K. Datta & G.A. Jones (eds), *Housing and Finance in Developing Countries*. London: Routledge.

Bolnick, J. & D. Mitlin (1999)Housing finance and empowerment in South Africa. In: K. Datta & G.A. Jones (eds), *Housing and finance in developing countries*. London: Routledge.

Bowden, P. NGOs in Asia: issues in development, *Public Administration and Development*, vol. 10, pp. 141-152.

Copestake, J. NGO-state collaboration and the new policy agenda - the case of subsidized credit, *Public administration and development*, vol. 16, pp. 21-30.

Douglas, M. (1995)Urban environmental management at the grass roots: towards a theory of community action. East-West Centre Working Papers,

Environment Series, no. 42. Honolulu: East-West Center.

Garilao, E.D. (1987).Indigenous NGOs as strategic institutions: managing the relationship with government and resource agencies, *World Development*, vol. 15, supplement, pp. 113-120.

Hulme, D.(1994).Social development research and the third sector: NGOs as users and subjects of social inquiry. In: D. Booth (ed.), *Rethinking social development: theory, research and practice.* Essex: Longman scientific & technical.

Igel, B. & H. Srinivas (1996).The co-optation of low-income borrowers by informal credit suppliers: a credit delivery model for squatter housing, *Third World Planning Review*, vol. 18, no. 3, pp. 287-305.

Patel, S. (1999).Interpreting gender and housing finance in community perspective: the SPARC, Mahila Milan and NSDF experience. In: K. Datta & G.A. Jones (eds), *Housing and finance in developing countries.* London: Routledge.

Patel, S., J. Bolnick & D. Mitlin (2000).Sharing experiences and changing lives. Paper presented at the 'Urban Community Exchanges' meeting at DFID, London on 26 January.

Sanyal, B. & V. Mukhija (2000).Institutional pluralism and housing delivery: a case of unforeseen conflicts in Mumbai, India. Report prepared for the Management Development and Governance Division of UNDP.

Seibel, H.D. (1997). Upgrading, downgrading, linking, innovating: microfinance development strategies - A System Perspective -. Economic and sociology occasional paper no. 2371. Columbus: Ohio State University.

Smets, P. (1995). Poor and in need for a house in the city! The government is there to help, but who is really helping who?, *Nagarlok*, vol. XXVIII, no. 4, pp. 78-92.

Private housing finance in India: reaching down-market? *Habitat International*, vol. 21, no. 1, pp.1-15.

1999 Housing finance trapped in a dilemma of perceptions: affordability criteria for the urban poor questioned, *Housing Studies*, vol. 14, no. 6, pp. 821-838.

SPARC (1996). Construction finance related experiences of SPARC, NSDF and Mahila Milan. Paper presented at the workshop 'Women and shelter finance', 22-24 January, Ahmedabad.

Another mela for housing in Hyderabad, 29th 30th 31st May 99. Available: sparc.ilbom.ernet.in!sheela@ilbom.ernet.in May 24 at 3:57:39 pm.

Steinberg, F. Non-governmental organizations (NGOs) and community based or-ganizations (CBOs) in India's Habitat sector: Coming to the forefront? Paper presented at the high level policy seminar on Integrated Human Settlement Strategy. Society for Development Studies, New Delhi.

Turner, J. (1976). Housing by people: towards autonomy in building environments. London.

Why not take a Cybernetic approach to Sustainable Development? Planning and Environmental Management in North West England during the 1990s

Michael Clark

INTRODUCTION

To what extent is correction part of the planning process? Might additional powers and resources cure mistakes or overcome unforeseen circumstances? Could this process become routine? This paper explores the contradiction between two different approaches to managing plan implementation and rectifying mistakes. Recent managerial and political emphasis on *quality* and measurable indicators of *performance* suggest that bureaucratic procedures will automatically adjust in a way that might be seen as *cybernetic*, or at least *intelligent*. But underlying administrative and political imperatives emphasize *flexibility* and decision makers' *freedom of action*. This creates several risks:

Mistakes will be acknowledged, but not acted on:
- Unacceptable situations will be treated as chronic when immediate corrective action is feasible,
- Put another way *future orientation* excludes short term solutions and is arbitrary in its choice of options,
- Opportunities for routine repair and remediation will be lost

SUSTAINABILITY IMPERATIVES FOR SYSTEMATIC INTERVENTION

Town planners, economic planners and development officers, and environmental managers are constrained by, and may reflect, the assumptions of the throw away (or demolish and rebuild) society. But these assumptions are challenged by sustainable development. Sustainability requires a holistic approach, the identification, recognition and control (or internalisation) of undesirable effects, or *externalities*, and adoption of a long-term perspective in which future opportunities or interests are not sacrificed for short-term gain. The language of sustainable development has been widely adopted within town planning. *Local Agenda 21* led to numerous initiatives, encouraged work already underway towards the same broad goals, and has been associated with attempts to address long term planning issues at a city or regional scale. Might *cybernetics* contribute to the process of learning about and perhaps controlling our relationship with the environment on which we all depend, or to the institutional and political mechanisms for sustainable development?

INTERPRETATIONS AND APPLICATIONS OF CYBERNETICS

Cybernetics is here used to describe self-repairing systems based on negative feedback. This use is derived from Ellis's suggestion that all quality assurance should:

- specify standards,
- identify critical functions and procedures necessary to achieve these,
- rely on consumers to establish if standards are met,
- show what standards are to be achieved, and which procedures must be followed,
- adopt a cybernetic approach to setting standards and procedures, with negative feedback leading to appropriate, effective action, and
- involve all personnel, and be committed to development and training. (Clark, 1998, based on Ellis, 1993, 7-8).

Cybernetics' dictionary definition is rather wider:

'Study of systems of control and communication in animals and electrically operated devices such as calculating machines. [f. Gk kubernetes steersman, ICS]' (Fowler & Fowler, 1964, 303) specifically, the interaction between automatic control and living organisms, especially humans and animals.'
(McGraw-Hill Dictionary of Scientific and Technical Terms, in Straube, 1995, 1)

Cyberspace, the non-dimensional world of instant electronic communication, 'a world without geographical distance' (Winger, 1997, 252), adds confusion to the poorly mapped jungle of mathematical, philosophical, biological and managerial applications of systems thinking, and the idea that this may contain some sort of environmental or behavioural response, which might amount to a learning situation.

THE PLANNING CONTEXT AND THE
CYBERNETIC PARADOX

Any self-repairing systems based on negative feedback require a mechanism for fault identification or recognition and an understanding of the system and its causal relationships (Steinbruner, 1974). This implies agreement on the extent of any problem, the scope of options that might be considered, and the priorities and criteria by which alternatives will be assessed. Systematic attempts at repair may be, and frequently are, substituted for by other actions that include amelioration: intervention to deal with the symptoms or consequences of the fault, but no effective treatment of its root causes. Much regulation and welfare provision may be criticised as being an institutionalised form of problem serving: relevant professions come to depend on a client (under) class, and cease to look for solutions, whether to crime, tooth decay or poverty (Blair, 1973; Higgins, 1978). Problems may also be met by displacement activity, ranging from the tendency to put off unwelcome tasks to more systematic spatial or temporal relocation. Many attempts at planning may be categorised as temporal and spatial displacement, as can much environmental regulation:

'Rather than rectify the externalities of industrial production... [the first wave] of environmental polices tended to displace pollution across both time and space.
... prescriptive strategies presumed strong causality between the perpetrators of ecological harm and the actual sources of impact that proved difficult to achieve in practice.'
(Cohen, 1997, 108-9)

Cybernetic self-repair implies automation, the lack of conscious or rational human input. This has long been recognised as politically difficult. The benefits of increased productivity achieved through automation are offset by the distributive and human consequences of mass production, and by its tendency to exclude technologies that are not capital intensive and increasingly Global in scale. Marx anticipated that automation and the control of technology would alienate labour from capital:

'... once absorbed into the production process of capital, the means of labour undergoes various metamorphoses, of which the last is the machine, or rather, an automatic system of machinery ('automatic' meaning that this is only the most perfected and most fitting form of the machine, and is what transforms the machine into a system).

This is set in motion by an automaton, a motive force that moves of its own accord. The automaton consists of a number of mechanical and intellectual organs, so that the workers themselves can be no more than the conscious limbs of the automaton. ..... In no respect is the machine the means of labour of the individual worker. Its distinctive character is not at all, as with the means of labour, that of transmitting the activity of the worker to its object; rather this activity is so arranged that it now only transmits and supervises and protects from damage the work of the machine and its action on the raw material.' (Marx, c. 1857 in McLellan, 1980, 141-142)

An additional paradox, which any enthusiast for routinised correction of faults must address, is that it is generally better not to rely on automated correction, especially in highly complex and uncertain systems. Cybernetic repair tends to be less robust that rational choice, as its learning ability is limited (if existent at all), and necessarily reflects the information and assumptions provided during programming.

'Cybernetic mechanisms which achieve uncertainty control do so by focusing the decision process on a few incoming variables while eliminating entirely any serious calculation of probable outcomes. ....

The cybernetic decision maker is sensitive to information only if it enters through an established highly focused feedback channel, and hence many factors which do in fact affect the outcomes have no effect in his decision process.' (Steinbruner, 1974, 66-67)

Arguably any attempt to overcome uncertainty by fragmenting decisions into small segments, which are treated sequentially, according to established procedure, amounts to an *instrumental* rather than *causal* learning process, which means that much bureaucracy operates on cybernetic, rather than rational, principles:

'The cybernetic paradigm ... emerges as something more than a dissent from ideas of rationality. It begins to appear as a fundamental and ubiquitously used process of decision.' (Steinbruner, 1974, 86)

Which begs the question, if the machinery of Government is to a large extent automated, why can't or won't it deal with its own failure?

LESSONS FOR PLANNING?

Cybernetics is unlikely to deliver simple solutions, and its incorporation within established decision making systems may account for some of their limitations. Also the drive for more routinised performance appraisal, and adoption of systems such as Strategic Environmental Assessment, may fail to meet expectations because of the inherent weaknesses of arms' length and automated decision making. Despite the limitations exposed by the cybernetic paradox, good design incorporates the features necessary for fault rectification:

- monitoring against agreed performance standards
- 'trigger' mechanisms
- repair capability (resources, power, intelligence)

Although elements of these are found within their documentation and procedures, planners (dealing with Town Planning, Regional Planning and Economic Development Planning) tend to substitute *future orientation* for *performance reinforcement*. If the tendency to focus on new plan preparation and on 'rolling programmes', with a medium term time horizon, is accepted as having higher status than addressing the limitations of existing programmes, is this a fault of planning systems, or does it merely reflect political and operational reality? Practicalities require planning intervention to be highly constrained. Much of what town planners actually do falls into a few, broad but far from comprehensive, categories:

preparation and implementation of development plans to guide and regulate development proposals originating in the private sector or (in most places outside the UK) land use zoning (similar to plan led development control, but with 'legal certainty')

EIA to ensure the implications of a proposal are fully recognised before approval. Economic development is similarly characterised by preparation of indicative plans or strategies, by attempts to understand the underlying trends in employment and commercial activity, and by attempts at co-ordination. De-regulation and privatisation of much social and economic infrastructure (transportation, energy, water, education, health, housing) have made it difficult for land use planners and economic development departments to co-ordinate infrastructure spending or regulation. Compared with town planners and economic development officers, environmental managers generally operate at a smaller scale, and relate to more immediate circumstances (i.e.. in 'real time'). Their spatial and temporal focus is greatest when responsible for a particular (valued and/or threatened) habitat, site or area, but they also operate at a larger spatial scale, and over longer time horizons, when acting as regulators. Environmental managers' effectiveness is frequently curtailed by their weak enforcement powers and inadequate resources or status, as well as by their having to rely on volunteer labour (Clark & Netherwood, 1999), indicative management plans, and collaboration with firms and landowners operating to different agenda.

Attempts at integrated economic and environmental planning or assessment have been the exception rather than the norm (Roo & Miller, 1997), and have had to cope with politically difficult economy/environment trade offs, and with failure to achieve either adequate safeguards for crucial environmental assets or universal acceptance that the environmental sacrifice which results is necessary. Subsequent legitimisation crises are reflected in the popularity of tunnel and tree squatting protesters such as 'Swampy' (an objector to the A30 road scheme in Devon in 1996 and the Manchester Airport second runway in 1997), and encourage the acceptance and use of 'direct action', especially where this exposes the inadequacies and injustices of site-specific decision-making, including EIA. Such procedures may appear as little more than a set of tightly controlled 'closed questions', intended to justify a particular course of action and form of investment, and 'rigged' to exclude alternatives, maximise the benefits associated with development and minimise the costs.

Failure to achieve consensus over unpopular schemes has been paralleled by more fundamental limitations. It is difficult for development plan led land use planning to achieve its objectives under conditions of low development pressure, as seen in the stagnation which has affected much of Europe and North America in recent years. The 'rust-belts' (areas of early industrialisation: former mining and steel making towns, fishing ports, etc.) and many outer estates (large municipal 'overspill' welfare housing schemes) and 'inner cities' have experienced de-industrialisation and out-migration, and a lack of commercial investment or public sector finance to provide the redevelopment and new building required for either development plan led or land use zoning based planning to be effective. At the other extreme, it is difficult to revise planning policies quickly enough under conditions of high development pressure, or to regulate effectively and maintain standards. Development control and infrastructure co-ordination failures favour 'non-planning' and permissive options (London Docklands, the 'Tiger' economies), and support popular (journalistic and political) confusion of the problematic symptoms of rapid growth (congestion, pollution, scarcity and high cost of accommodation) with its causes.

Such limitations are only partly addressed by measures to streamline planning procedures and to ensure comprehensive coverage. In Britain's case in the 1990s, by up to date development plans corresponding to national or regional guidance. 'Macro'/Global agenda invite criticism of restricted interpretations of planning and environmental management, and require a broader interpretation of 'environmental planning' than allowed by the British land use planning system (Hall, Hebbert and Lusser, 1993). This was subsequently evident in increasing use of terminology such as governance. Not only is planning once more being approached in ways which acknowledge, for example, the two way relationship between land use and transportation, or the possible links between environmental protection and health, but its recommendations are also coming under the sort of strategic scrutiny outlined by Kozlowski and Hill's 'Ultimate Environmental Threshold' (UET) method, and operationalised by early forms of Strategic Environmental Assessment (SEA) such as the routine environmental appraisal of development plans (Kozlowski and Hill, 1993; Department of the Environment, 1993).

Sustainability appraisal has tended to replace and broaden the scope of SEA. In the new planning system introduced by the Planning and Compulsory Purchase Act 2004 it is required for Regional Strategic Guidance (RSS), and for Local Development Documents, prepared in line with Local Development Schemes that themselves draw on RSS, and on the authority's Community Strategy (HMSO, 2004; RTPI, 2004)

SUSTAINABILITY IMPERATIVES AND PLANNING

The 1992 edition of Planning Policy Guidance Note 12 called for environmental appraisal of development plans, and the recommended methodology incorporated 'Sustainable Development' language and concepts within official documentation in an attempt to apply the principles agreed at the Rio Earth Summit (Department of the Environment, 1993). Despite the Guide's complexity and difficult implementation (Clark, 1993), by late 1994 environmental appraisals had been completed by 40 (17%) out of 234 English and Welsh local authorities, and another 140 (60%) were carrying them out (Therivel, 1995). This was a period of quite remarkable and wide-ranging enthusiasm for the rhetoric of sustainable development, as illustrated by the (UK) Liberal Democrats' 1993 Consultation Paper on Sustainable Economy (Box 1).

BOX 1

'There is widespread agreement on certain national and international policy goals:

The rate of the use of renewable resources must not exceed the rate of regeneration.

The rate of depletion of non-renewable resources must not exceed the rate of development of renewable substitutes.

Irreplaceable biological resources must be protected.

Waste generation and pollution must not exceed the assimilative capacity of the environment.

Implementing the precautionary principle where there are good grounds for judging either that action taken promptly at comparatively low cost may avoid more costly damage later, or that irreversible effects may follow if action is delayed.'

We can pursue these goals through policies 'based on the principle that people should have the information to make decisions for themselves ... market mechanisms that leave people free to choose.' Where radical reforms cannot be achieved by the market, 'standards and controls to protect future generations from the excesses of the present' become necessary. 'Policies are also needed to provide conditions that are conductive to the essential technological development and innovation that are necessary to achieve quality lifestyles that are sustainable.' (UK Liberal Democrats 1993)

We now have a Sustainable Development Commission, another for Integrated Transport (2005), and a what cynics might see a s a plethora of similar bodies, each with a (non negotiable) mission to change unacceptable behaviour. While these appear to be at the heart of Government, it is questionable if their influence matches their apparent status. The Sustainable Development Commission's May 2005 websites show frustration at the slow pace of progress:

PRINCIPLES AND IMPLEMENTATION
We invite government and business to interact with us and consider how we can help mainstream sustainable development into your activities. We particularly like to work at a strategic level, in long-term partnerships, helping organisations and departments to deliver sustainable development, raising awareness and providing examples of best practice.' (Sustainable Development Commission 2005b)

'WORK STREAMS: GOVERNANCE ON THE FRONTLINE'
Local government across the UK spends £40 billion a year on services, products and salaries. Clearly, its potential for implementing sustainable development practice and transforming citizens' quality of life is enormous. Yet too few local agencies have made doing so a priority, or have developed joined-up policy and people-led sustainable development practice. ...The problem is that while commitments to sustainable development principles exist at all levels of government – national, regional and local –

they are often unclear or inconsistent, with the result that the delivery of frontline sustainable practice in communities is patchy at best.' (Sustainable Development Commission 2005c)

Planning documents with titles such as <u>Lancashire Structure Plan 1991-2006, Greening the Red Rose County</u> emphasize commitment to sustainability in the early 1990s, and were influenced by key officers' involvement in bodies such as the County Planning Officers Society's Local Agenda 21 Task Group (Bell, 1995). More instrumental application of sustainability criteria is illustrated by the Environmental Appraisal chapter of Preston Borough Council's October 1995 Local Plan (Public Consultation Draft). Here the approach is similar to that recommended by the Good Practice Guide, with, for example, environmental stock being identified in terms of the three categories of Global Sustainability, Natural Resources and local Environmental Quality, and listed against indicators of positive impact. So, in the first category, transport energy forms two 'stock' categories, under trips and modes. Indicators are reduces trip length and number of motorised trips, increases public transport share, and attraction of walking and cycling. In the second category, Minerals Conservation is indicated by reduces fossil fuel and mineral consumption, and increases reuse/recycling of materials. The third category is illustrated by Public Access/Open Space, positive impact being improves urban green space and safeguards/improves access to urban open space; urban fringe or countryside areas for recreation (Preston Borough Council, 1995, 114).

A CREDIBILITY GAP?
Indicators invites criticism if the clear policy statements they produce cannot be matched by action. Preston illustrates the problem. The Council's 1995 Draft Local Plan's Environmental Appraisal makes a number of very strong commitments. For example, access to public open space varies enormously across the Preston urban area and there is:

"...a serious shortfall in recreational green space in the Borough. The Local Plan will need to identify opportunities to improve provision, preferably where provision is poorest".
(Preston Borough Council, 1996, 67)

The Local Plan's <u>Deposit Draft</u> recommended that developers meet the full costs of 8.5ha/1,000 population green space for new housing, or pay a commuted sum of £662 'in lieu' per person accommodated (Preston Borough Council, 1996, 59). Although the House builders' Federation objected the principle survived the inquiry process, to be implemented once the plan is adopted (Planning Inspectorate, 1998, 148). But 'Commuted' charges are

unpopular and may, if hypothecation is not absolute, be little more than use of planning powers raise funds. Despite such initiatives British local authorities have insufficient powers to make drastic changes to a far from equitable or satisfactory situation. There is competition from other, more pressing, objectives for the funds necessary to gain access to private land, or to provide new playgrounds or parkland, and even existing 'urban green space' in recreational use may be out of bounds to those it might benefit most. In these circumstances planners could be criticised for engaging in weak rhetoric. They have correctly identified a problem, but cannot change the status quo.

Environmental commitment, and the language of sustainable development, are easy to criticise. The gap between aspirations and what is feasible is too large, and this is made worse by routinised procedures, such as the methodology suggested in the 1990s for environmental appraisal of development plans, as these favour the rhetorical use of sustainable development terminology. The answer to this criticism may be that sustainability is a learning process. We should be concerned with the direction of change, rather than absolute measures of achievement. However, it is difficult not to be impatient when the trends appear opposite to what is being prescribed. Weak planning powers, commercial pressure and changes in what is technically feasible, and competitive, have favoured changes in lifestyle.

Retailing reflects and facilitates the globalisation of markets and of systems of production and distribution, and encourages, perhaps necessitates, greater car dependence and use, and larger scale, longer distance road transport of finished products from increasingly centralised and automated warehouses. By the mid 1990s, much professional and political thinking had become wary of the adverse effects of retail change. But the legacy of previously approved planning permissions and development plans meant that it was not possible to halt development of a major new regional shopping centre at Trafford Park on the outskirts of Greater Manchester, or the shift of trade from town and city centres to out of town retail complexes such as the complex in Warrington near the M62 and M6 motorways, for car users (off-peak) one of the most accessible locations in the most heavily urbanised part of North West England (itself one of the most densely populated regions in the World). During the same period, housing allocations in development plans responded to, and encouraged, a property market that reflected increasingly complex mobility patterns and growing dependence on cars and on trips not easily served by public transport.

In these circumstances, it is perhaps best to regard planners' endorsement of sustainability objectives as a longer-term commitment and statement of good practice. A more cynical interpretation suggests that the 1990s saw little more than adoption and incorporation of fashionable phrases and sentiments. First 'environmental' was used in the sense of ecological preservation, but with only limited capacity to control the damage caused by economic expansion: Manchester's second runway, continuing growth in road and air traffic, additional development on green fields, and associated increases in car and truck mileage. Then 'green' was used in the wider context of 'sustainable development'. But, again, without the powers or the will necessary to bring about the major lifestyle changes this would require.

39 STEPS TO SUSTAINABILITY?

More popular involvement was encouraged by Local Agenda 21. Lancashire's 1989 Green Audit and 1991-93 Environmental Action Programme (LEAP) largely pre-date the Rio

Earth Summit, but were adapted to contribute to the LA21 process and helped in the search for practical indicators (Lancashire County Council, 1997, 146-149).   These closely reflect the characteristics of a 'sustainable community' identified by the Local Government Management Board's Sustainability Indicators research project (ibid, 148), and a set of selection criteria drawn up by the Lancashire Environment Forum Green Audit Working Group. These identify effective indicators as those, which are:

- Important
- Relevant and Useful
- Available
- Able to Show Trends / Make Comparisons
- Understandable and Communicable
- Lead to Setting of Targets or Actions
- (from, Lancashire County Council, 1997, 150)

 Lancashire's Second Green Audit in 1997 reviewed the county's performance against the following list of sustainability goals and indicators (BOX 2). The importance of the 39 indicators was discussed in terms of sustainable development before the audit explained each statistic or map, and outlined its trends and its links to other indicators. Readers were asked to return a questionnaire indicating how much, if any, progress has been made towards these goals, and the audit summarised replies to the same questions from the Lancashire Environment Forum, the 'stakeholder organisations' group responsible for the Specialist Working Groups which carried out much of the work for the LEAP document and 15 year action programme.

BOX 2. Your Assessment of Progress Towards Sustainable Development in Lancashire

Respondents were asked to place a tick, cross or? Alongside each indicator, and to give a brief reason for each assessment). Lancashire Environment Forum comments are included here as + (moving towards sustainability goal), - (moving away from sustainability goal) and? (Trend Unclear).

CARRYING CAPACITY:
More efficient Use of Resources and less Waste (Sustainability Goal)
Household Waste Production -; Household Waste Recycling + ;
Household Electricity Consumption -; Town growth - ; Derelict land + (Indicators 1 - 5)

Lower Levels of Pollution
Air Quality -; River Quality +; Bathing Waters + (Indicators 6 -8)

A More Diverse Natural Environment
Protecting Wildlife Areas +; Wildlife Diversity? (Indicators 9 - 10)

QUALITY OF LIFE:

Basic Needs for Everyone Which are Met More Locally
Basic Services Within walking Distance -; Distance Travelled to Work -; Homelessness - ;
Prosperity and Deprivation ? ; Lead in drinking Water? ; House Prices? ; Poverty? ;
Children in Poverty? (Indicators 11 - 18)

More Opportunities for Work in a Diverse Economy
Unemployment +; Long Working Hours? ; Earnings Gap -; Employment Diversity? ;
Income Distribution -; Day Care for under-Fives? (Indicators 19 -24)

Improvements in Health
Low Birth Weight +; Death Rate +; Years of Life Lost? ; Long-Term Illness -(Indicators 25
- 28)

Access to Facilities, Goods, Service and People Whilst Protecting the Environment
Mode of Travel to Work -; Transport Investment - (Indicators 29 -30)

Less Fear of Crime and Persecution
Property Crime -; Violent Crime - (Indicators 31 - 32)

Access to Education, Training and Information
School-Leavers' Exam Results +, School-Leavers' Destinations? , School-Leavers' Literacy?
(Indicators 33 - 35)

People Having a Say in Decision Making
Voter Participation -; Community Groups + (Indicators 36 - 37)

People Valuing the Neighbourhoods and Communities in Which They Live
Community Cohesion - ; Quality of Life ? (Indicators 38 - 39)

(adapted from questionnaire inserted in Lancashire County Council, 1997, and ibid xi
and 139-141)

Lancashire Environmental Audit's sustainability goals and indicators show strong
convergence between 'green' objectives and more general political targets and standards.
Sustainability has become a virtuous 'catch all' to accommodate everything worthwhile,
both as a means for development (health, education, community cohesion...), and the sign
that it is taking place. Blowers has established the importance of intra as well as inter
generational equity as necessary conditions for sustainability (1993, 7). Under right-wing
Central Government in the UK between 1989 and 1997, it was logical for local politicians
to include a welfare or Socialist agenda within their interpretation of sustainable
development to help counter the 'hollowing out' of the public sector and the loss of local
control (Patterson & Theobald, 1995). But, before sustainability is too strongly associated

with the 'old left', it should be recognised that it is open to criticism as a form of weak reformism. It may be sham or token, a confusing smokescreen which conceals worsening conditions, and which substitutes meaningless actions in place of effective policies. And it may disable those with a genuine understanding of the problem (radical Greens, 'neurotic' consumers and residents), while favouring political realism and the status quo.

In part the Lancashire audit's indicators show what is available to measure, and they, and the wider goals, also reflect some of the values, attitudes and priorities identified by 'non-expert' focus groups who were approached in an attempt to reduce the professional and class bias of earlier work. Their scepticism, unfamiliarity with the term 'sustainability', lack of confidence in local government and reluctance to act independently 'to advance sustainability' offset the second Green Audit's generally positive and purposeful tone (ibid, 149-150), and raise the possibility of a disabling credibility gap. They may also help explain a shift towards indicators that are focussed on local demands and anxieties, and are instrumental and achievable, and away from those which might only be achieved by dismantling Western industrial society, as we know it.

CONCLUSION

Sustainable development is about devising mechanisms for repairing the effects of over-development, and countering the false economics of globalisation. This is no simple task in a world whose aspirations largely subscribe to the promises, and continuing rise in material living standards, associated with industrialisation and mass production. There is a sentimental backlash against the damage done by industrial growth, but it is fickle and little more than a minor irritant when compared with the power of capital or the State, or the all-pervading attractions of consumerism. Similarly the intra and inter generational injustices associated with globalisation are readily countered by the selfish and optimistic perceptions of the great bulk of the population.

In this context, self-repair depends on education rather than campaigns or minority or extreme forms of political mobilisation. This amounts to a form of 'cultural cybernetics', which draws on the relatively objective, and critical position provided by a systematic viewpoint to changes attitudes and expectations, and realises and express values which would otherwise go un-noticed.

'...a society's potential to make the jump to ecological modernisation is surely predicated upon other cultural characteristics in addition to a resoluted respect for scientific rationality. A factor of special importance is the ability to formulate political consensus around problem situations....

Social capital ... a society's degree of associativeness and trust among its members.' (Cohen, 1997, 116)

Activity in Lancashire, and in numerous other parts of the world, illustrates how the suspect concept of 'sustainable development' and the unlikely motivation of Local Agenda

21 have made a start in establishing priorities and lines of communication. So have parallel attempts to apply strategic environmental assessment to plans and policies. At this early stage, all are flawed. LA21 is under-resourced, over-reliant on volunteers and good will, and liable to loose political clout if owned, as was intended, by the 'grass roots' communities and under-represented individuals it is to mobilise and exploit (Clark & Netherwood, 1999). Sustainable city initiatives do not take place in a vacuum, and tend to look beyond existing plans and commitments partly because of the political difficulty of criticising what has already been agreed.

A cybernetic approach would require more rigorous testing of the status quo: the identification of unacceptable conditions, including gross social injustices, establishment of priorities and a clear programme of action in which a far wider range of factors would be regarded as variables than has become the norm in our, plan or zoning led, traditions of incremental development control. This seemed too radical for planning professions in the UK in the 1990s, not helped by the widely reported failure of bold Socialist ventures, worldwide. But this observation may miss the roots of changes now working their way through more widely cast forms of intervention and involvement: new forms of *governance,* embedding of principles such as sustainability and social justice, and better attempts at policy integration and evaluation. The inadequacy of 'planned' solutions has its roots in the poor responsiveness of automated systems, partly because of bureaucracy's reluctance to accept signals that had not been anticipated in advance. Any future attempt at cybernetic control needs to give more attention to *robustness* (Alexander, 1964), and to recognise political realities.

The logic of integrated approaches may not necessarily be rewarded by their adoption or acceptance, but they are part of the process of political mobilisation and education, which will establish what, is acceptable, and what justifies intervention. While there is an enormous amount of circumstantial evidence to suggest that the planet is 'going down the tube', that globalised production is increasing the rate of environmental destruction, the largely rhetorical use of the language of sustainable development is starting to provide the political context for more effective intervention and leadership. This requires a move beyond hectoring or congratulatory hype, to agreement and implementation of targets and standards. We require a cybernetic system of negative feedback loops. under human control, that cut in before the limits at which nature or human conflict provide more drastic forms of system regulation.

BIBLIOGRAPHY

Alexander, C. 1964: *Notes on the Synthesis of Form.* Harvard: Harvard University Press.

Allison, E.W. & Allison, M.A 1995: Using culture and communications theory in postmodern urban-planning - a cybernetic approach. *Communication Research*, 22.6, 627-645,

Balakrishna, S. 1994: Policy analysis - cybernetic and other approaches. *Journal of Rural Development*, 13:4, 477-487.

Bell, G. 1995: Green counties colonise sustainable development. *Planning*, 1110, 17th March.

Blowers, A. 1993: The time for change, Ch 1. in Blowers, A. (Ed.), *Planning for a Sustainable Environment*. London: Earthscan.

Clark, M. 1994: Moving nearer to sustainability goals, review. *Environmental Appraisal of Development Plans: a Good Practice Guide*. HMSO, 1993, *Town and Country Planning*, 63:6, June, 177-8.

Clark, M. 1998: Quality Assurance for Planning and Environmental Management, the case for Re-Regulation. Ch. 12 in Kivell, P., Roberts, P. & Walker, G. *Environment Planning and Land Use.* Aldershot: Ashgate.

Clark, M. with Netherwood, A. 1999: Beyond volunteering and rhetoric: implications of Local Agenda 21 initiatives in Wales. Ch. 4 in Buckingham-Hatfield, S. & Percy, S. (Eds.) *Constructing Local Environmental Agendas.* London: Routledge.

Cohen, M.J. 1997: Risk society and ecological modernisation. *Futures*, 29:2, 105-119.

Department of the Environment, 1993: Environmental Appraisal of Development Plans: a Good Practice Guide. London: HMSO.

Ellis, R. 1993: Quality assurance for university teaching: issues and approaches, Ch.1 in Ellis, R. (Ed), *Quality Assurance for University Teaching.* Milton Keynes: The Society for Research into Higher Education & Open University Press.

Elohim, J.L. 1994: The systemic, cybernetic and synergetic alternative in quality management. *Systems Research*, 11.1, 15-45.

Flood, R.L. & Romm, N.R.A. 1995: Enhancing the process of methodology choice in total systems intervention (TSI) and improving chances of tackling coercion. *Systems Practice*, 8:4, 377-408.

Fowler, H.W. & Fowler, F.G. (Eds) 1964: *The Concise Oxford Dictionary of Current English*. Oxford: Oxford University Press..

Hall, D. Hebbert, M. and Lusser, H. 1993: The Planning Background. Ch.2 in Blowers, A. (Ed.), *Planning for a Sustainable Environment*. London: Earthscan.

Kozlowski, J. & Hill, G. 1993: Towards Planning for Sustainable Development. A Guide for the 'Ultimate Environmental Threshold' (UET) Method. Aldershot, Avebury.

Kravchuk, R.S. & Schack, R.W. 1996: Designing effective performance-measurement systems under the Government Performance and Results Act of 1993. *Public Administration Review*, 56:4, 348-358.

Lancashire County Council, 1997: Lancashire's green Audit 2: A Sustainability report: Lancashire's key environmental, social & economic indicators, their inter-relationships and trends. Preston: County Planning Dept

Lee Donaldson Associates, 1994: Preston Shopping Study appended to Preston Borough Council, Preston Local Plan, Deposit Draft. Preston: County Planning Dept

Liberal Democrats, 1993: Sustainable Economy, Consultation Paper No. 3.

Marx, K. c. 1857: The Labour process and Alienation in Machinery and Science, - Grundrisse, 583-592, in McLellan, D. 1980: *Marx's Grundrisse*, second edition, London, Macmillan, 141-149.

Overman, E.S. & Loraine, D.T. 1994: Information for control - another management proverb. *Public Administration Review*, 54:2, 193-196.

Patterson, A. and Theobald, K.S. 1995: Public sector restructuring and local environmental practices, paper presented at the *Annual Conference of the Institute of British Geographers*, University of Northumbria, Newcastle, 3rd January, draft copy, mimeo.

Planning Inspectorate, 1998: Inspector's Report, Preston Local Plan, Report on Objections, Vol 1, Policy G10 - greenspace provision in new housing development.

Preston Borough Council, 1996b: Preston Local Plan, Deposit Draft, An Audit of Greenspace.

Preston Borough Council, 1995: *Preston Local Plan; Public Consultation Draft*, October. Preston: County Planning Dept

Preston Borough Council, 1994, *A Census Atlas for Preston*. Preston: Preston Borough Council.

Rhodes, R.A.W. 1996: The new governance - governing without government. *Political Studies*, 44:4, 652-667.

Roo, G. de & Miller, D. (1997), Transitions in Dutch environmental planning: new solutions for integrating spatial and environmental policies', Environment and Planning B, Planning & Design, 24, 427-436.

Rudall, B.H., 1995: Contemporary systems and cybernetics. *Kybernetes*, 24:6, 5.

Straube, K. 1995: *An Annotated Bibliography of Cybernetics as Applicable to Space Stations*, May 17, http://www.pacifier.com/~kstraube/biblio.html#top

Therivel, R. 1995: Environmental appraisal takes off in development plans arena, *Planning*. 1108, 3td March, 6.

Winger,A.R. 1997: Finally: a withering away of cities. *Futures*, 29:3, 251-256.

Part Four

Contested Space and the New World Order

Housing for the Urban Poor in Cape Town: A Post Apartheid Dream or Nightmare?

Erik Bähre

INTRODUCTION

With the abolishment of apartheid and the first democratic elections of 1994, the African National Congress (ANC) put great emphasis on the eradication of the inequalities between Whites, Coloureds, and Africans. Central to the abolition of the inequalities was the eradication of poverty through development. Poverty-stricken Africans, and to a lesser extent coloureds, had to have better communal facilities, such as sanitation, roads, adequate policing, and health care. More jobs had to be created and the appalling housing situation of many Africans had to change. The development aims of the new government were consolidated in the national Reconstruction and Development Programme (RDP) (ANC 1994). The new government appointed a special temporary RDP minister without portfolio, Mr. Naidoo, and between 1996 and 1999 the numerous RDP projects became integrated into the portfolios of the other ministers or were stopped.

One of the most prominent parts of the RDP was the housing grant for the poor. From 1994 to 1999 one million low-cost houses had to be built, of which only a fifth was accomplished by the beginning of 1998 (Mail and Guardian 1998, 4). In cities such as Cape Town, the housing shortage had already been tremendous under apartheid (see e.g. Cole 1987; Cook 1992). Under apartheid only Africans with a 'pass' were allowed to live in urban areas and others were forced to live in the impoverished homelands. The 1923 Urban Areas Act especially, restricted the residence of Africans in urban areas. Africans were only allowed to live in the city as workers and even family members were not permitted to live with them. This resulted in an urban population of mainly men, often living in migrant hostels under poor conditions (Ramphele 1991, 1993; Robertson 1990). The inability to enforce the pass-laws, the abolition of these laws in 1986, and the end of apartheid led to an increased growth of the urban population and women in particular (James 1999). The growth of the urban population increased the already existing housing shortage and increasingly more people, and Africans in particularly, have established illegal squatter communities between existing formal settlements or on the outskirts of Cape Town.

The aim of this paper is to explore some of the consequences of the post-apartheid development policy on housing. I think that the most fruitful way to do this is to look at the impact of this policy in a particular township, Indawo Yoxolo, and analyse the different reactions, negotiations, and conflicts that are part of such policies. In 1995, Indawo Yoxolo was a small informal settlement tucked away between some bushes and without any communal facilities, houses, roads, etc. By 1998, large parts of Indawo Yoxolo had transformed in townships with tar roads, streetlights, schools, two public phones, and clearly demarcated plots with an electricity meter, a toilet, a tap, and a small house for the poor. The new township Indawo Yoxolo was not only built for the residents of the already existing squatter camp. Also African residents of other squatter camps in Cape Town could, under certain conditions, which will be outlined below, apply for a plot. The building of Indawo Yoxolo was therefore one of the many government attempts to deal with the massive growth of the African urban population in Cape Town.

This paper will show that a particular understanding of 'community' is central to the RDP. This understanding of community and the development practices that result from it, however, is problematic can contribute to conflict.

HOUSING POLICY: THE POLITICS OF COMMUNITY

In 1991, when the apartheid regime had already started to crumble, political organisations, grassroots organisations and government bodies in Cape Town had established the Development Planning Committee (DPC), consisting of different political parties, government institutions and community-based organisations.[i] Their aim was to provide serviced residential plots, houses, education, health, employment and other resources to the, mainly African, poor in some of the most destitute areas of Cape Town. Within five years the DPC wished to develop and upgrade 34,500 sites and improve the housing situation of more than 35,000 poor families. People from 21 informal settlements, eight areas of backyard shack dwellers and residents of three hostels had to benefit from this project and another 6200 Coloured families who were on a waiting lists for housing could obtain access to the housing scheme (DPC 1994, 8).

In 1993-94, the DPC and its projects became part of the national RDP. Because the DPC became part of the RDP, one has to understand the way the RDP was managed and what its central policies were. The RDP policy guided the housing process in Indawo Yoxolo, and the role of the DPC in the management of the process.

To build houses and infrastructure for the poor, the RDP ensured a subsidy of maximum R15,000[ii] for the poor (see table 1). Private sector building companies, and in some instances NGOs, could be contracted to build roads, develop plots, and establish electricity connections, sewerage systems, toilets, and of course houses. The applicant would be allowed to occupy and own a plot in the new neighbourhoods. A lot of emphasis put was on public services and underground infrastructure, which meant that often little of the subsidy was left to build a house for the applicant, which led to many complaints about small matchbox houses.

Monthly income applicant and spouse	Subsidy
less than R800	R15,000
R800 - R1500	R12,500
R1500-R2500	R 9,500
R2500-R3500	R 5,000

Table 1: Individual housing subsidy provided for through the RDP
Source: Masakhane (1995, p.4).

The DPC had secured extra funds from the Provincial Administration of the Western Cape and the Cape Metropolitan Council. This made it possible to raise the RDP subsidy for housing from R15,000 to a maximum of R17,250 for each plot and have more money for infrastructure and community facilities (DPC 1996a).

Central to the RDP, and therefore to the building of townships such as Indawo Yoxolo, was community participation. Community participation had to be achieved through the establishment of local community representative bodies in which all local political organisations and community-based organisations had to be represented. The community-based organisations had to participate in the development projects and discuss its implementation in their community.

The focus on community participation is in line with contemporary global development thinking. Experiences in development all over the world had shown that top-down development - development projects designed without the involvement of the ones to be developed - could end up in major disasters. An approach that would ensure the involvement of the community would do more justice to the wishes of the poor and would hopefully improve the changes of a successful development. Moreover, community participation fitted very well with notions of empowerment, governmentality and democratisation. Since the late 1980s, due to disappointing experience with structural adjustment lending, the end of the Cold War, and the dominance of neo-liberal thought, democracy was regarded as increasingly important (Leftwitch 1994, 366). In South Africa's context, in which the vast majority of its population was withheld the right to vote, an active approach towards promoting democratisation was seen as crucial for development (ANC 1994, .119-135).

Just like the RDP, the DPC focused on community participation for development (DPC 1994, 4). Community representation had to be secured by a Project Committee consisting of representatives of numerous community-based organisations. This Committee had to be responsible for the implementation and management of the projects. They had to inform and consult the community about the DPC plans and, most notably, the Project Committee had to decide on the rules and procedures for the allocation of sites and manage the process (DPC 1994, 14). Families who lived longest in a particular area were to go first to the new plots and that those older than 21 years and living with dependants would be given priority (DPC 1996d, .1). The Project Committee became a powerful intermediary between the community, the DPC, government, and private construction companies. The role of the Project Committee was especially powerful in prioritising people's applications, as it was difficult to ascertain how long the squatters had lived in a particular area. The Project Committee also had a say in the recruitment of labour for the housing projects: at least 50% of the labourers had to be recruited among residents of Indawo Yoxolo.

The results of the DPC and RDP policy on housing and development in general seemed to be a continuation of the forms of rule under colonialism and the apartheid era. Of course, the ideologies and aims of the post apartheid government differed tremendously from the colonial and apartheid era; instead of repression, the new government aimed to liberate and empower people; instead of exclusion, the post-apartheid government made efforts to make resources available to non-whites; instead of dehumanising non-whites, the government tried to emphasise humanity. The continuation of policy, therefore, lied not in its aims and ideologies, but in the management of projects.

Under colonial times, South Africa, as many other parts of Africa, was governed by indirect rule. 'Natives' were controlled by separate institutions and laws, which were administered by a chief representing a tribe. The British colonial authorities strictly controlled this tribal chief. If such a tribe did not exist, the colonial government would create one in the process of indirect rule (Gluckman 1971, 40; Mamdani 1996, 62-65; Vail

1989,.11-15). The system of apartheid resembled this form of indirect rule (Mamdani 1996,.8). Under apartheid, the homelands had their African rulers who collaborated with the National Party and the urban townships had their illegitimate town councils (cf. Shubane 1991,.65). The pretence of legitimacy of these chiefs under colonialism and rulers of homelands depended on the notion of tribe, race or ethnicity. Mamdani (1996,.90) argues that:

> 'Control and representation were two sides of the same coin, which would eventually make for a single fit: the mode of representation, whether racial or tribal, would shape the lines along which natives would organize and in turn avail the state corresponding avenues of native control'

Also in the post-apartheid era control of people and their representation seemed to coincide. The persistence on a naïve notion of community - although this notion was continuously contradicted in the media and by experience - served this form of rule. In the post apartheid era, with its emphasis on development, the seemingly non-political notion of community had taken over the functions of the terms race and tribe. The notion of community allowed the state to control and rule of groups of people via local bodies (cf. Ferguson 1990; Scott 1998).

Of course, under apartheid not everybody accepted the forms of rule based on race, and this rule not always functioned. Many neighbourhood organisations, in South Africa often known as 'civics' and organised in the 1980s in the United Democratic Front (UDF), were engaged in boycotts, stay-aways and protest marches against the state (Bähre 1996; Jacobs 1992, 23-24; Matiwane and Walters 1986,.72).

But after the 1994 elections, the role of the protesters against the government was expected to change. The local government transition act 209 (1993) ensured that 'civics' were represented in the local government.[iii] Furthermore, civics had a major say in the RDP fora. Thus, due to the political changes taking place in South Africa, civics had to change drastically from organisers of boycotts and other forms of protest against the government, into community organisations represented in local government and implementing government policy, such as the RDP housing projects (Bähre 1996; Seekings 1992, .216). In the post-apartheid era, however, new forms of resistance against government rule and development have emerged. Not all the residents of Indawo Yoxolo agree, or keep quiet, about development practices and housing projects. Let us look at the way this form of rule takes place in Indawo Yoxolo and how powerful yet problematic inclusive notions of community are.

THE PROJECT COMMITTEE

In Indawo Yoxolo, the township where the research took place, the local DPC was made up of representatives of residents of the areas that were eligible for a plot in Indawo Yoxolo. Opponents of the Project Committee preferred to call them the 'Old Committee' because they favoured a new committee, or the 'Big Five'. The Big Five are the five wild animals that can be found in South Africa's game parks: leopard, lion, elephant, rhino and buffalo. The adoption of the name Big Five for the Project Committee emphasised the power and danger of this group, but was also a mockery about their status. Moreover, the name Big Five reminds one of the big men paradigms (see Thoden van Velzen 1973 for a critical analysis of the big men paradigm).

The five wild animals that were controlling Indawo Yoxolo were Mr. Bula, Mr. Zantsi, Mr. Nqasa, Mr. Posa, and Mr. Mtontsi. They were dangerous and it was best to avoid them as much as possible. I once had a brief conversation with Mr. Nqasa. His reputation was that of 'the gun' of the Big Five: stupid enough to kill and get caught and involved in all kinds of dirty business, also outside of Indawo Yoxolo. His reputation was that he was not the brain of the organisation, but that he was willing to murder people. Mr. Nqasa was a big man of about forty years old, but possibly younger. He was always nicely dressed and had a small, trendy mobile phone and one could notice his gun bulging from under his jacket or sweater. It was very uncomfortable to meet him. I was playing soccer with two kids in front of my research assistant's place while teenagers were playing street theatre where they pretended to rape a girl. Mr. Nqasa made a chat with my research assistant and I joined them. We shook hands, talked a bit about the weather, made some jokes, laughed a bit, and after that he strolled away. To an outsider it must have looked like one of those ordinary conversations neighbours have all the time. But I knew that he had recently killed

Mr. Mabeqa: the man who had introduced me into Indawo Yoxolo and who was, together with my research assistant, one of the key figures that opposed the Big Five. Mr. Nqasa, of course, also knew that I knew about his murder and Mr. Nqasa also knew that he and the other Big Five members had threatened to kill my research assistant as well. But we managed to pretend a friendly and open conversation about the weather.

Mr. Zantsi had the reputation of being the most powerful and smartest of the Big Five and some told me that whenever the Big Five resorted to violence to maintain their position, he was 'accidentally' away for a visit to his home in the former homeland Transkei. Due to my attempts to stay away from the Big Five, I had actually never seen him, except once in the distance when he and some others drove with two cars to the old Indawo Yoxolo. Mr. Bula, the third member of the Big Five was also a powerful man who threatened and blackmailed people. The other two members of the Big Five, Mr. Posa, very much at the margins of the group, and Mr. Mtontsi, a poor drunkard, were not such powerful people.

Together, the Big Five formed a collective clientelism. Instead of relationships between individuals (patronage), collective clientelism is characterised by less personal relationship of a group of leaders with settlers of a community (Burgwal 1995, 27-28, 144; Van der Linden 1997, see also Barth 1959, 7). The Big Five attempted –often successfully- to control any initiative in the area, such as the building of schools, the appointment of teachers, the distribution of RDP plots to applicants, plans to build speed humps to slow down traffic, and they would ask for bribes to receive a plot. Their control was to the extent that they supported schoolteachers who took away the children's lunch so they were forced to buy sweets and chicken feet from the women –also Big Five supporters- who had their little food stalls at the school ground. They co-operated with certain factions of the ANC, and at times also with other political parties, such as the National Party and United Democratic Movement. But the Big Five were particularly powerful because they were the DPC's local Project Committee.

THE OPPOSITION
The Big Five managed to stay in control over development but they were not unchallenged. As more people moved from the informal settlements around the Cape Flats to the serviced Indawo Yoxolo, politics in Indawo Yoxolo changed.

The most prominent leader of the opposition against the Big Five was Mr. Mabeqa, an ANC comrade who previously lived in Guguletu and moved to a plot in Indawo Yoxolo with his wife and teenage daughter. Because of his central position, I will call the opposition Mr. Mabeqa's group. Most of the supporters of Mr. Mabeqa's group lived in the serviced Indawo Yoxolo, which made them less dependent on the Big Five's willingness to put them on the housing list that would entitle them with the housing grant.

Politically, they were related with certain fractions within the local and provincial ANC. They also had some unclear relationships with the South African National Civic Organisation (SANCO), the civic body that was successive to the UDF. They claimed to be the legitimate SANCO committee in Indawo Yoxolo, which the Big Five, however, contested. The most important political stronghold of Mr. Mabeqa's group was their relation with councillor Gqoli. Mr. Gqoli was the only candidate for the local government elections of May 1996 for ward X of the Central Substructure.[iv] This comprised of three informal squatter camps including the squatter area without communal facilities and clearly demarcated plots that were going to be part of the developed Indawo Yoxolo.

The developed area of Indawo Yoxolo was not part of councillor Gqoli's ward X but part of ward Y. The councillors of ward Y were unknown to the residents of Indawo Yoxolo and they might have represented only other parts of ward Y. Because the councillors of ward Y were unknown, and because Indawo Yoxolo was divided between two wards (Ward X for the old squatter area and ward Y for the serviced area) Mr. Mabeqa's group tried to promote councillor Gqoli as the legitimate representative of the whole area.

The co-operation between councillor Gqoli and Mr. Mabeqa's group could have been motivated by the 'competition' between the local government structure and the RDP structure. The representatives of local government were elected but the Project Committee had much more control over resources and had a major say in the development of Indawo Yoxolo. Therefore, the local government was circumvented by the parallel structure of the RDP legitimised by community participation and community development. The Project Committee's control over the development project could undermine local government. The Big Five did not acknowledge councillor Gqoli as the legitimate councillor. Instead, they supported councillors from the illegal squatter camps where they had lived before or adjacent wards.

FUTURE DWELLING
Instead of only focusing on the potency of these politically powerful Big Five and their social position, as often is done in an analysis of big men, political security has to be taken into the analysis as well (Thoden van Velzen 1973). Challenging the relationships with development offices, government institutions, and political parties, largely played out the struggle between the Big Five and Mr. Mabeqa's group. Moreover, the success of the Big Five in maintaining their position was to some extent a consequence of the actions of these institutions.

Future Dwelling co-ordinated the DPC development projects in Indawo Yoxolo. Future Dwelling was a private sector company that managed the relations with the private sector, subcontractors, and government institutions. The role of Future Dwelling as a provider of resources was central to the position of the Big Five. Future Dwelling was aware of the problems caused by the Big Five. In 1996, there even had been a workshop organised with the participants of the RDP projects to discuss the illegal payments for plots.

The DPC workshops, and later its statements in newsletters, did not stop corruption and I heard of applicants paying bribes of up to R1, 200 in return for a place on the housing list. But not everybody was able, or willing, to pay such large sums of money. This confined them to the squatter camps that were part of Indawo Yoxolo: the Big Five only allowed them to live on a plot after they had paid a bribe. In September 1997, the Big Five had tried to kill an opponent for not paying a bribe by shooting at him through the window of his shack in the squatter area of Indawo Yoxolo.

The opposition had made numerous attempts to challenge the relation between the Big Five and Future Dwelling. They had called meetings with Future Dwelling and at times also other development agencies. This, however, had always been unsuccessful. Future Dwelling would either fail to show up and if they would be present they were not willing to reconsider the co-operation with the Big Five. In November 1997, Mr. Mabeqa and other opponents of the Big Five, had finally managed to meet with the director in the office of Future Dwelling to discuss the violence and corruption in Indawo Yoxolo. There were no Big Five supporters present and therefore I could easily join the meeting. The director of Future Dwelling was unhappy about this meeting, but the presence of the residents of Indawo Yoxolo, and the support of their community leaders forced him to meet them.

They told the director about the problems they had with the DPC's local Project Committee, i.e. the Big Five. Moreover, they had problems with Mr. Gwayi, their liaison officer responsible for the contacts between Future Dwelling and the Project Committee in Indawo Yoxolo. They repeated the allegations, which they had expressed earlier at a local town council meeting that the liaison officer of Future Dwelling had sided with the Big Five and was also involved in corruption. They held Future Dwelling accountable for its support to the Project Committee. Instead of challenging the corruption and violence in Indawo Yoxolo, Future Dwelling was actually supporting the Big Five through the co-operation with their liaison officer.

Furthermore, they told the director that the Big Five were never properly elected and that the Project Committee did not include the new residents of Indawo Yoxolo. They told him that he was not the only one ignoring these problems. Also Mr. Mhloma, from the Department of Education, persistently ignored Mr. Mabeqa's group although they were the only legitimate SANCO committee in Indawo Yoxolo and instead kept on working with the Big Five. After these allegations, the response of the liaison officer present at the meeting, Mrs. Dlamini, was that Future Dwelling wanted to wait until a larger ANC investigation into the housing and the RDP issues in the Cape Metropolitan Area was finalised. The director added:

> 'Things have changed in Indawo Yoxolo since we started. All political groups have to be included which represent the whole community. It has to be an inclusive community committee and should be elected. Then we have an accredited RDP forum in Indawo Yoxolo. It must include the entire community.'

Mr. Mabeqa and his supporters tried to explain that the tensions with the Big Five were too high to form a single committee. They asked the director how they could co-operate with someone who had threatened and tried to kill them? This was impossible, but the director kept on repeating his 'formula' that the Project Committee had to be inclusive and completely ignored the political problems in Indawo Yoxolo.

The director refused to take any actions concerning the allegations of corruption that were put towards his liaison officer and said: 'One can not change people's jobs based on some rumours'. He promised that the liaison officer would stop working in Indawo Yoxolo and that another liaison officer would replace him. In practice, however, it seemed that the liaison officer kept control over the situation in Indawo Yoxolo. Some complained to me that the new liaison officer relied heavily on the previous liaison officer's advice and that she continued to work with the Big Five and ignored Mr. Mabeqa's group. The ongoing support of the Big Five eventually led to rumours that Future Dwellings, including its director, were also involved in corruption. There were also increasing rumours about the ANC's involvement because the investigation into housing and RDP issues never seemed to be finalised. The slow investigation process was considered, at least by some, as a deliberate attempt of the ANC to hide corruption scandals. Although the National Party was the largest political party in the Western Cape Province and in the Cape Metropolitan Area, and thus might be considered, at least too some extent, responsible for the problems in Indawo Yoxolo, there were at this stage no allegations towards them.

The reason for Future Dwelling's approach seemed to be politically motivated. Future Dwelling co-operated with the Big Five because they were the most powerful group in Indawo Yoxolo and were therefore likely to be successful in carrying out the development projects. Although Future Dwelling used the rhetoric of inclusive community representation, their main concern was to get the job done. Similar to indirect rule, the Big Five's willingness to use violence was only a bonus because it made them more powerful. Thus, Future Dwelling provided the Big Five with the parameters necessary to be powerful men (cf. Thoden van Velzen 1973). The main challenge to the Big Five's opponents seemed to be to influence the distribution of resources and to undermine the political security which the Big Five received from Future Dwelling and the ANC. The project of rule, which, at least in Indawo Yoxolo, was so intrinsically interwoven with community participation, made it very difficult of the unbound weak to challenge the position of the big men. Although it might have been unintended, the control over the development process led to a control over people through violence and intimidation. Other objectives of the development process, such as empowerment, or democracy, did not lead to any changes by Future Dwelling, the ANC, and the Department of Education.

ANC

The opposition also made several attempts to challenge the support the Big Five received from the ANC. Some of the complaints about the Big Five had reached the provincial body of the ANC. In October 1997, the ANC of the Western Cape Province established a Commission of Inquiry into the allegations of corruption and violence in Indawo Yoxolo. The information on the proceedings and results of the Commission of Inquiry is from the Commission's confidential report to the ANC. The Commission of Inquiry interviewed 27 residents of Indawo Yoxolo who testified about the intimidation, violence, and corruption of the Big Five. They told the Commission that they were forced to pay bribes of up to R700 to Big Five members in exchange for a plot to which they would have been entitled to in the first place. The Big Five also 'stole' plots from its owners and sold them to people who did not qualify for a RDP grant, but who were willing and able to bribe the Big Five. They also complained about the violence of the Big Five. One of the 27 complained that he was beaten with a firearm butt and another man had been shot. Another person testified that a Big Five member threatened him with a gun.

When it was the Big Five's turn to respond to the allegations they blamed councillor Gqoli. They were unhappy that Mr. Gqoli openly supported Mr. Mabeqa's fraction and felt he had no right to interfere in Indawo Yoxolo. To the allegations of bribery, they replied that they had collected a small amount of money from residents (R50 per household) to cover their administrative expenses: 'for tip-ex and petrol', as some of them put it. They denied that they sold houses illegally and told the Commission that they wanted to help people who had plans to sell their house to others.

After the Commission of Inquiry had heard the allegations and the Big Five's response, they established a report for the ANC of the Western Cape Province. The Commission concluded that it frequently happened that comrades were accused of crimes without being guilty of misbehaviour. They stated, however, that the illegal selling of plots by the Big Five was probably true because this was known to happen in other informal settlements in the Western Cape, such as Crossroads. The Commission felt it had sufficient evidence that four comrades were involved in the illegal selling of plots in Indawo Yoxolo, even after the Commission of inquiry had already started its work.

The Commission recommended expelling two Big Five members for six months and Mr. Zantsi for life. He was accused of, amongst others things, harassment, beatings with a firearm, and the illegal sale of houses. The Commission did not report the crimes to the police and the crimes did not seem to be the reason for the disciplinary actions that they recommended. Mr. Zantsi, for example, was not expelled for his crimes, but for publicly challenging the ANC and for giving the impression that he supported rival political parties. The ANC of the Western Cape enforced the Commission's recommendations. After one year, however, Mr. Zantsi was re-admitted to the ANC. It was not so much the criminal activities of the Big Five that concerned them, but, similar to indirect rule, the ANC could use a loyal Project Committee to establish control over this area. Thus, the ANC was able to give political security, one of the parameters of the big men paradigm, to the Big Five in return for their political loyalty.

In February 1998, a member of the Big Five, Mr. Nqasa, had murdered Mr. Mabeqa who had led the opposition against them. Others who had been critical about the Big Five's rule were intimidated or killed. This had, at least temporarily, caused the disappearance of any opposition to the Big Five. Through violence, terror, and the continuous support from Future Dwelling and fractions within the ANC, the Big Five were able to maintain their powerful position. Mr. Nqasa was imprisoned for the murder but about a year later he was 'working' again in Indawo Yoxolo.

These problems were not only confined to Indawo Yoxolo. The eruption of violence in Cape Town led to an independent investigation by the Cape Town City Council, which was released in December 1998. The tenure of the report was that the violence was related to the ANC dominated development projects. City manager and local electoral officer Mr. Boraine stated that the distribution of resources in a poor area made a few people very powerful. Although the problem was recognised, the report failed to point out that development policy created the parameters for such powerful brokers. Instead, the report focused on the community as an independent area with warlords, a possible 'third force' and intolerant politicians (Steenkamp and Bateman 1998) Yhe development project itself was not regarded as part of the problem and hardly any reference was made to the role of development planning.

CONCLUSIONS

With the collapse of the apartheid state, the hopes that the ANC and many Africans had about the future were high, maybe too high. Before, and some years after, the 1994 elections people expected the new government to solve many of the racial inequalities of the past. Adequate housing for the poor was regarded as one of the key issues in this transformation process. But, the building of houses for the large numbers of poor Africans was a tremendous task. Many of the policy requirements for development proved to work out differently in practice and had caused, or contributed to, political conflicts, violence, intimidation, and corruption. Numerous development policies, development workers and journalists adopted a seemingly unproblematic image of the community as a homogenous group of people. A person was not seen to represent himself, but everybody in 'the community', in a powerful and naive way. Such simplistic images of community served a form of rule similar to indirect rule in colonial Africa: The goals might have been different, but the means to achieve them seemed similar.

It seems a contradiction that a political party that is rooted in the struggle for democracy and freedom has been able to neglect the oppressive aspects of the development process. Unfortunately, at least some government agencies and development institutions did not wish to deal with the problematic use of 'communities'. Instead of dealing with the establishment of violent power brokers in places such as Indawo Yoxolo, and instead of listening to the objectives raised by opposing groups, they kept repeating their mantra of adequate housing for the poor through community participation. Notwithstanding numerous protests by the victims of this policy, the projects were not adjusted and powerful and violent brokers were not seriously challenged. To some degree, the management of housing for the poor was continued along repressive lines of rule of the past. This means that, both on a theoretical and policy level, more attention should be paid to the possibilities that poor people have to question or challenge the delivery of housing, and their involvement in the development process.

NOTES

[i] The forum consisted of the African National Congress, Cape Provincial Administration, South African National Civics Organisation, Western Cape Regional Services Council, Western Cape United Squatters Association, Cape Town City Council, Western Cape Civics Association, Ikapa Town Council, Umzamo Development Project, Crossroads Town Council, and at a later stage the Pan African Congress joined (DPC 1994, 1).
[ii] R1 (one Rand) is approximately 0.15 Euro.
[iii] See the Provincial Gazette Extraordinary 4943 (1995) for the participating civics in the Western Cape Metropolitan Area.
[iv] The local government elections in the Western Cape Province and Kwazulu Natal (the only provinces where an ANC victory would not be sure) were postponed for half a year. In the Western Cape was a political battle over electoral borders because the way the borders were drawn had important consequences for the election results and tax revenues.

BIBLIOGRAPHY

ANC 1994: The Reconstruction and Development Programme: A policy framework. Johannesburg: Umanyano.

Bähre, E. 1996: "We organise each other": Financial Self-help Groups and Civics in the Townships of Cape Town, South Africa. M.A. Utrecht University.

Bähre, E. 2002: "Money and Violence: Financial Mutuals among the Xhosa in Cape Town, South Africa". PhD University of Amsterdam.

Barth, F. 1959: Segmentary Opposition and the Theory of Games: A Study of Pathan Organization. Journal of the Royal Anthropological Institute 89, 5-21.

Burgwal, G. 1995: Struggle of the poor; Neighborhood organization and clientelist practice in a Quita squatter settlement. PhD. University of Amsterdam.

Cole, J. 1987: Crossroads: the politics of reform and repression 1976/1986. Johannesburg: Ravan Press.

Cook, G. P. 1992: Khayelitsha: new settlement forms in the Cape Peninsula. In D. M. Smith, (ed.), The Apartheid City and Beyond; Urbanization and Social Change in South Africa, p. 125-135. London, New York, Johannesburg: Routledge and University of Witwatersrand Press.

DPC 1994: Unpublished Business Plan, November 1994

DPC 1996a: Development Planning Committee Bulletin no. 1, February

DPC 1996b: Development Planning Committee Bulletin no. 3, March/April

DPC 1996d: Development Planning Committee Bulletin no. 3, June

Ferguson, J. 1990: The Anti-Politics Machine; 'Development', depolitication and bureaucratic state power in Lesotho. Cambridge: Cambridge University Press.

Gluckman, M. 1971: Analysis of a social situation in modern Zululand. Manchester: Manchester University Press.

Jacobs, B. 1992: Heading for Disaster? Work in Progress. December:23-25.

James, D. 1999: Bagagsu (those of my home): women migrants, ethnicity, and performance in South Africa. American Ethnologist 26 (1), 69-89.

Leftwitch, A. 1994: Governance, the State and the Politics of Development. Development and Change 25, 363-386.

Linden, J. van der 1997: On popular participation in a culture of patronage; patrons and grassroots organization in a sites and services project in Hyderabad, Pakistan. Environment and Urbanization 9 (1), 81-90.

Mail and Guardian 1998: Whatever happened to the dream of low-cost housing? February 20-26.

Mamdani, M. 1996: Citizen and Subject: Contemporary Africa and the Legacy of Late Colonialism. Princeton: Princeton University Press.

Masakhane (1995): Home truths.

Matiwane, M. and S. Walters 1986:   The   Struggle   for   Democracy: A   study   of community organisations in Greater Cape Town from 1960's to 1985. Cape Town: Centre for Adult and Continuing Education, University of the Western Cape.

Ramphele, M. 1993:   A bed called home: Life in the Migrant Hostels of Cape Town. Edinburgh: Edinburgh University Press.

Ramphele, M. 1991:   The politics of space: life in the migrant labour hostels of the Western Cape. Doctoral thesis. University of Cape Town.

Robertson, M.K. 1990: Black Land Tenure: Disabilities and Some Rights. In. A. J. Rycroft, A. J. Boulle, M. K. Robertson, and P. R. Spiller (eds), Race and the Law in South Africa, p. 119-135. Cape Town: Juta and Co.

Scott, J. C. 1998: Seeing like a state: How certain schemes to improve the human condition have failed. New Haven and London: Yale University Press.

Shubane, K. 1991: Black Local Authorities: A contraption of control. In M. Swilling, R. Humphries, and K. Shubane (eds) Apartheid city in transition,. p. 64-77. Cape Town: Oxford University Press.

Steenkamp, W. and C. Bateman 1998: Crossroads conflict; "warlords" arm for '99 election. Cape Times, December 11.

Thoden van Velzen, H.U.E. 1973: Robinson Crusoe and Friday: Strength and weakness of the big man paradigm. Man 8 (4), 592-612.

Vail, L. 1989: Introduction: Ethnicity in Southern African History. In L. Vail (ed.) The Creation of Tribalism in Southern Africa. 1-21. London: Currey.

The Changing Nature of the Informal Sector in Karachi Due to Global Restructuring and Liberalisation

Arif Hasan

INTRODUCTION

This paper is not the result of scientific research on the effects of liberalisation on the informal sectors and settlements of Karachi. It is more the result of observation and dialogue with informal sector operators and residents of informal settlements. This interaction between the actors in the informal sector drama and myself has been made possible by my association with the Orangi Pilot Project-Research & Training Institute (OPP-RTI), its replication in seven Pakistani cities, and the work of the Urban Resource Centre (URC) in Karachi. The OPP-RTI is a community financed and managed settlement-upgrading project and operates from Orangi Township in Karachi. The Township has a population of 1.2 million (about 12 per cent of the city) and is the largest informal settlement in Pakistan. Settlement in Orangi began in 1965. The Township is also the hub of much of informal sector activity in the city and was created by middlemen through the illegal subdivision and sale of state land. The URC, on the other hand, analyses government plans from the point of view of various community organisations, informal service providers and interest groups operating in Karachi. Its forums, supported by research, have created a space for interaction between interest lobbies and communities on the one hand and politicians and bureaucrats on the other. Statistics in this paper are given as endmotes and most of them are derived from the research work of these two organisations.

The informal sector in Karachi, as in other Pakistani cities, has served the physical and social infrastructure needs of low and lower middle-income communities and settlements. In the last decade, new needs have surfaced and they have been accompanied by major changes in the global, and thus in the local, economy. For the vast majority of Karachi population the formal sector cannot service these needs as its products are unaffordable to them and its organisational culture far removed from their own. In addition, these changes have redefined the relationship between the various actors in the informal sector drama. This paper represents an attempt to understand these changes and to identify the directions they are likely to take. However, before attempting this, it is important to understand the causes for the emergence of the informal sector in Karachi and its scale and manner of operation.

The regions that were brought together to form the state of Pakistan after independence in 1947 had endured just over one hundred years of British rule. The elite, who took over from the British, were educated in Britain and their view of development, as in other matters, reflected that of their colonial masters. As such, the new state adopted the British post-war "welfare state model" as its model for development. According to this model, the state was responsible for providing subsidised housing, health and education and jobs to its citizens. In addition, it was to determine the parameters within which private enterprise was to function and industrialisation was to take place. This model was not successful in the Pakistani context for a variety of reasons. The necessary institutional framework for its planning and implementation did not exist in fact. Revenues to subsidise the planned social and physical infrastructure could not be generated. The organisational culture of the post-colonial establishment was one of control through the coercive force of the state rather than of dialogue, discussion and interaction with urban interest groups. One could argue quite effectively that such interest groups were not even constituted in any organised form until the late 1970s.

The failure of the state to provide proper housing, health and education and jobs for its citizens was accompanied by an urban population explosion. Three reasons account for this. Firstly, the migration from India at the time of the partition of the Sub-Continent in 1947 more than doubled the population of a large number of towns in the Sindh and Punjab provinces (Government of Pakistan, 1951)[1]. Secondly, the eradication of malaria, small pox and cholera and the promotion of immunisation programmes decreased infant and child mortality in a big way. Thirdly, green revolution technologies and mechanisation forced landless labour and small peasants to migrate to the cities. Thus, the demand-supply gaps in housing, transport, health, education and jobs increased, and with these the state's inability to service this demand. By the late 1970s most state initiatives in these fields had declined and those that remained operative were being run at an increasing subsidy which the state was unable to provide. The helplessness of the administration to provide, and hence administer, these basic services came to fuel corruption.

Traditionally, middlemen have always existed in Pakistani society and they have provided lower income groups, at a considerable price, with finance during difficult times and with access to the corridors of power and hence to patronage. Historically, their activities have been small in scale as compared to the larger social and economic context. It was initially these middlemen who came forward to bridge the housing and employment demand-supply gaps in Karachi. Since the gaps were considerable, they employed apprentices from various communities, and these in turn became the new informal sector entrepreneurs. Today, it is the third generation of these entrepreneurs that are active in informal sector activities in Karachi. The relationship that their predecessors established with government officials and agencies for support has long since been institutionalised. The size of under-the-table payments to be made to different government functionaries, through whom and at what time, has also been formalised.

The vast majority of Karachi people live in informal settlements (Sindh Katchi Abadi Authority, 1996)[2]. These have been developed on government land, illegally occupied by developers with the support of government servants and protected through bribes by the police. Almost all these settlements have residents' organisations (created by the

148

developers) that constantly lobby government agencies for infrastructure and security of tenure. The developers hire journalists to write about the "terrible conditions" in their settlements and engage lawyers to help regularise tenure. These informal developers have developed many of Karachi's important link roads and commercial areas. Loans, material and advice, for the construction of homes, are provided by small neighbourhood contractors who become the architects, housing banks and engineers to low-income households (Hasan, 2001)[3]. Similarly, over 72% of Karachi's population travel in individually owned mini-buses that have been purchased using informal loans with large interest rates from moneylenders. Since these buses have no terminals, depots or workshops, they use the roads for these purposes and informally pay the police and the local administration for permission to do so (Hasan, 2000)[4]. Another important sector is related to the recycling of solid waste. Instead of taking solid waste to land fill sites, municipal waste collectors, in defiance of rules and regulations, take the solid waste to informal recycling factories spread all over the city. In the process even organic waste, which cannot be recycled, does not reach the landfill sites. Here again large sums of money exchange hands illegally (Urban Resource Centre, 2001)[5].

As settlements consolidate, private schools are established within them. They far outnumber government schools and are affordable to the residents because neighbourhood-educated women teach in them on low salaries (OPP, 1999)[6]. Most of these schools begin as one-classroom affairs in people's homes and some of them expand to become large institutions. They are established by entrepreneurs, public-spirited individuals and/or neighbourhood community organisations and remain unregistered and unrecognised till attempts at their registration are made long after their establishment. Private medical practitioners (qualified, unqualified and/or traditional), establish health clinics in the informal settlements, despite being unregistered with any government agency or medical council. Entertainment and recreation also develops in informal settlements. Video machines, table football and carom and card game tables are set up by entrepreneurs without permission. The profits from these activities are shared between the entrepreneurs and the law enforcing agencies.

The most important informal sector activity, however, is related to generation of employment. Garments, leather goods and carpets are all produced in the informal settlements. Middlemen provide training, materials, equipment and cash for the production of these items. The production takes place in people's homes, on a contract basis. The manufactured items are taken to the factories where a label is placed on them before they are packed in alternative packets. In this way, exporters and industrialists are able to reduce production costs and prevent the unionisation of labour and the application of labour laws and minimum wage. Various parts for the light engineering and the electronics industries are also produced in a similar manner on lathe and rubber moulding machines in informal settlements. Spare parts for machinery, cars, tractors, and diesel engines are also manufactured in these settlements and their price is about half that of industrially produced products. It is because of these spare parts that the transport and services sector to agricultural machinery is affordable to the operators and hence to primary producers.

The success of the activities of the informal sector in Karachi described above, has much to do with the availability of cheap government land, protection to local industry provided by high import duties, the pioneering spirit of the first generation of migrants and entrepreneurs and the helplessness of state institutions in the face of an increasing demand-supply gap in physical and social sector infrastructure. However, with liberalisation and other related developments all this has started to change.

Economic liberalisation has been accompanied by structural readjustment, the communications revolution and major sociological changes in society and, as such, its effects cannot be seen in isolation from these developments. Structural adjustment has meant reduction in import duties on all manufactured goods. By 2003, these duties will cease to exist. It is already becoming apparent that the Pakistani light engineering industry cannot compete with products from South East Asian countries. Consequently, lathe machine operators in the informal settlements are not receiving sufficient orders or are being asked by the contractors to lower the quality and prices of their products (Alimuddin *et al.*, 1999). Structural readjustment has also meant a huge increase in utility charges, especially electricity. As a result, carpet and textile power looms, most of which function through contractor funded orders, in informal settlements, are working on reduced profits or closing down (Ibid). According to a recent newspaper report, illegal electrical connections to informal workshops have increased alongside the cost of the bribe to acquire these connections (Daily Jung, 2000).

One of the major objectives of the structural adjustment programme is to help Pakistan service its international debts more effectively. Thus, the devaluation of the Pakistan rupee, so as to increase imports, is an essential part of the structural adjustment plan. The rupees constant devaluation has caused large-scale inflation and a search among the marginalized and lower income groups for additional employment. It has increased the use of child labour and forced a larger number of women out to work so that their incomes considered as more than a "bonus". Most workingmen now have more than one job. Teachers give tuition in the evenings, government servants drive taxis, policemen fleece shopkeepers and motorcyclists and white-collar workers work evening shifts as part-time employees in the service sector in addition to their full time jobs.

Under structural adjustment, Pakistan has also undertaken to privatise profitable government institutions and utilities and to sell state assets, mainly related to land, real estate and industries. As a result, land that was not considered valuable has now become an important commodity. It can no longer be easily encroached upon and, where it is transferred to private ownership, it is protected. This deprives informal sector developers of raw land for development at places appropriate for their clients. The government has also undertaken to privatise health and higher education. All this is adversely affecting low-income groups, especially those who had an element of upward mobility. Many non-establishment development experts believe that Pakistan, as a result of these issues, has double digit inflation and recession (Khan, 1998).

Privatisation has also meant employment on merit rather than through political patronage or quota systems. It has also meant the dismissal of many government employees. With privatisation of education, merit means those who can afford education and this marginalizes poor communities still further. For these people, an alternative source of education and skill despite limited means and circumstances becomes a necessary for survival.

This inflation and recession is taking place at a time when the older squatter colonies have been consolidating and such colonies constitute the majority of informal settlements. These are no longer purely working class settlements. The younger generation in them is overwhelmingly literate (Government of Pakistan, 1998)[7]. Many of them have become doctors, engineers, college teachers, bank managers and white-collar workers. Many of the small workshops and looms established by the first generation of entrepreneurs and artisans through middlemen support, have now developed direct links with the formal sector industries and exporters whom they service. Similarly, schools (begun as informal ones) have developed links with NGO and government support agencies and some health clinics have started to access government facilities in population planning and immunisation. Interest groups have organised themselves to present their claims and protect their gains. So there are now vocal transporters' organisations, loom operators' associations, neighbourhood groups, sports and cultural clubs (that manage to access government funds), and hawkers associations. Almost every sector of informal activity now has an organisation registered under the Societies Act. Increasingly these organisations are being led by second or third generation of city dwellers who have broken with their rural culture and background. They are better educated than their parents or grandparents and more comfortable than them in dealing with those in power. Instead of seeking access through middlemen and touts of political parties they approach the establishment through the power of their organisations who increasingly have yearly audits and elections.

Due to the changes mentioned above, there has been great change in people's lifestyle, supported by the communications revolution. Nuclear families are replacing joint family systems. Clan and tribal organisations, that the migrants had brought with them have ceased to be effective and are being replaced by new community organisations or by a dependence on state institutions. The communications revolution has made the television and video an important entertainment tool. The television is the main source of information for the vast majority of Karachi households, (Ibid)[8] more than 50 per cent of whom have access to some form of cable. Thus, video shops and cable operators, all too expensive in the formal sector for the lower and lower middle-income population, have become a necessity. Santa Barbara, The Bold and The Beautiful, MTV and a variety of news is now available in homes in all low-income settlements of Karachi and in the teashops and eating places located within them. These have brought about a clash of values and cultural confusion. It has also brought about a generation gap, which seems unbridgeable and is one of the major reasons for an increase in honour killings of women in first generation urban families. Vocabularies have also changed. Words of respect for elders or for those of a higher class have been substituted by "uncle" and "auntie" and that too in the English language equivalent. The whole feudal vocabulary, which the migrants had brought with them, has simply vanished with the new generation.

Liberalisation and the communications revolution has also introduced the corporate culture to Karachi. There is a great demand for information technology professionals, operators and technicians not only for the local market but also for employment abroad. The training for these professions is provided both by government and private institutions. In the case of government institutions, this training is affordable to low income groups but is on too small a scale to service the demand. As such, only those who are exceptional students can get into government institutions. Private institutions are far too expensive and only the rich can afford them. Thus, a large gap has been created between demand and formal sector supply.

The corporate culture has introduced a feel of affluence in the city, which was unknown before. Golf clubs and various recreational and cultural facilities have been developed and are sponsored by companies for their clients, employees and for advertisement purposes. Unlike previously, these activities are performed in new locations in elite areas or five star hotels and not in municipal or public buildings in the inner city. As a result, the inner city as a space for multi-class entertainment is dead. These corporate sector promoted activities and the glamour and pomp that surrounds them is in sharp contrast to the physical and social conditions in lower and lower middle-income settlements. There is an increasing feeling of insecurity among the promoters of these activities and so they and the corporate sector employees and clients are surrounded by security systems and armed guards. This is in sharp contrast to the Karachi of the pre-liberalisation period.

Liberalisation has also meant the introduction of fast food chain stores and the popularisation of various consumer items. McDonalds, Pizza Hut, and others have opened branches all over the city. Huge advertisements, colourful and well lit, dominate the urban landscape and dwarf badly constructed, badly lit businesses and homes. New post-modern buildings of the corporate sector, with posh interiors, contrast sharply with the sedate government buildings of earlier decades. Since many young people from Karachi's informal settlements work in this environment, ties, white or blue shirts and the "corporate hair cut" are becoming common phenomena and everyone knows what a credit card is and wishes to acquire one.

What has been described above is really the emergence of a First World economy and sociology with a Third World wage and political structure. It is the emergence of new aspirations related to consumerism and the desire to belong to the "contemporary" world as portrayed in the media, but without the means of achieving these aspirations and desires through formal institutions and processes. Thus the most important role (and it is a new one) that the informal sector is trying to play today and probably in the foreseeable future, is to help bridge this aspirations-means gap. In Karachi a whole new world has emerged to do just this.

Although the younger generation has new aspirations, state culture and family pressures prevent or hinder them from pursuing their desires. There is a major conflict between the individualism of the young, and the conservative social values of the older generation that seek to protect the joint family and clan systems. This is one of the major reasons, apart from the financial ones, why many young Pakistanis wish to emigrate. (Daily Dawn, 2000)[9] Getting a visa, a job and establishing connections after one migrates to a First World country is not an easy job for young Karachi people from low or lower middle-income settlements. Middlemen have emerged to cater for this need, helping to acquire genuine and or forged visas and arranging jobs abroad. Newspaper reports suggest that these operators have contacts in visa sections in embassies and that large sums of money exchange hands in this trade. To acquire an American or Japanese visa, young Pakistanis are reported as paying up to Rs 200,000 (US $3,333) to middlemen. An entire street in the inner city of Karachi deals with arranging the necessary emigration and employment papers and, from observation, one can see that the number of middlemen and clients involved is increasing every day.

All Karachi neighbourhoods, including low income and even marginalized ones, have not one but many video shops in them. All these shops rent out pirated videos. Video copies of Indian films arrive in Karachi even before their official release in India, videos of American films arrive well before release in Karachi. All attempts at curbing this piracy have failed. If they were to succeed, most people in Karachi would never be able to hire videocassettes, and similarly for audiocassettes. More recently, cable television has also made a big appearance in Karachi. Most of the cable companies are illegal and informally use the telephone network for providing home connections. They service all areas of Karachi irrespective of class. Telephone department officials and the police are informally paid by the cable companies to let this happen. The cost of a cable connection varies from Rs 450 per month for a connection from a legal company to Rs 150 from an illegal one. At a modest estimate there are over 150,000 people involved in the video and cable-related trade.

All low-income settlements (formal or informal) have video halls in them. These are large asbestos roofed shacks, which show video films of all types. The films are advertised on the notice board outside along with the names of the stars and are held at regular hours. In the interval tea and chips are available. Under the law this is an illegal activity but it provides to the male-only day wage labour that lives around the port and wholesale markets with their entertainment. The video hall operators consider this a "joint venture" between them, the police and the excise department officials.

New aspirations and exposure through the media to a new and glamorous world has led to the opening of a number of "beauty parlours" and tuition centres for spoken English. Neighbourhood beauty parlours are multiplying in the low-income settlements and they advertise various hairstyles that are named after Indian film stars. Being well groomed and speaking English has become an added asset for a woman in the marriage "market" in Karachi's older informal settlements. The pioneering beauticians are trained informally through existing hairdressers in upper middle-income beauty parlours. Now their apprentices, themselves multiplying in number, are taking over the informal settlements. This trade has become so important that popular radio programmes now give regular beauty tips for women and the trade operators.

The most important informal sector activity today is related to information technology. Training schools, actually no more than tuition centres, have opened up informally in all low and lower middle-income areas. These centres have no admission requirements in terms of qualifications for admission and offer no exit qualifications either. Their trainees are employed having been tested by the prospective employers. If they are well trained the employers prefer them to qualified persons since they can pay them a much lower salary for doing the same work. Similarly, there is a whole sector that deals with pirating computer software and marketing it to both informal and formal outlets. All attempts at curbing this activity have also failed and, as a result, both international companies and the government have simply given up. The cost of such software can be as little as 5% of its original value. Without this sector information technology would also be unaffordable to the lower or even middle-income groups in Karachi.

New lifestyles promoted by the media and the corporate sector have also had an influence on the lifestyles of the poorer sections of the population. They consume *Seven-Up*, *Coca-Cola* and beef-burgers and are interested in designer shirts and brand name perfumes. However, these are all unaffordable to them. So fake *Seven-Up* and *Coca-Cola*, costing half the price of the real one, is manufactured in informal factories and marketed in a big way in the original bottles. Fake brand name perfumes and fake designer shirts are also manufactured and marketed. A cheap alternative to the beef burger is available in every Karachi locality.

This new informal sector activity, the result of liberalisation and related changes, really tries to serve the better off and the slightly upwardly mobile residents of old consolidated or consolidating informal settlements. At the same time, this process also marginalizes a large section of these settlements and deprives them of employment and access to diminishing government subsidies and benefits. This division has increased crime such as armed robberies and car and purse snatching in Karachi. These "criminal" activities are not easy to carry out in Karachi's affluent areas due to the presence of the police and private sector guards and security systems. However, they continue to happen and grow in the lower income settlements. So residents of many of these settlements organise informal neighbourhood policing systems and try to get approval from the government for operating them. So far such approval has not been forthcoming and these neighbourhood-policing systems continue to operate and grow in defiance of state rules and regulations.

Apart from the emergence of these new informal sector activities, the old ones have also undergone a change. Informal developers are now forced to develop their settlements very far from the centre of the city because land in the centre has become an important asset to its owners. The diminishing purchasing power of the new migrants to the city means smaller lots of land, narrower lanes and less open space. Health and education institutions established by the informal sector in the older settlements have come of age and struggle to become formal institutions and try increasingly successfully to access government poverty alleviation funds (also a by-product of structural adjustment policies) and related programmes. However, they find it difficult to establish themselves in the new settlements. This is because these settlements, unlike the older ones when they were first established, do not dominate the politics or the economy of the city. They also contain a smaller percentage of the city population and so politicians are less interested in them. They are also far away from the city to be ignored more easily by local government and entrepreneurs. Given inflation and recession, their buying power is also limited.

The future of the informal sector in Karachi is difficult to predict. However, some trends are clear. The links between the informal workshops and the formal sectors of industry are slowly being eroded except in the case of those industries (such as garments) which have an export potential. It is feared that even these links will cease when formal sector garment factories are established through local and foreign investment programmes. The process has begun. Since these industries have much more sophisticated machinery, they will be far less labour intensive and cause further unemployment.

The informal sector is now moving into producing cheap consumer goods for the poorer sections of the population. This means less profit and marginalization from formal sector processes and economy. At the same time, the state sector is rapidly shrinking, especially in the provision of physical development and social services. This means that politicians will not continue to offer favours and patronage. It was through the system of favours and patronage that informal settlements were established and informal entrepreneurs were able to function. Favours and patronage are being replaced by cash payments for protection of activities that are in defiance of state regulations. All this means the marginalization of all those without merit or skills or access to expensive private sector education.

The above trends are creating unemployment, which will increase until formal sector private investment finally replaces the informal sector job market. This is nowhere in sight yet and as a result, the rich-poor divide continues to increase, leading to violence and crime. The worst affected are those sections of the new generation of consolidated lower and lower middle income settlements whose aspirations to belong to this new world cannot be fulfilled. Also, badly affected are those entrepreneurs and contractors who had established a working relationship with formal sector businesses and industries. It is important to note that these groups are potentially the most powerful in political terms. Their marginalization is creating a new situation.

It is therefore understandable that the present situation of inflation, recession and increasing marginalization of these groups, is being blamed on liberalisation, the WTO, structural adjustment, and World Bank and IMF policies. The press (especially the populist newspapers), politicians of various shades, NGOs and now even transporters and solid waste recyclers' associations, backed by academia, are all participating in this debate and issuing statements against globalisation. Seminars, symposia and workshops are regularly held on the subject and they endorse these views. The anti-WTO, World Bank and IMF protests in Seattle, Melbourne, Chang Mai and Prague, electrified the residents of lower middle-income settlements in Karachi and various interest groups operating in the city.

The informal sector and the frustrated potentially-upwardly-mobile sections of Karachi, look forward to joining this movement against the "New World order". How all this will resolve itself is an important issue for the future of Pakistan. So far there has been no proper research into the long-term effects of liberalisation on the city. So far, there has only been observation and discussion. This paper is another contribution to this debate.

NOTES

[1]Karachi's population increased from 450 thousand in 1947 to 1.137 million in 1951. According to the 1951 census 48.6 per cent of Pakistan's urban population had originated in India.

[2]According to the Sindh Katchi Abadi (squatter settlement) Authority, over 50 per cent of Karachiites live in 716 informal settlements which grow at twice the annual urban growth rate of Karachi.

[3]According to the 1987 "Yakoobabad Case Study" by the author, 93 per cent of Yakoobabad residents had taken materials and or cash on credit from small contractors to build their homes.

[4]Of the 13,200 mini-buses in Karachi, 6,000 are unregistered since there is a ban on the registration of mini-buses. In addition, the mini-bus operators pay Rs 780 million (US $13 million) a year as bribes to the city administration to use the roads as bus terminals, depots and workshops.

[5]According to Urban Resource Centre (URC) figures, the solid waste recycling industry's annual turn over is Rs 1.2 billion (US $20 million). It pays about Rs 220 million (US$ 3.6 million) informally every year to various government agencies to permit it to function.

[6]In Orangi Township, there are 72 government schools and 682 private schools most of which began as informal one-class affairs.

[7]According to the 1998 census results, 74.04 per cent of the Karachi age group of between 10 and 24 is literate as compared to a total Karachi figure of 67.42 per cent. In the 1981 census, 61.10 per cent of the age groups of between 10 and 24 were literate.

[8]According to the 1998 census, 79 per cent of Karachi households said that their main source of information was the television.

[9] According to a survey reported in Daily "*Dawn*" Karachi (November 2000), 38 per cent of Pakistanis wish to migrate. The figure for Karachi therefore must surely be higher. Author's interviews with persons wishing to migrate (unpublished)

BIBLIOGRAPHY

Alimuddin, S, Hasan, A, Sadiq, A (1999), The Work of the Anjuman Samaji Behood, Unpublished report, December.

Daily Dawn (2000), November, Karachi, Pakistan.

Daily Jang (2000), October, Karachi, Pakistan.

Government of Pakistan (1951), Population Census Reports.

Government of Pakistan (1998), Population Census Reports.

Hasan, Arif (2000), Understanding Karachi, City Press, Karachi.

Hasan, Arif (2000), Housing for the Poor, City Press, Karachi.

Khan, Akhter Hameed (1998), July, Orangi Pilot Project Programmes, OPP, Karachi.

Orangi Pilot Project (OPP)(1999), September, 79th, Quarterly Progress Report, Karachi.

Urban Resource Centre (2001), Solid Wastes Studies/Papers, unpublished report, Karachi

Structural Analysis of the Housing Pattern in Squatter Settlements

Hülya Turgut

INTRODUCTION

Turkey, as a developing country, has been undergoing a migration process since the 1950s. Migration from rural to urban areas or from small towns to big cities has created many problems that the governments or local authorities had not faced before. The most severe problems have arisen in Istanbul since it is the most attractive city for all the citizens. Istanbul had been one of the most important capitals of the Mediterranean basin for almost sixteen centuries, starting from the foundation of Constantinople in the 4th century A.D. and ensuring up to the end of the Ottoman Empire in the 1920s. Istanbul has had to face three major transformations in its history because of its unique location.

The "Islamisation" of the Byzantine city following the Ottoman conquest meant the establishment of new urban policies, a new type of urban administration, new institutions and organisations, as well as the promotion of new building types. In the nineteen century another transformation took place. In this government-sponsored transformation modernisation efforts recast the traditional urban policies based on Islamic law, replaced the urban administration, institutions and organizations with new ones adopting European precedents, and introduced another set of building types, this time conforming to the requirements of a modern Westernized lifestyle (Çelik, Z., 1991, 16).

The last and perhaps the most depressing transformation has taken place in the second half of this century. Starting from the Ottoman period in the 19th century, Istanbul has experienced migration from different parts of Anatolia and Thrace at gradually increasing speed. The background of these newcomers has been the most powerful factor in the reshaping of the city during the last three decades. Istanbul has been struggling with the population growth since the 1900's to save its values against these uncontrollable developments. The changes, which have occurred in Istanbul in the second half of this century, reflect the social and cultural differences of its population within the transition process

Migration from rural areas to towns and metropolises both means a change from rural to urban life as well as a change from rural production to industrial production. The characteristics of this transition period from tradition to the futuristic are reflected in the physical environment. Squatter settlements are a continuation of rural life styles, which develop in urban areas and change through time. Such an urbanization starting with migration to towns from rural-agricultural-traditional areas and ending in an urban, industrial-modern society can be analyzed for its values of culture-space interactions according to different scales, leading to a better understanding of Squatterisation as a fact, not only as a problem area (Turgut, H. et al, 1995). The settlement and spatial organization of squatter areas differ significantly from those of legal housing areas. The primary determinants of the housing patterns in squatter settlements begin with the acquisition of land on which to build and continue with the organization of living and working activities within the combination of culture-rooted behavioral characteristics and resource limitations. On the other hand, efforts for upgrading of squatter areas have failed because they have not been based on a participatory process involving squatters and users. Squatter settlements, which had tremendous potentials in terms of being transformed into settlement areas within the Istanbul Metropolitan region, have today assumed an unhealthier, multistory, and fixed housing pattern. The success of an implementation of alternative housing patterns to be recommended for the low income urban sector relies on the continuity of the planning, building and utilization which extends from the individual housing unit to the settlement. Decisions regarding equipment, space, unit housing and settlement must be suitable to the socio-cultural/behavioral characteristics of the population if this continuity to be possible. Conducting planning activities related to the squatter areas without first performing structural analyses of the culture and space interaction in these settlements is only a futile attempt doomed to failure (Turgut, H., 1998).

In the first part of this paper a theoretical framework is established, explaining and discussing culture, continuity and change in the process of urbanization.

THEORETICAL FRAMEWORK
In the last decades the squatter phenomenon has been studied and interpreted by different researchers having various perspectives. As these researchers have taken into account different aspects of this phenomenon in relation to their background, the definitions and the interpretations have differed from each other to a large extent. This differentiation demonstrates the complexity and the multidimensional nature of the problem. According to the first definition we have chosen "Squatterisation is a transition process from rural to urban life, a transitional life style and its reflection to space". The second defines this from the viewpoints of distribution of wealth (income), social structure and social security rather than only being a shelter (Arslan 1989, 34-37). The third approach takes into account the aspects related to ownership, legislation and construction processes and defines this phenomenon as "the casual buildings, which have been built on lands or plots without having any ownership and the right to built on it in terms of building legislation and laws." These definitions show that the fact of squatter settlements and the squatting process itself are complex subjects due to their socio-cultural, psychological, economic, political and physical attributes. We cannot isolate these different attributes from each other; for example, we cannot study the subject as if it is only a social problem or just a shelter or socio-economic and political problem. We have to have a holistic approach in order to reach much more comprehensive definitions and interpretations (Saglamer, G. et al, 1994).

After having summarised the different definitions and the interpretations of squatter settlements and the emergence of this phenomenon in big cities, we would like to focus on structural analysis of culture, continuity and change in squatter settlements.

Squatter settlements are among those housing patterns, which have the most visible reciprocal interactions between user groups and their cultures. The housing pattern in the urbanization process contains the spatial setting which is appropriate to the cultural, behavioral, socio-economic characteristics of the user group and their alterations in the course of time. Layout patterns and spatial organizations of squatter housing show dramatic differences from legal housing patterns.

Cultural, behavioral, socio-economic and spatial characteristics formed in the process of urbanization can be grouped as structural components composing housing patterns. Cultural components consisting of norms, customs, mores, life-style, family and kinship structure form the "Cultural Setting"; behavioral processes such as "personal space", "territorial behavior" and "privacy" form the "Behavioral Setting"; components of "dimension", "location" and "form" the "Spatial Setting"; characteristics of "income", "profession", "education" form the "Socio-economic setting". In this structural analysis of housing pattern, each sub-system - output form an input for the other sub-system and, together, they form the "Housing Pattern" (Turgut, H., 1996).

In the forming process of housing patterns, which consist of cultural, behavioral, spatial and socio-economic dimensions, the temporal dimension gains significance. According to the definition of Altman, Oxley and Werner, homes contain temporal qualities of linear, cyclical and spiraling time, which reflect dynamic, flowing and changing relationships between people and environments. (Altman, I., Oxley, D., Werner, C.M., 1985.) Linear time deals with the continuum of past, present and future. Cyclical and spiraling features of homes refer to repetitive and recurring activities and meaning, with cycles potentially recurring daily, weekly, monthly, annually or in some other regular or semi-regular fashion.

Changes in cultural, behavioral and environmental components, which have these temporal qualities form the housing patterns in historical perspective. The structural analysis of squatter housing pattern in the process of urbanization made above is summed up in Figure 01. As described in Figure 01, there is a transactional relationship among spatial, cultural, behavioral, socio- economic components.

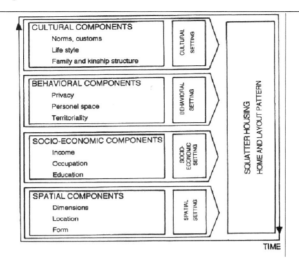

Figure 01. Structural Analysis of Squatter Housing Pattern in the Process of Urbanization

CASE STUDIES: ANALYSIS OF SQUATTER HOUSING PATTERNS

As the aim of this paper is to focus on the transition process of migrant poor in Istanbul, the information, which will clarify this process have been analysed in this part of the paper.

Analysis made by author, are exemplified with field studies from squatter settlements of P_nar, Gültepe, Akadlar. In order to collect the necessary information, measured drawings have been prepared with the schematic site plans, observations and interviews have been carried out and questionnaires have been applied.

The migrants from Anatolian villages moved to these areas and built their squatters illegally without tenure, plan and permit. The tolerance and non-involvement by the state encouraged the inhabitants and squatter sites were enlarged, improved, developed or rebuilt. During these periods layout and settlement patterns have changed dramatically, from temporary shelters to permanent housing blocks, reflecting alterations in cultural, behavioral and spatial dimensions. At the beginning, the squatter houses, which were built on state, municipality, foundation or private lands, were given title deeds in one way or another. Starting from the beginning, the newcomers gradually began to accept the urban life style and the flats have become for them the symbol of being a citizen. As ownership gives them comfort and as they wanted to obtain rent from their land, they have tended to build multi-storey buildings on their plot in order to rent them out. The squatter inhabitants who have not obtained the title deeds of their plots tend not to build multi-storey buildings because of this problem.

To explore this evolution of formation, three housing patterns have been presented;

- Original squatters as temporary dwellings (Late 1950's-to recent days.)
- Acculturation example as semi permanent dwellings (Late 1960's to recent days)
- Multi-storied rental housing blocks as permanent dwellings (Late 1980's to recent days)

Starting from the Neolithic period, many dwelling types and settlement forms have emerged in Anatolia. The individual shelter was the first step in this process. As subsequent steps, individual shelter began to constitute groups to set a social environment and they also acquired different characteristics to meet the requirements, which mainly emerged as a consequence of social and cultural developments.

TEMPORARY DWELLINGS
In its simplest form, a dwelling unit contains a single space, which houses all sorts of activities. The number of rooms is obviously a function of the well being of inhabitants as well as cultural constraints. The migrants who are settling as low-income groups in big cities also have a low-income origin in their native towns. Therefore, they usually use simple space organizations in the first phase of Squatterisation (Saglamer, G., 1993).

The dwelling units, which contain up to 3 spaces, have very simple layout organizations. The rooms are not specialised for certain activities in this phase and have multi-functional use with minimum furnishings. They have very low standards of building material and construction. All houses have individually drainage and waste disposal systems and the toilets are generally located in a corner of the garden. The inhabitants still maintain their rural life style and rituals, high level of privacy and territoriality (Figure 02).

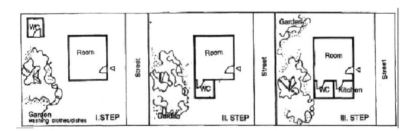

Figure 02. Examples of Temporary Dwellings

SEMI-PERMANENT DWELLINGS
In the second step of Squatterisation the dwelling units, which have more than 3-4 rooms, have generally been obtained by adding one group of spaces to the other. Thus instead of setting up complex space organizations, users preferred simple groupings of spaces for their changing requirements. Adding an individual unit or a group of spaces to the existing

layout demonstrates the feature of expandability of the dwellings in rural and squatter settlements.

This phase covers horizontal development of the squatter settlement. There is still rural type of space organization but the house is no longer a temporary shelter. Squatter house has a more specialized space organization based on functional needs.

The inhabitants start to change their rural life style and the level of privacy and territoriality tend to decrease (Figure 03).

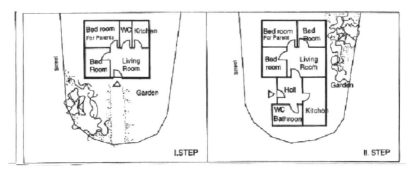

Figure 03. Examples of Semi-Permanent Dwellings

PERMANENT DWELLINGS

In the third phase, the inhabitants start to build their dwellings with the idea of building a multi-storey apartment block. After the first floor is built, the family moves in. They built the second floor as a rental flat or a flat for close relatives. After attaining sufficient financial resources, the second and the third floors are added and the owner family moves up to upper floors as a status symbol.

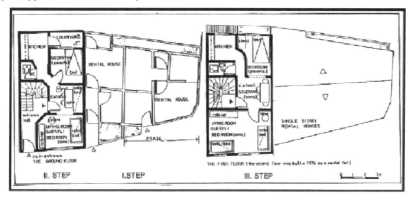

Figure 04. Examples of Permanent Dwellings

The new life styles, which the migrants start to adopt in big city, effect the formation of the new apartment blocks and these multi-storey blocks demonstrate the radical changes in migrants life in terms of socio-cultural and economic dimensions. The extended family of the traditional living pattern has been replaced by the nuclear family; relatives who used to live in the group have been excluded from the household. Expectations and preferences for the future have began to form an urban way of living. Rural norms, customs, values and habits have lost their effects on the family-life.

The main feature of spatial setting shaped in this phase is the certain level of "Space spacialisation" with a high-density use of furnishings. The multi-functional nature of the rural space organization has left its place to spacialized space organization (Figure 04).

CONCLUSION

The Squatter Housing Patterns and the case studies represented in this paper helped us to explore the transition process in terms of the cultural, behavioral, socio-economic, politic, spatial and morphological settings in an historical perspective.

In the last decade the multi-storey apartment blocks became the major informal housing type in Istanbul. Most of the newcomers have opportunities to buy plots with shared title deeds and built apartment blocks on it without any permission from local authorities. Although these buildings contain flats like the ones the urbanized population use, there are many important differences between these flats. Informal housing block still have rural features in their space organisations, forms, texture and color of the facades.

The speed of changes in physical environment, which emerged because of economic and political factors, is less than the speed of the changes in socio-cultural concepts in the continuum of space. Transition process has to struggle with this phase difference until the process ends.

BIBLIOGRAPHY

Arslan, Rıfkı, 1989, "Gecekondulasmanin Evrimi", *Mimarlik* 89/6, no. 238, 34-37.

Altman, I., Oxley, D., Werner, C.M., 1985. "Temporal Aspects of Homes: A Transectional Perspective", I.Altman,C. Werner (edit.), *Home Environments: Human Behavior and Environment,* vol.8, New York: Plenum Press.

Çelik, Zeynep, 1993, *The Remarking of Istanbul*, University of California Press.

Saᴼlamer, Gülsün, 1993, "Continuation of Vernacular in Squatter Settlements", Marjorie Bulos, Necdet Teymur (Edit.), *Housing: Design, Research, Education* , Avebury, 207-220.

Saᴼlamer, Gülsün; Turgut, Hülya; Inceoglu, Arda; Aksoy, Meltem; Paker, Nurbin, 1994 "Is Informal Housing The Destiny Of The Urban Poor? ", *An International Symposium on People, Place And Development*, Cardo-University of Newcastle upon Tyne, 1-2 December 1994, 606-615.

Turgut, Hülya; Aksoy, Meltem; Paker, Nurbin; Inceoglu, Arda; Sa□lamer, Gülsün, 1995, "Home and Street, Relationships of Home-Street in Squatter Settlements and Urbanization", *VII. International Building and Life'95*, pp. 153-163.

Turgut, Hülya, 1996, Determination of Culture- Space Interaction in Squatter Settlements, Example: "Pinar Settlements, Ongoing Research Project, Istanbul: ITU, Faculty of Architecture.

Turgut, Hülya, 1998;"Culture, Space and Urbanization/ A structural Analysis of the Housing Pattern in Squatter Settlement" *IAPS 15 Conference,*Eindhoven, Holland, 14-17 July, 1998.

Part Five

From Multiple to Multicultural Built Environment

Oldham: Separate Development

Iain Jackson

INTRODUCTION

Oldham is worthy of study beyond provocative journalism, not only because of the thrilling discontent residing within this key part of east Manchester, but also because of its unique topography, its unusual social makeup and the typology of its urban fabric. This, when coupled with the housing problems, the unresolved social issues and the significance of our urban centres, renders Oldham a notable source in identifying current problems within predominantly northern towns.

Oldham's historical success is largely owed to cotton, the spinning of which was perfectly suited to the moist air of the Pennines. The textile industry thrived within the town and the Industrial Revolution enabled larger quantities of cotton to be produced, at greater speeds, in large mills that still form Oldham's familiar townscape. The mills had an insatiable appetite for workers and this large demand for labour ensured a steady rise in Oldham's population reaching a steady plateau of 221,400 in 1981 (Ethnic minorities in Oldham, Report of the Chief Executive's policy unit, Oldham Metropolitan Borough, September 1993, p. 4).

Despite the industrial gritty impression of the town, Oldham is still predominantly countryside with approximately two thirds of the borough remaining as arable farming land and moors.

This paper will address the current housing situation within the town, and the need for clear bold design decisions to be made regarding the future development and sustainability of our urban centres.

Although the story of immigration into this country is a familiar one I think it merits comment. Following the end of the Second World War workers were recruited from the 'Commonwealth' to meet the shortage of labour facing the British manufacturing/transport industry. At its peak in 1947 around 40,000 people entered the UK from the New Commonwealth and Pakistan. The 1962 Commonwealth Immigrations Act imposed a system of employment vouchers, which restricted entry only to people "likely to be of use to the country", subsequently the number of immigrants dramatically dropped below 2000 by 1972 from over 31,000 in 1963 (Ethnic minorities in Oldham, Report of the Chief Executive's policy unit, Oldham Metropolitan Borough, September 1993, p. 1-2). In 1991 there were 19,100 people of non-white ethnic origin settled in Oldham, making up nearly 9% of its population (Ethnic minorities in Oldham, Report of the Chief Executive's policy unit, Oldham Metropolitan Borough, September 1993, p. 3).

The immigrants arriving in Oldham settled in the Glodwick and Westwood districts, close to the mills. These districts contain wards that now have a population of over 75% Asian origin.

The housing in these areas was purpose built residences for the mill workers and date to approximately 1870-1920. They are almost exclusively all terraced houses in a back-to-back row formation with rear alleys separating the back yards.

Many of these houses, following years of zero maintenance are dilapidated, as well as being severely overcrowded. 29% of Bangladeshi households and 15% of Pakistani households live in accommodation containing more than 1.5 people per room (excluding kitchens and bathrooms), which has other connotations beyond general discomfort and sanitation. Long term implications such as space for children to complete homework and so on are extremely important.

The reports compiled by Oldham council state that a higher percentage of Asian working class families are owner occupiers relative to their white counterparts (Ethnic minorities in Oldham, Report of the Chief Executive's policy unit, Oldham Metropolitan Borough, September 1993, p. 26-27)[i]. However, the condition of these houses is generally considered to be unfit. Overall, 52% of Asian houses are considered unsatisfactory with 11% of dwellings requiring critical external repairs costing above £1250.00 (Ethnic minorities in Oldham, Report of the Chief Executive's policy unit, Oldham Metropolitan Borough, September 1993, p. 27). Although this amount may seem negligible it is worth considering that house prices have dropped to around £5000 in some areas and so represents ¼ of the house value. In Burnley, another northern town reduced to rioting, houses can be found at £1500-2000, with currently 4000 houses empty and boarded up (Community Cohesion, A report of the Independent Review Team, Chaired by Ted Cantle, The Home Office, 2001 P.43). Many owner-occupiers have mortgages/loans for much larger amounts and are trapped in 'negative equity'. The south-east of England is generally the opposite, land is at a premium and more houses are required than ever before. In a press release from 1999 *The Department of Environment, Transport & Regions* (DETR) stated that between 1996 and 2021 it expected the number of households to increase by an incredible 3.8 million[ii]. To meet this requirement it is vital that existing housing stock that is derelict or underused and suitable must be redeveloped and reused. 3.8 million additional new 'Barratt Homes' is probably not the answer – a firm commitment to redeveloping our 'brown field' sites must be engaged, if we are to protect the remaining 'green field' sites, maintain a density in our urban centres and resist a suburban sprawl.

Land value is of course crucial. A drop in land value in simple terms could indicate over supply, however in this case it is more likely to indicate a low demand for the commodity (illustrated by the extent of vacant properties in Burnley). Low land values in residential terms and a flooded market in simple economics reveals that the area is no longer a desirable dwelling place, for a whole variety of reasons. The knock on effects soon follow – shops close down, local schools struggle to remain open and the area quickly becomes vacant, as tenants move on. However, in areas of high owner occupancy, such as the Asian districts of Oldham, the exodus is slowed down. It is not as easy to 'up sticks and go'. The residents are trapped in houses that need repairing, have too few bedrooms and are worth less now than when they first bought them. Coupled with the fact that the population of urban areas has until recently been falling the situation (Ethnic Minorities in Oldham, report of the chief Executive's Policy Unit, Oldham Metropolitan Borough, 1993, P.4)[iii]. The effect is that neighbourhoods become run down, properties continue to fall into disrepair and residents become increasingly dissatisfied. The dissatisfaction has vented itself by attacks on the authorities and 'the others'.

This is where the local council has to make some brave decisions.

Redevelopment of certain areas, involving the demolition of districts could be the most appropriate action, rather than building on fresh sites. More generous space standards, durable materials, environmentally friendly design with quick procurement would vastly improve the housing standards[iv]. Good design can transform not only the visual condition of a space but also the confidence of inhabitants, investors and visitors. An increase in housing density can be exploited enabling land to be dedicated to sports, relaxation and community buildings. However, the housing market must also be sensitive to other economic projections for the area, and cannot be the sole factor in deciding the future of a region. With this in mind, the mills could be redeveloped as mixed-use buildings, offering commercial space on the lower stories with residential/home working above. Oldham has a rich heritage and where possible buildings, such as the mills should be salvaged. The mills act as local landmarks and provide a unique typology that is distinctive to Oldham. Once restored the mills will provide a sense of place and could be a crucial component in attracting investment.

In Liverpool 'The Tea Factory' has recently been converted from a derelict back-street warehouse (not too dissimilar from the scale and age of the Oldham mills) into a successful mixed-use bar/retail/offices/residences and external Public Square with landscaping. Many other inner-urban properties are currently under conversion and a further example of regeneration in Liverpool is the proposal, still on the drawing board, for Kensington. Kensington is located just outside Liverpool City and contains one of the main roads into Liverpool. It is a key district acting almost as a gateway to the city and for many, forms the first impression of Liverpool. It is vital that this area is visually seductive, projects an image of the city that entices business and satisfies the housing needs of local residents.

Physically, Kensington has many parallels with the previously mentioned districts of Oldham. The housing stock is largely back-to-back terrace housing although a hierarchy exists on the main roads with grander period properties built at a greater scale and generally split into flats/surgeries. A group of residents in the area has formed *Kensington Regeneration,* in conjunction with the local council and other funding bodies. After generous public consultation and employing a firm of architects they have developed a scheme that will radically transform Kensington. The proposal, revealed at a public meeting, stated that certain streets containing derelict properties could be 'filled up' with residents from other streets, thereby completely filling the terrace in certain streets whilst completely vacating the properties in other streets. The empty properties would then be demolished and the land converted into gardens, parks and a variation on the traditional street labelled 'green runs'[v]. This is a radical, low energy solution that will require the co-operation of many and sometimes opposing parties. The area differs to Oldham in that a vast majority of the properties are owned by housing associations that have a vested long-term interest in the area. This method will clearly reduce the housing stock and the density of the area, which according to CABE,

In some places housing market renewal will only be addressed through a reduction in overall housing stock and a related decline in population. It will be important to plan positively for this outcome, ensuring that optimum population levels are maintained and local services provided that sustain and enhance the lives of the community[vi].

This maybe key to the development of Oldham. A falling population and overly crowded dwellings may benefit from a reduction in housing stock in vulnerable areas in favour of better-suited, more responsible residences. However it could be argued that this approach lacks confidence and optimism for a return to past population levels/occupied dwellings and subsequently remains a short-term solution when bearing in the back of our minds the 3.8 million housing deficit. Equally is the Kensington approach trying to force the terrace typology to work, instead of biting the bullet and demolishing the lot in favour of a new build solution that would be more inline with the housing requirement projections of the future?

As is often the case, the fall in the land value of certain areas has not stopped the desirability and demand in other areas, and this is true within Oldham. Saddleworth has a vast white majority and is an affluent area of the borough (Ethnic minorities in Oldham, Report of the Chief Executive's policy unit, Oldham Metropolitan Borough, September 1993, p. 8)[vii]. Demand for housing remains consistently high and may contribute to the lack of demand and vacation elsewhere. Stringent planning laws prevent the construction of new properties, which keeps demand and prices buoyant.

The continued separation of 'cultures' in Oldham has been cited as a reason for recent troubles and to some extent the housing market has intensified the Asian and White split in housing districts. In 1990 the Commission for Racial Equality produced a report titled, *Racial Discrimination in an Oldham Estate Agency*. The report described how an estate agent, in the centre of Oldham directed and encouraged certain people groups looking to purchase property towards certain districts within the town. The segregation began right at the top of the chain. The premise for buying property from this agent was not what type of property one may desire, nor was it the price of the property – but on the colour of one's skin! (Commission for Racial Equality, Racial Discrimination in an Oldham Estates

Agency, 1990.) Asian customers were directed to the Asian districts – without being shown properties in other areas and White customers were shown the opposite.[viii]

Following the series of 'disturbances' in Oldham, Burnley and Bradford, the Government, under the direction of the Home Secretary formed a 'Community Cohesion Review Team' led by Ted Cantle. The Review Team visited the above towns as well as some others to,

'..seek the views of local residents and community leaders in the affected towns…to bring about social cohesion and also to identify good practice in the handling of these issues at local level. (Community Cohesion: A report of the Independent Review Team chaired by Ted Cantle, Home Office 2001, P. *Foreword*'.)'

The outcome was an eighty page comprehensive report that spoke frankly about the range of issues affecting the 'communities'. Although the term, 'community cohesion' is sickly and is not a prerequisite for a successful neighbourhood, the report compiled sixty-six recommendations placing a high emphasis on education, open debate and strong local leadership. In terms of housing the report stresses that, 'funding for housing improvements can distort regeneration programmes as it is capital intensive' and that 'a more consistent and focussed approach on people, rather than on property needs [is required] (Community Cohesion: A report of the Independent Review Team chaired by Ted Cantle, Home Office 2001, p. *26).*

These comments highlight the complexity of the situation. Although the housing stock is dilapidated and often unsuitable 'The Review Team' placed most concern on the relationships between the disparate people groups, rather than the physical makeup of the houses. This is significant especially as regeneration is often expressed in X million pounds worth of investment, a large proportion of which is usually spent on construction.

Whilst I strongly think that the housing situation in Oldham needs careful review and possibly drastic action to be taken, I agree that property alone will not dissolve the years of hatred that has recently manifested itself through rioting. During the last two decades vast amounts of funding have already been awarded to Oldham, largely aimed at the most deprived areas. A Local councillor has labelled the millions of pounds worth of investment a 'drop in the ocean.'[ix] £120m in current and imminent regeneration funding has been allocated to the borough, yet only £500,000 has been given to go round the fifty community groups that exist within Oldham[x].

If we are to go with The Review Team's notions then clearly the balances are perverted, or the community groups are massively under-funded.

Poor urban design and construction has been blamed for the many social problems the town has encountered. Poor design can incubate and harbour anti-social behaviour, forming an alibi for criminal activity. Design approaches such as balcony access to flats, incomprehensible planning of estates, poor lighting and inappropriate sitting of high-rise blocks are no longer appropriate design solutions. Architects now work with the police at the early design stages to ensure that their schemes are not providing hiding places, escape routes, possible mugging points and so on. These interventions are clearly having an effect not only on our towns and cities but also on the physical makeup and appearance of buildings, streets and estates, hopefully making them safer and more enjoyable places in which to live and socialise.

I agree that additional resources should be invested into developing community relations, community buildings and youth projects, and that housing/urban regeneration is by its nature, very expensive. Nevertheless, to assume that the built fabric will magically sort itself out is myopic. Oldham is in a fragile position where most areas need attention, including the built fabric, the community buildings and the identity of the town.
Whilst The Review Team is focusing on the 'people side' of Oldham nearly 1/3 of Bangladeshi families still live in cramped unsuitable conditions. In a speech from 26 July 2001, Lord Falconer, the Housing Minister said,

'These riots had many complex causes. I have no doubt that poor quality housing is at least one of the defining characteristics of racial disadvantage (The Guardian newspaper, Thursday July 26 2001)'.[xi]

The Housing Associations, council and developers need to ensure that Oldham rectifies its current housing problems and in the same stride grasps the opportunity of attracting as many people from 3.8 million housing shortfall as possible through quality accommodation and employment. The Review Team Report makes two further recommendations with regard to housing strategies. The first states,

> 'Housing agencies must urgently assess their allocation systems and development programmes with a view to ensuring more contact between different communities and reducing tension. They must also consider the impact on other services, such as youth provision and health. It is also essential that more ambitious and creative strategies are developed to provide more mixed housing areas, with supportive mechanisms for minorities facing intimidation and harassment' (Community Cohesion: A report of the Independent Review Team chaired by Ted Cantle, Home Office 2001, P. *51).*

The second recommendation makes a connection between school catchment areas and the impact this may have on housing policies and programmes (Community Cohesion: A report of the Independent Review Team chaired by Ted Cantle, Home Office 2001, P. *51)*
Both of these suggestions raise some crucial points, again linking the factors of race, housing and education. This is where I find that the report a little too broad. It recommends a separate funding method and thought process for 'people' and 'buildings' yet still makes comments like the above that clearly involve an interdependency and careful synchronisation of many delicate components.

The redevelopment of our urban centres is crucial, and the redevelopment must be design lead with quality materials, techniques and standards. It cannot be substituted or made a scapegoat for political and social malnutrition. Design is important but it is not enough, other economic factors need to kick in, as mentioned above, investment in people and the community, health, education and social services.

Recent trends in urban design have seriously fallen short of hard-edged quality regeneration. Harperhey in Manchester is to be 'regenerated' with a whole array of schemes from a new college to better shopping areas and improvements to the streets. However, Harperhey has become victim to the recent trend in urban design. The new discipline of 'Urban Designer', has developed a fascination with the placement of banners and flags along the streets seemingly at every available opportunity. I fail to see how a broken district or town can possibly gain a sense of identity, worth and pride through the addition of elaborate street lamps with flapping banners every five metres. If the banners had an event to advertise it would be understandable, however to seriously propose the addition of these items as a serious piece of urban regeneration, when the economy of the area is non existent, seems platitudinous and patronising to the people living there. Our streets represent approximately 80% of public open space in urban areas and must be well-designed, carefully considered and easy to use[xii]. The streets can be tailored and made individual to a district or town through simple interventions such as suitable paving, cycle paths, street furniture and signage, without flying the flag of ornament and surface cosmetics. The revenue devoted to these schemes could be used for real community building exercises and on much needed youth services.

Oldham's trump card could be its location once again. Its close proximity to Manchester (possibly the giant of urban renewal) and the final stretch of the M60 motorway has brought Oldham considerably 'closer' to Manchester and the surrounding districts. Oldham can take advantage of its ready labour force and its low land values can be exploited in attracting new (well-designed) construction and vital employment. The East Side of Manchester has been in decline for many years and when compared to south Manchester only a few miles away it is very much the poor relation.

The physical problems and the racial polarity of the housing market needs to be quickly addressed with sincere local politics, fair distribution of resources and a firm commitment to transforming Oldham's ghettoised estates. CABE recommends that the people of the communities should be at the centre of the housing renewal decision making,

'Start by listening to what local people have to say; their personal histories and stories about the neighbourhood, the things that work/do not work their likes/dislikes. The wealth of knowledge and insight gained will be invaluable in shaping strategies'[xiii].

This seems a sensible approach and would inform specific parameters in the brief/action plan ready to be implemented. To ensure that quality is maintained CABE recommends that all those who have an impact on the built environment agree to sign up to best practice in the preparation of briefs, identification of budgets and the appointment of good contractors and designers. The parties involved will include the private house builders, Housing Associations, the Local Authority, parks and leisure departments as well as other specialists[1] (hopefully this will be seriously implemented and not just another 'tick the right boxes paper chase exercise').

The local council must begin to deliver; £120m grants cannot be considered 'drops in the ocean', but significant starting points which trigger and entice additional funding and investment. The governmental reports that have been produced in the last 2-3 years contain useful, practical advice compiled by teams of experts and based on the views of local residents with genuine interests in our towns. Oldham alongside the neighbouring towns of Rochdale and Ashton-Under-Lyne must present a positive, almost Newfoundland approach in attracting employment and much-needed breathing space for Manchester and the Northwest.

NOTES
[i]78.9% of Pakistani's and 85% of Indian's own their own home in comparison to 67.2% White homeowners.

[ii]DETR press release 29/03/1999

[iii]The population of Oldham fell by just over 2000 people between 1981 and 1991: Ethnic Minorities in Oldham, report of the chief Executive's Policy Unit, Oldham Metropolitan Borough, 1993, P.4

[iv]Average floor space in new German homes can be as much as 50% greater than English equivalent house types with lower construction costs. Source: Towards an Urban Renaissance, DETR, E & F Spon, 1999, P.67.

[v]Green runs are stretches of parkland that link important public buildings such as schools, community centres and 'one-stop shops' together, enabling safe pleasant routes for pedestrians, pushchairs and cyclists.

[vi]Commission for Architecture and the Built Environment: Building Sustainable Communities: Actions for Housing Market Renewal. www.cabe.org.uk

[vii]Saddleworth has a white population of over 99%. Source: Ethnic minorities in Oldham, Report of the Chief Executive's policy unit, Oldham Metropolitan Borough, September 1993, p. 8

[viii]Unfortunately the Commission did not send an investigator of mixed race. It would have been interesting to see which district they were sent to.

[ix]Oldham Labour Councillor Mohammed Azam quoted in Cover Story, http://www.newstartmag.co.uk/oldham.html, viewed 11/05/2003

[x]Cover Story, http://www.newstartmag.co.uk/oldham.html, viewed 11/05/2003

[xi]"Falconer: 'Minorities end up on worst estates'", The Guardian newspaper, Thursday July 26 2001. Viewed on http://society.guardian.co.uk./Print/0,3858,4229011,00.html

---

[1] Commission for Architecture and the Built Environment: Building Sustainable Communities: Actions for Housing Market Renewal. www.cabe.org.uk P.5

[xii]Designing Streets for people: an inquiry into the design, management and improvement of streets. Pre-consultation draft, The Institution of Civil Engineers, P.4
[xiii]Commission for Architecture and the Built Environment: Building Sustainable Communities: Actions for Housing Market Renewal. www.cabe.org.uk P.1

BIBLIOGRAPHY

Aldo Rossi, The Architecture of the City, MIT, 1982

Ungers, The Dialectic City, Skira, 1997

Commission for Architecture and the Built Environment: Building Sustainable Communities: Actions for Housing Market Renewal. www.cabe.org.uk

Community Cohesion: A report of the Independent Review Team chaired by Ted Cantle, Home Office 2001

Designing Streets for people: An inquiry into the design, management and improvement of streets. Pre-consultation draft, The Institution of Civil Engineers

Ethnic minorities in Oldham, Report of the Chief Executive's policy unit, Oldham Metropolitan Borough, 1993

Urban Task Force, Towards an Urban Renaissance, E & F Spon, 1999

Todorovic & Wellington, Living in Urban England, attitudes and aspirations, DETR, 2000

Commission for Racial Equality, Racial Discrimination in an Oldham Estate Agency, Commission for Racial Equality, 1990

Web Site Sources

http://www.newstartmag.co.uk/oldham.html

The Guardian Newspaper : http://society.guardian.co.uk./Print/0,3858,4229011,00.html

Emerging Problems of Urban Regeneration in the Multiply Deprived Area of Bijlmermeer (Amsterdam)

Karen Leeming and Tasleem Shakur

Many contemporary European urban policy initiatives recognise that their needs to be a consolidated, area based approach when tackling the regeneration of regions with multiple deprivation. However, within the individual countries of the European Union the differing social and economic histories, the structure of local and national governments and the composition of the urban fabric mean that interpretations of how this approach is achieved can be diametrically opposite. Within the UK the avowed focus of the regeneration of areas with multiple deprivation is the preservation of communities and engagement of these existing residents within the planning and implementation of urban renewal initiatives (Ginsberg, 1999; Social Exclusion Unit, 1998; 2001). Conversely, within the Netherlands, there is a belief that the approach adopted by countries such as the UK maintains a high proportion of low-income households within areas of multiple deprivation that in turn leads to physical and social monotony and low social cohesion. To counteract this, the focus of Dutch housing policy since 1997 has been urban restructuring (Priemus, 1998). This policy diversifies the housing stock within areas of multiple deprivations in order to encourage social mix and to decrease the numbers of low-income housing. The reasoning behind the policy is that new inhabitants who are wealthier than existing residents will act as a social and economic catalyst and will demolish the homogeneity generated by an economy overwhelmingly based on low income (van Beckhoven & van Kempen, 2003). This paper examines how urban restructuring has impacted upon a large area of multiple deprivations on the outskirts of Amsterdam and some of the effects it has had on existing residents[1].

BIJLMERMEER: THE BACKGROUND CONTEXT

The focus of this study is an area called Bijlmermeer (or the Bijlmer), which is situated, in the sub-municipality of Zuidoost several kilometres to the south east of the city of Amsterdam in the Netherlands. Bijlmermeer is a large-scale housing project that was built on polder land during the 1960s to ameliorate the severe post-war housing shortage within Amsterdam. It has undergone several changes in administrative control over the years and is now under the control of the City of Amsterdam, and has formed part of the Southeast municipal district since 1987.

Bijlmermeer was intended to be a modernistic, model satellite town to Amsterdam and was designed to house 50,000 people (Catling, 1998) utilising the 'Functional City' concept of the Swiss architect Le Corbusier (Stadsdeel Zuidoost, 1994). Le Corbusier advocated clear demarcations between living, working, recreation and traffic areas, and the resulting design for Bijlmermeer was as a car-free zone with tall buildings in park-like surroundings *(figures 1 & 2)*. Cars were diverted via raised roads, and parking was in peripheral and rooftop car parks with access to them via internal corridors and external footbridges (Kwekkeboom, 2003).

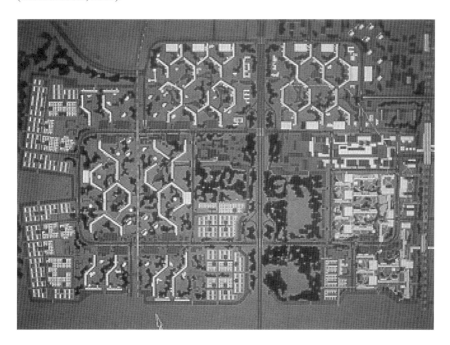

Figure 01: The original plan for the Bijlmermeer, Municipal Urban Planning, 1968.
Source: Bruijne, D., van Hoogstraten, D., Kwekkeboom, W. & Liutjen, A., 2004: 10

Figure 02: Bijlmermeer under construction 1971. Source: Bruijne, D., van Hoogstraten, D., Kwekkeboom, W. & Liutjen, A., 2004: 10.

Bijlmermeer was largely based upon high-rise (10 floor), deck-apartment blocks built in a honeycomb pattern interspersed with green spaces, cycle and pedestrian paths, and shopping centres between the blocks. Unfortunately the original plan was altered due to budget restrictions and many of the refinements of the plan that were geared towards providing a pleasant environment and 'quality of life' were abandoned or compromised. For example, larger but fewer lifts were installed, long access galleries or walkways were added, and the covered street part of the design was raised one floor with the ground floor becoming a storage facility (Kwekkeboom, 2003; Projectbureau Vernieuwing Bijlmermeer, 1987).

The housing was originally intended for the predominantly white, Amsterdam middle-classes, and a small number – who are still in residence today – did move in. However, by the time that the development was finished, the housing preferences of the majority of the Amsterdam middle-classes had veered from expensive gallery apartments such as those in Bijlmermeer, to lower-priced, low-rise developments in the suburbs in new towns such as Almere, Lelystad and Purmerend (Luijten, 1997; Projectbureau Vernieuwing Bijlmermeer, 1987; Webbink, 2000).

SPIRAL OF DECLINE

Within a relatively short space of time it became evident that the development had major problems. For example, the large amount of parkland surrounding the blocks meant that it was both difficult and expensive to maintain, and so it became run-down and a dumping ground for garbage, litter and the discarded equipment of the drug trade and was generally avoided as a leisure site by residents.

Additionally, the apartment blocks proved difficult to manage. This was partly due to their sheer size. During the building of the development it had been decided to increase the numbers of apartment units in order to increase the potential income from rents. These were incorporated by such means as adding extra floors to the buildings (Projectbureau Vernieuwing Bijlmermeer, 1987). The finished complex had 18,000 housing units, 13,000 of which were in high-rise blocks, with an official population figure just short of 50,000 (Dukes, 2002). However, due to the numbers of 'unofficial' residents, others have estimated the population to be in excess of 100,000 (Markovic, 2000).

Other reasons for the apartment blocks being difficult to manage were the changes that were made to the original design. For example, there were too few elevators to service the buildings properly, and the existing elevators were extremely large – holding around 100 people. This meant that if elevators were vandalised or put out of action then it affected large numbers of residents. Also, the aisles and walkways, such as those leading to the car parks, were dark and often sited in obscure places and they became sites for drug selling and drug taking and of crimes such as mugging, with the open parkland allowing for a speedy escape (Webbink, 2000). Additionally, the high rents of the area meant that many of the apartments remained (officially) empty and this contributed to the budgetary problems of the Management Company leading to a reduction in maintenance and security that exacerbated the existing problems.

Consequently, rather than becoming a modernistic, model satellite town to Amsterdam, Bijlmermeer became a place where those with multiple social and economic disadvantages and few options were encouraged to locate.

ETHNIC CONTEXT

Initially, the area became home to the many immigrants who moved to Amsterdam in the run up to Surinamese independence in 1975. In July 2001 one of the Bijlmermeer project managers estimated that Surinamese residents formed 25%-30% of the population. However, a recent study by RESTATE (Aalbers, van Beckhoven, van Kempen, Musterd and Ostendorf, 2003) puts the figure for the Southeast as a whole slightly higher at 31%, with 40% in Bijlmer-Centre and 33% in Bijlmer-East.

Later additions to the Bijlmermeer population include immigrants from other Dutch colonies such as the Netherlands (or Dutch) Antilles, North Africa, and more recently Asia and Eastern Europe. The area now has such a multiplicity of nationalities that it is difficult to obtain reliable statistics. For example, one project manager refers to a survey of residents held in the late 1990s when making decisions regarding ethnic populations. This survey indicates that there are just over 80 different nationalities in the area, however, the manager of a community project geared towards promoting and improving the image of Bijlmermeer believes the figure is nearer to 150. A third, unofficial survey, indicated that the figure is over 160, albeit with only one or two representatives from some nationalities. The residents and the officials who took part in the study for this paper suggested that the huge discrepancies between the official and unofficial figures are due to a combination of four factors.

The first is to do with legitimacy: If residents are living in Bijlmermeer illegally, such as by multiple occupancy or squatting, then they are less likely to respond to official surveys as this may bring them to the attention of the housing authorities and lead to eviction. There is some supporting evidence for this factor. On the 4th October 1991 an Israeli El Al cargo plane crashed into two of the apartment blocks killing the crew, an unidentified passenger and at least 43 people on the ground. Investigators found that due to the high numbers of illegal immigrants living in the development, and their unwillingness to co-operate with the authorities, it was impossible to ascertain the exact numbers of residents killed (Smith, 2000). The crash may also have been a contributory factor in some residents wanting to leave Bijlmermeer.

A second factor concerns the ability to speak Dutch: Many of the immigrants – especially the more recent – are unable to speak Dutch and may have difficulties in responding to surveys accurately. The third factor is the high rates of illiteracy amongst residents, which means that they tend to ignore written or postal questionnaires, and the fourth factor is a distrust of any officials who ask questions. So residents may be able to speak Dutch and are living in the Bijlmermeer legitimately, but refuse to participate in detailed surveys because either they cannot or because they are afraid of what the information may be used for.

Bijlmermeer not only houses an extremely diverse population with differing cultures, languages, experiences and needs, it is also the site of severe social and economic problems. For example, until recently, the crime and labour market inactivity rates within the area were amongst the highest in the Netherlands (Catling, 1998; Markovic, 2000), and although these rates are falling, they are still considerably higher than the average in Amsterdam (Aalbers *et al*, 2003). Additionally, there is a high concentration of drug problems that is in part fuelled by the movement of the drug scene away from the red light district of Amsterdam into parts of Bijlmermeer (ibid).

The severity of these problems and the ways in which they manifest themselves has meant that for most white residents – although not all – moving out of the area has been a high priority. However, the same is not true for the many Surinamese and Guyanese residents – provided that they live in a block with a low crime rate – who believe that the area has a lot to offer provided that the problems are tackled (Catling, 1998). Those white residents who do not want to leave are, in the main, original residents of the development. This group are sometimes known as the 'Bijlmer Believers', and they have tried to focus the attention of the authorities on the advantages of the original design plan of Le Corbusier, whilst forcing them to tackle the problems blighting the area (Webbink, 2000).

RENEWAL OF THE BIJLMER

In 1992, it was decided that the problems of Bijlmermeer needed to be addressed and the Nieuw Amsterdam Housing Association, Southeast City district (the district council for Zuidoost) and the City of Amsterdam set up a Steering Committee for Renewal of Bijlmermeer and the Projectbureau 'Vernieuwing Bijlmermeer' (Bijlmermeer Renewal). The renewal strategy was based upon three elements: spatial renewal; management renewal; and social renewal (Projectbureau Vernieuwing Bijlmermeer, 1987).

The spatial renewal involves somewhere between 50-60% of the original high-rise area (as the plans are responsive to ongoing feedback from the redevelopment, the Projectbureau cannot give a definite figure at this time). The project – which is expected to be completed at some time between 2007 to 2010 – encompasses the demolition of some of the housing blocks, the redevelopment of others into smaller units, the development of new housing (see fig 3), and the division of tenants into one third social rental, one third premium rental and one third owner occupier (Webbink, 2000).

The management renewal element is geared towards the actual management of the residential and living environment and intends to concentrate on improving the quality of life within the area by involving the residents in the decision-making processes.

**Figure 03: New Layout plan of K-South block based on the Urban Renewal Plan of
Bijlmermeer 1996. Source: Projectbureau Vernieuwing Bijlmermeer 2002: 115.**

One part of the social renewal element is to tackle the high levels of labour market
inactivity in the district. It proposes to do this by ensuring there are co-ordinated links with
the nearby business district of Holendrecht/Amstel III – which is one of the largest in the
city – and the adjoining leisure and entertainment complex containing the Amsterdam
ArenA, a multiplex cinema, and the Mojo Concert Hall. This part of the social renewal
element has the avowed intention of employing local people in construction work and
training a further 2,000 residents for watch duty work (Projectbureau Vernieuwing
Bijlmermeer, 1987).

Fortuitously for Bijlmermeer, as it was formulating this renewal strategy the European
Commission launched a new initiative to target areas of extreme deprivation. The URBAN
initiative was introduced in 1994 and advocates an integrated approach to regeneration. It
is also area-based, and has a strong emphasis on local participation in project design and
implementation.

THE 'BLACK AND WHITE' CONFLICT

The renewal strategy already in place in Bijlmermeer meant that it matched all of the criteria and the URBAN Bijlmermeer Programme was launched in September 1995. However, from the beginning of the programme there were major problems concerning local participation in the decision making process. The majority of the representatives in the organisational set-up of URBAN-Bijlmermeer were white, and the vast majority of residents of Bijlmermeer are from non-white ethnic minority groups (Dukes, 2002). This led to black politicians together with representatives of other agencies and groups forming the *Zwart Beraad* or 'Black Consideration' group (Leistra, 1996). Increasing confrontation between *Zwart Beraad* and white district councillors led to the suspension of the URBAN-Bijlmermeer programme from May 1996 to January 1997 and the headlining of the problems in local newspapers as the "Black and White conflict"(Dukes, 2002).

Resolution of the conflict included the replacement of the Steering Committee by the Uitgebreid Bestuurlijk Overleg (UBO) with 4 seats for ethnic minority groups and a seat for religious institutions, and the inclusion of two seats for ethnic minority groups on the Supervisory Committee URBAN-Bijlmermeer (Dukes, 2002). Project criteria were also changed to include the stipulations that:

The project should be multicultural and would therefore help to reinforce the multi-ethnic community.

The project should be developed/created by residents' groups, from the bottom-up.

Additionally, a two million guilders "Fonds voor Onderop" or "bottom-up Fund" was established by the UBO for community projects. Also, under recommendations from *Zwart Beraad* and the UBO ethnic minority organisation, a Multiculturalisation and Participation Bureau was initiated in 1997 to stimulate and support grass roots projects in the area, as well as monitoring the quality and progress of programs from a multicultural viewpoint (Dukes, 2002; Kwekkeboom, 2003).

The URBAN-Southeast Investment Programme ran from 1995-1999 and the area received a new tranche of funding when it was given Objective Two status by the European Union (Vernieuwing Bijlmermeer, 2003). This is a major subsidy programme geared towards ensuring economic and social parity within the EU.

COMMUNITY INVOLVEMENT IN THE RENEWAL PROCESS

Involving the community within the regeneration process has proven difficult for several reasons. First is because of the multiplicity of nationalities, languages and cultures, and attempts to circumvent the problems that arise from this has included both formal and informal approaches. Formal approaches have included having interpreters present at information points and during public enquiries, publishing literature in several languages and making presentations to individual ethnic groups. Informal approaches include contacting people via stalls at markets and festivals, and at sport and games facilities

(Webbink, 2000). Second, the high turnover of residents and the social and economic problems of the region has led to limited involvement by the residents in promoting social cohesion and place-attachment (Aalbers *et al,* 2003). Third, and perhaps more interestingly, is the belief by a number of residents that it is pointless to get involved because the decision-making authorities do not have their interests in mind. Instead they believe that the authorities are more interested in ensuring that they move out of the Bijlmer because they do not fit into the planners' image for the future of the area.

WELCOMING DIFFERENCE OR WILY DISPERSAL?

On first appearances, the policy of urban restructuring actively welcomes the differences between social, cultural, national and economic groups. It assumes that these differences will produce dynamism within a community that will act as a regenerative catalyst for areas with multiple deprivation. However, there is an increasing body of research that contests this approach and argues that the residents of these areas would increase their social and economic standing if policies were geared to renewing and supporting the *existing* communities in the area and not fragmenting them, dispersing them and introducing a wider social mix (Atkinson, R. & Kintrea, K. 1998; Bolt, G., Burgers, J. & van Kempen, R. 1998; Reijndorp, 1996, 1997) and that urban restructuring does not necessarily promote social cohesion and contact within neighbourhoods (van Beckhoven & van Kempen, 2003). Some residents of the Bijlmer go further, they believe that the policies are there to actively and widely disperse the poor, especially those who are black and from minority ethnic groups so that they are no longer a potential 'threat'.

"We live on the streets and they don't like it, because we're poor they think we'll riot" (non-white resident).

"We frighten them, I think it's because we like loud – clothes, music, talk" (non-white resident).

"We're not wanted. We live outside, our culture is outside and this outside culture is off-putting to the middle classes. The Council allowed the place to deteriorate so much so that they have an excuse to move people out and redesign the place. At same time they're making people work for benefits so that the place is kept clean. These are things to attract the middle classes. No street culture, low buildings, and clean" (non-white resident).

"We're not target for all this money. The target groups are elites, not people residing in area (non-white resident).

"It's all elements to attract the middle classes. Limited street culture. Low-rise buildings, and kept clean cheaply by people on benefit" (non-white resident).

"They leave it, they leave it, and they leave it. And then they have to do something, they have to take the people away because they say there are too many people outside" (non-white resident).

The low numbers of socially rented accommodation available after refurbishment of high-rise blocks fuels this belief as does the strict allocation process for the accommodation that is available. To have a chance of being re-housed within Bijlmermeer a resident must be an urban renewal candidate. To become an urban renewal candidate they must have been renting a home within the Bijlmer high-rise buildings for two years – essentially they must be 'legal' tenants in order to have any rights to re-housing. However, even if they are urban renewal candidates this does not mean that they will be re-housed in a similar sized home or even within Bijlmermeer. The reduction of the numbers of social housing available within Bijlmermeer has ensured that the numbers wishing to remain will by far exceed the numbers of social housing available. Urban renewal candidates are only given *priority* when the supply of suitable[2] rented housing is searched, and if there is not housing available in Bijlmermeer then they are offered suitable accommodation elsewhere in Amsterdam.

Those tenants who have been renting a home within Bijlmermeer for less than two years – and there is a tacit acknowledgement that this will include the 10-15% of residents who are living in Bijlmermeer illegally – are categorised as semi-urban renewal candidates and as such are not eligible for automatic re-housing. This group, which includes some of the most socially and economically excluded as well as most vulnerable groups, are given removal expenses of 4,500 Euro and help in searching the housing lists of Amsterdam and its' environs for suitable accommodation. At present, there is evidence that a large number of those Bijlmer residents who are *sans-papiers*[3], and those who have legal residency in the Netherlands but who are living illegally in Bijlmermeer are continually moving from high-rise buildings undergoing renovation into unrenovated high-rise blocks (Aalbers *et al*, 2003) rather than move from the area. This is possibly because they have access to jobs, albeit low-paid and insecure, through the many informal networks of the alternative economy.

Several residents also alleged that one of the reasons a number of people wanted to move away from Bijlmermeer was because of the El Al cargo plane crash in 1991. When the plane crashed its cargo was said to be flowers and perfume, this was later changed to non-toxic chemicals. Finally, the Israeli government admitted that the plane was carrying 190

litres of Dimethyl Methylphosphonate (DMPP) one of the primary components in the manufacture of the deadly nerve gas Sarin, as well as approximately 24 pieces of depleted uranium ranging in weight from 6 to 30 kilogrammes that were acting as a counterbalance weight (Reydt, 1999; Sancton, 2001; Uijt de Haag, Smetsers, Witlox, Krüs & Eisenga, 2001). A large number of people (estimates veer from 300 to over 800) who were near to the crash site, either because they were rescue workers or because they were residents, have experienced a number of health problems in the interim. Whilst the majority of these complaints may be related to Post-traumatic Stress Disorder, there are also a number that have suffered physical complaints such as auto-immune diseases, genetic faults and rare diseases and cancers (Reydt, 1999; Sancton, 2001; Smith, 2000). According to Sancton

(2001, 4) many Bijlmermeer residents believe "that authorities have been slow to respond because the victims are mostly poor immigrants[4]". The sum total of the handling of the aftermath to the crash has been that a number of residents now believe that it was a significant dispersal factor for several reasons. First, the area housed a large number of unregistered tenants or 'illegals' who have limited rights when expressing housing preferences under the regeneration programme's criterion, second, there was the perceived possibility of contracting a disabling or fatal disease, and third, that the authorities were reacting to the events very slowly.

In other parts of Bijlmermeer, even those residents with a middle income (gross earnings of approximately 20,420 to 38,571 Euro per annum) who are interested in buying rather than renting a property within the area are finding that they are being priced out of the market. In the early 1990s the price of a house in the Bijlmer was much lower than surrounding regions, over the past ten years they have risen sharply across the board. For example, apartments in the renovated buildings are put up for sale as soon as the former tenants have vacated them and they are mainly in the price range 90,756 to 136,134 Euro. This has encouraged the Amsterdam City Council to help these buyers by extending the Amsterdamse Middensegment Hypotheek (AMH) or Amsterdam middle-sector mortgage to the Bijlmer. The AMH is a repayment free and practically interest free loan up to the value of approximately 45,378 Euro and gives prospective buyers the chance to buy at a reasonable price (Bijlmerbouw, 2001 4).

But for some, especially small businesses, this is too little, too late. Prior to renovation, a number of the retail premises in Bijlmer were empty and were targets of vandalism and in some cases arson attacks. Local shopkeepers were encouraged to move into the premises by low rents and taxes in order to both deter the vandals and to provide sorely needed services such as ethnic food stores. When the regeneration spread to the shopping parades, some of the tenants felt that the much higher taxes and rents of the new premises were a strategy to force them out so that firms offering more generic brand names that were attractive to the middle classes could move in. For some of these tenants, their fears have been realised and they have, 'They've done this to get security on the cheap', had to move out of the Bijlmer. Many of the unemployed within Bijlmermeer have problems with literacy and numeracy, many are semi-skilled or unskilled, have little job experience and have problems with self-esteem. The introduction of initiatives such as 'Dubbel Plus', which offers government subsidised jobs that pay between 30-50% more than standard social benefit to those who have been unemployed over a year, are registered with the Employment Office and are over 23 years of age, are geared towards providing some of the missing skills and experience (Aalbers *et al*, 2003). However, as many of the jobs provided are within the district police, the district cleaning department and the housing corporations, and because a number of residents who are enrolled in the scheme believe that they had no choice but to accept low paid jobs because otherwise they thought that they would lose their social benefit, this has fuelled a belief that they are being used as cheap labour as security guards, cleaners and caretakers to make Bijlmermeer more attractive to outsiders.

"Many of the people here don't get work. Then at the same time they make people work but they don't get any extra money, they get the same as when on social, you see…if you get 1500 guilders a month you get food and others, if you get 1750 you get nothing, you have to pay for the food you see" (non-white resident).

"You have to take job, no social if you don't" (non-white resident).

"They want it nice and safe, you see, but it costs too, too much, so they make us do it" (non-white resident).

"They've done this [subsidised jobs initiative] to get security on the cheap" (non-white resident).

It would appear that the types of job opportunities offered by the renewal process have also contributed to this belief as well. For example, one idea was to employ as many of the unemployed Bijlmer residents as possible on construction projects. However, even though training facilities were put in place, and there were thousands of applicants, the Job Centre did not manage to find enough recruits. The problems were similar with the development of the Amsterdam Arena and Arena Boulevard. Those from the Bijlmer who are employed tend to be in low paid and low skilled jobs such as cleaning (Reindorp, 1997).

CONCLUSION

Urban landscapes are the result of the power relationships between those who design them, those that govern and service them, and those who live there. Regenerating urban landscapes can be a measure by which the former two groups seize back control of neighbourhoods from the latter group and re-impose their cultural norms and values.

There is no doubt that the multicultural neighbourhood envisaged by the urban renewal managers of Bijlmermeer is one that welcomes different cultures and nationalities – it has to given the size of the ethnic population there. However, the indications coming from some of the residents are that it is a multicultural vision that is geared to producing a sanitised version of the neighbourhood that already exists by dispersing those elements of the existing community that do not promote this vision. The social engineering that is taking place in Bijlmermeer is promoting a social mix that it is believed will produce a more harmonious, tolerant and positive community, but, this form of society is also one that can be viewed as a strategy to prevent ethnic resistance (van der Horst, 2003) or even a strategy that 'is dangerously close to the old saying 'urban renewal = Negro removal'' (Priemus, 1998, 308). Especially given that within the Netherlands, the idea of active dispersal and de-concentration of ethnic minorities goes back to the 1970s and is still a policy feature of some political parties today (van Beckhoven & van Kempen, 2003). Urban restructuring does not promote social cohesion, instead it is more about the restructuring of the physical environment in the hope that it will:

'...contribute to [the] social and economic vitality of the city as a whole' (van Beckhoven & van Kempen, 2003, 871). The implications for the high-rise parts of Bijlmermeer are that urban restructuring is both welcoming difference *and* utilising (maybe not so) wily dispersal techniques that ensure that ex-residents cannot move back into social housing in Bijlmermeer once they have moved away because they do not contribute to this 'social and economic vitality'. Or, as one resident phrased it:

'...once you've gone, it's bye, bye'.

NOTES

[1] Based on a number of informal, semi-structured interviews, human geography field trips and a few research visits (funded by both individual students and EdgeHill College) that were held over a period of three years (2001-2004) with residents of Bijlmer-Central and Bijlmer-East.[i]

[2] Suitable in this case meaning one that is judged appropriate for the residents' income, household size and existing terms of residency.

[3] Without legal residence status in the Netherlands

[4] Within the Netherlands the terms 'minority' and 'immigrant' are usually interchangeable (Mollenkopf, 2002)

BIBLIOGRAPHY

Aalbers, M., van Beckhoven, E., van Kempen, R., Musterd, S., & Ostendorf, W. (2003) *Large Housing Estates in the Netherlands. Overview of developments and problems in Amsterdam and Utrecht*, RESTATE report 2e, Urban and Regional Research Centre, University of Utrecht.

Atkinson, R. & Kintrea, K. (1998) Reconnecting Excluded Communities: The Neighbourhood Impacts of Owner Occupation, Edinburgh, Scottish Homes.

Bolt, G., Burgers, J. & van Kempen, R. (1998) "On the Social Significance of Spatial Location; Spatial Segregation and Social Inclusion", *Netherlands Journal of Housing and the Built Environment*, Vol. 13, No. 1, 83-92.

Bruijne, D., van Hoogstraten, D., Kwekkeboom, W. & Luijten, A., (2003) *Zuidoost Amsterdam Southeast*, Amsterdam, THOTH Publishers.

Catling, C. (ed.) (1998), *Amsterdam*, APA Publications

Ginsberg, N. (1999) "Putting the social into urban regeneration policy", *Local Economy*, May, 55-71.

Kwekkeboom, W. (2003) "Rebuilding the Bijlmermeer 1992-2002", In: Bruijne, D., van Hoogstraten, D., Kwekkeboom, W. & Luijten, A., *Zuidoost Amsterdam Southeast*, Amsterdam, THOTH Publishers, 75-113.

Leistra, G. (1996) "Bijsturen in de Bijlmer", *Elsevier*, November 11th, p38.

Luijten, A. (1997) "A barrel of contradictions: The dynamic history of the Bijlmermeer", *Archis*, 3, 15-13.

Mollenkopf, J. (2002) *Assimilating Immigrants in Amsterdam: A Perspective from New York*, Amsterdam, Amsterdam Study Centre for the Metropolitan Environment.

Priemus, H. (1998) "Redifferentiation of the Urban Housing Stock in the Netherlands: A Strategy to Prevent Spatial Segregation?" *Housing Studies*, Vol. 13, No. 3, 301-310.

Projectbureau Vernieuwing Bijlmermeer (2002) *Finale Plan van Aanpak, I Defintieve Versie*

Reijndorp, A. (1996) "Bevordert herpositionering de leefbaarheid?" *Nieuw Tijdschrift voor de Volkhuisvesting*, 2, No. 6, 6-9.

Reijndorp, A. (1997) "Between city and state: Social renewal in the Bijlmermeer", *Archis*, 3, 56-63.

Smith, G. (2000) "Uranium Skies: What Was Aboard Flight 1862?" *Earth Island Journal*, Winter, Vol. 14, No. 4, 1-7.

Social Exclusion Unit, (1998) Bringing Britain Together: A National Strategy for Neighbourhood Renewal, Cm 4045, London, The Stationery Office.

Social Exclusion Unit (2001) A New Commitment to Neighbourhood Renewal: National Strategy Action Plan, January, London, Cabinet Office.

Stadsdeel Zuidoost, (1994) *From Bindelmere to Southeast City District*, Amsterdam, Stadsdeel Zuidoost Communications Department.

van Beckhoven, E. & van Kempen, R. (2003) "Social Effects of Urban Restructuring: A Case Study in Amsterdam and Utrecht, the Netherlands", *Housing Studies*, Vol. 18, No. 6, November, 853-875.

van der Horst, H. (2003) "Multicultural Theming in the Netherlands: Pacifying, Essentializing and Revanchist Effects", In: Ingram, S. & Reisenleitner, M. (eds.) *Placing History: Themed Environments, Urban Consumption and the Public Entertainment*, Wien, Turia and Kant, 1-24.

OTHER SOURCES

Bijlmerbouw: Informatiekrant Vernieuwing Bijlmermeer, Winter, 2001, English summary, 4.

Bruijne. D, Van Hoogstraten. D, Kwekkeboom. W. & Luijten. A.(2004). Zuidoost, Southeast Amsterdam.   The Netherlands : Thoth

Dukes, T. (2002) The European Community Initiative URBAN: Help or Hinder for Local Participation? The case of URBAN Bijlmermeer (Amsterdam, the Netherlands), http://www.by-og-byg.dk/eura/workshops/papers/workshop5/dukes.htm

Markovic,I.(2000)*Going*   *Dutch.*
http://www.europmag.com/Numero_hors_200/Immigration/Ntherlands/Immig_neth.ht
m

Reydt, P. (1999) "Dutch government rocked by parliamentary report into 1992 El Air crash", 27 April, http://www.wsws.org/articles/1999/apr1999/hol-a27.shtml

Sancton,   T.   (2001)   "Burning   Questions!,   Friday,   March   16, http://www.time.com/time/magazine/printout/0,8816,22329,00.html

Uijt de Haag, P.A.M., Smetsers, R.C.G.M., Witlox, H., Krüs, H.W. & Eisenga, A.H.M. (2001) "Risk analysis of depleted uranium following an aircraft crash", 16 March, *Cyclone Fluid Dynamics*, http://www.cyclone.nl/bijlmer/bijlmer.htm

Vernieuwing Bijlmermeer (2003) *The development of Amsterdam Southeast*, Amsterdam, Vernieuwing Bijlmermeer/Arena Boulevard.

Webbink, J. (2000) *Renewal in Tomorrow's Town*, Projectbureau Vernieuwing Bijlmermeer, September, (Unpublished project overview).

The Architectural Fairyland of China (1984 onward): Problems and Recommendations

Erica Liu

INTRODUCTION

Chinese cities are changing fast. The lifestyle of people changed drastically. Fashion used to be exclusively dominated by Chairman Mao's style; unisex loose fit earth-colored cotton suits, it is now overwhelmed with a rainbow of colors and designer brands. Girls are taking to high heels, fashionable dresses, color-dyed hair and make-up. Old couples practice Western-style ballroom dancing in parks with loud music. The noise is still there, but its content is very different. Entrepreneurs and middle classes, whom have been condemned as "the tail of capitalism" "monster and demon"[i] in Mao's days, are back in strength. They flourish in every city. In the countryside, enterprising peasants are setting up small factories and transport businesses. And the Government advice, as told by the tourist guide, is "Get rich by working hard. Have no fear of becoming prosperous." On the cityscape, the old doom dusty streets with huge hoardings that were covered with the propaganda of Mao are now adored by advertisements for Playstation computer games and Nike trainers. The highways leading Beijing International Airport to the city have miles of greenbelts that remind visitors of Europe. Chinese cities are essentially full of international style modern architecture as a result of modernisation and globalisation. Glassy skyscrapers that dominate the center of cities have MacDonald, KFC, PizzaHut, Hardrock Café, Starbuck Coffee and cyber café on their ground and first floors.

GLOBALISATION AND ARCHITECTURAL FAIRYLAND

The implementation of the open and reform policy in the 1980s brought a new prosperity to the economic and cultural developments in China. After the success of the Special Economic Zone of Shenzhen, the Central Secretary Department and the State Department of China held a series of meeting with regional governors from 26 March to 6 April 1984, and confirmed to open a further fourteen harbor cities including Shanghai, Tianjin, and Guangzhou, for foreign investment. Rapid growth in economy made urban planning a paramount concern. In the cities, modern high-rise commercial and residential buildings, parks, green belts, roads and highways were in great demand. In the countryside, satellite towns for industrial expansion were planned with new towns in Britain and the Netherlands as references. International student exchange programs were encouraged in universities and institutes. Famous architects such as I. M. Pei, John C. Portman and Yoshinobu Ashihara were invited to give lectures in universities and to participate in construction projects such as the Great Wall Hotel (1983) by Becket. Thriving practices gave strong stimulus to theoretical developments. Chinese architects were provided with a favorable social condition for creative activities. They looked for inspiration from the long-excluded foreign architectural theories - from modernist pioneers like Wright and Le

Corbusier to post-modernist masters such as Venturi, Johnson and Stirling, almost too much for ready digestion. Architectural styles were experimental at this stage, some interesting concepts were put forward, such as developing a national style that was "modern" and yet with ethnical characters. However, there were too many buildings trying to do too much, cut outs and curves and pagoda roofs that clash with modern glass. Frenetic and indiscriminate constructions on a massive scale often ended up in the "architectural hall of shame" - "Big Roof style", superficial revivalism, rows of glassy towers and concrete boxes, form without context. Examples of this were the Beijing Library, Citic International Building (1982), Jing Guang Centre (1995), Fu Hua Mansion (1996) and the Chinese Women Activity Centre (1996).

Under new leaderships and policies, China was keen to catch up with the economic growth that the capitalist countries enjoyed during the past decades. To create a modernized socialist state, foreign intervention or capitalist practices were unavoidable. Following the building boom in 1990s, many cities were in a state of architectural ferment. Government officials and developers welcomed modern chrome and glass towers, which symbolized economic advancement in the Western world and the open encouragement of capitalism in China. Although it would be a difficult balance between capitalist economic development and socialist rule, the delicate circumstances did create unprecedented opportunities for both foreign and home architects to create signature masterworks. The obsession of gigantic scale and novel ideas, ideas for a place like nowhere else in the world, was a reflection of broader socio-economic trends. With entry into the World Trade Organization in 2001 and Beijing's hosting of the 2008 Olympics ahead, the Chinese authorities were eager to demonstrate they were on par with other industrialized nations. Architecture covered with blue glass and cheap chrome in the late 1980s and early 1990s could no longer satisfy public taste. Lands were cleared for cutting-edge architectural designs. Like a blank canvas, any edifice designs or even the most ambitious architectural visions that may out dazzle that of the West were welcomed.

Modernisation and globalisation is turning China into a fairy ground for architects and urban planners. Experimentation and grand dreams are encouraged to foster state-of-the-art urban designs and space age cyber-cities. Celebrity architects such as I. M. Pei and Sons have just completed the Bank of China's new Beijing headquarters (Figure 01 & 2) and have, among other projects, drafted a master plan to redevelop Tianfu Square in Chengdu, second in size only to Tiananmen. Michael Graves, the American architect and designer of themed Disney hotels, has ambitious plans for the modern refurbishing of an old brownstone along Shanghai's Bund, which is a row of graceful colonialist-era stone buildings that are often cited as the zenith of Western architecture in China. Von Gerkan recently signed a contract for a $320-million exhibition center in Shenzhen to be completed in 2003. He is due to finish a daring $58-million convention complex in Nanning the same year. Paul Andreu, renowned for his designs of airports around the globe, designed a $300-million Beijing National Theatre alongside Tiananmen Square. The Theatre is the size of several football fields, the site will house three auditoriums inside a 56-meter-high translucent glass and titanium dome that appears to float on water.

Visitors will descend via escalators through the water into an underground lobby. The futuristic design of the building is controversial because it is located side by side with the Great Hall of the People, Tiananmen Square and the Forbidden City, which are the country's most lasting monuments. Huge firms such as Skidmore Owens & Merrill, which practically invented the skyscraper, have designed China's tallest building, the $540-million, 88-story Jin Mao Building, which houses the world's highest hotel in Pudong city, near Shanghai. Kohn Pederson Fox, creators of New York's World Bank Headquarters and Rockefeller Plaza West, has several projects under discussion, including a 182-hectare site on the outskirts of Beijing. Commissioned by the Chinese pharmaceutical giant San Jiu, the mega-town will combine research and agricultural areas with housing and services for up to 10,000 people. He also designed the $600-million World Financial Center, which schedules to be the world's tallest building when it opens near Shanghai in 2003 or 2004. The ghastly 95-story tower will be so high that a huge circular section will be cut through the top to relieve wind pressure. These will be followed in 2007-8 by the cloud-topping Shanghai World Financial Center and Union Square in Hong Kong, both buildings will be taller than 1500 feet. The most interesting design is perhaps the Chinese Network Television CCTV by Rem Koolhaas. The building is only 750 feet high but has a 5.5 million square feet floor space on which the building snakes off into a squared loop. In the suburbs, Dutch firm Kuiper Compagnons recently designed an award-winning community unit that set on canals outside Shanghai, which is inspired by the designs of Venice, Amsterdam and ancient Athens. Von Gerkan also unveils drawings of a science city filled with observatories, museums and a pyramid-shaped civic plaza for the new town design of Lang Fang, located 70 km from Beijing. The design is a lakeside metropolis that on paper looks like a modern Aztec capital.

Figure 01: The landscape design, the   **Figure 02: The arched portal viewed from**
China Bank Tower, I. M. Pei   **inside the China Bank Tower, I. M. Pei**

PROBLEMS & RECOMMENDATIONS INTELLECTUAL PROPERTY AND BUREAUCRATIC INTERVENTION

Although the design environment of architecture and urban planning is encouraging in China, these projects are too ambitious for a poor country. Many of the designs may never be built. Major construction projects are largely designed by Western professionals because developers prefer Western signatures on their blueprints, which are considered to be prestigious and therefore ideal for publicity purposes. As a result, novel designs with impressive details emerged. Nevertheless, intellectual property is still a problematic issue in the country. There is the peril that in many cases, unveiled designs are stolen and resold without the authorization of architect. For instance, the design scheme of a competition entry for the Beijing National Theatre has been used in the Shanghai Opera House without the acknowledgement or endorsement of the original design team.

Moreover, regulations often work against world-class standard. Professional work procedures are often interrupted by bureaucratic practices. Foreign firms are not permitted by law to do the complete design of a building. Parts of the work are allocated to a local company. Then a contractor, usually a state agency will take over and controls the project. Consequently, the architects who produce the original designs do not have control over the final products. Quality control is difficult. Take the China Construction Bank building in Beijing as an example. The architect designed its exterior walls with translucent green glass, but the contractor replaced it with a cheaper Darth Vader-type dark glass. The building thus lost its original appeal. Besides, developers often go bankrupt before the project finishes. The project will either be halted or sold to another developer who may change the building details according to their budget and requirements. Corruption, construction snafus, and bureaucratic interference make architectural practice a difficult task in China.

The bureaucratic practice is closely related to the internal theoretical struggle between the conservatives and the reformers within the Party. Like many Chinese political battles, the internal struggle is fought indirectly via cultural channels, such as architecture. Cradock (1994: 155) criticized that "t(T)he balance sought in the key Dengist formula: economic vigor but political obedience, or, to give it its approved name, socialism with market characteristics. Many would have called it not a balance at all, but a contradiction in terms." Economic development and multiculturalism inevitably increase the pressure for corresponding political freedom and spiritual liberalization. Modernization may carry the danger of political consequences. The freedom of choice of the people is still subjected to the level of tolerance of the authorities. Local developers and contractors intend to assert control over construction projects because of the finance and power involved during the building process. Construction projects sometimes became a power struggle between the locales and the foreigners, between the money-minded and the creative intention. To improve the situation, a clear hierarchy of leadership in construction projects is vital. Architects or planners who produce the original designs should lead their projects, while supported by contractors whose job is to build rather than to design. Alternative measures such as introducing different procurement methods may allow the local developers and contractors have a certain control over the project, while architects and designers take charge of the final design. Governmental policies may change to allow foreign design firms to franchise their practices to local companies. Hence, local designers are employed and trained by foreign expertise. This franchised practice may also joint venture with a team of local contractors. By doing so, overseas funds and loans may channel to sponsor the project. Both the architectural firm and the contracting company share the liability and the financial rewards of the project. The original scheme of the building remains controlled by the design team.

TRADITIONALISM VERSUS MODERNISM

Generally speaking, the development of modern Chinese architecture was crippled by the Cultural Revolution and then overwhelmed by the new economic reforms. On the one hand, native architects lurch toward representing the ideals of a quasi-capitalistic economy – promises of adventure, power, joy, growth and transformation. On the other hand, they grope for a sense of national identity, or a way forward that retains the Chinese heritage. According to Geertz (1973: 258), this "search for identity" is a "demand for progress" that included insight from both the past and the future. In other words, nationalism is linked with modernity, and nationalism also is inevitably linked with traditionalism. The new generation of Chinese architects often looked to the West for inspiration. Western architects such as Benjamin Woods and I. M. Pei, on the contrary, approached the subject with emphasis in what exists and is special in the country. They attempted to guide native architects to appreciate their architectural heritage from a different angle. Boston architect Benjamin Woods was widely praised for his sensitive redevelopment of a neighbourhood of traditional row houses in Shanghai. Pei, who has designed some of the most acclaimed structures in the world, from the Louvre Museum in Paris to the Rock and Roll Hall of Fame and Museum in Cleveland, created a harmony between Chinese traditions and modern structures in his famed Fragrant Hill Hotel (1982) in Beijing. The 350-room low-rise is set around gardens in Chinese courtyard style. Pei employed shrubs, screens and space to emphasis the importance of human proportion, nature and geometry, which were the key elements in traditional Chinese architecture.

Modern architecture with indigenous identity does not necessary mean revivalism or superimposing traditional accoutrements onto modern structures. A deep understanding and appreciation of the theoretical implications of architectural heritage are essential, especially in relation to society and institutional practice. In other words, authentic architecture requires a cultural leitmotif. According to Trilling (1974: 99-100), a leitmotif is a self-defining set of cultural ideals, and authenticity involves mastery or complete control – something is authentic when it manifests its self-definition.[ii] Take the Forbidden City in Beijing as an example. It has been built to serve the royalty, not the masses. The structure was all about the sequence of space, ritual and power. The progression of space from the surrounding streets to the City's main gates, courtyards, steps, platforms, then the court and palace was like a ritual. The hierarchical devices of steps and various ground levels created precinct and distinction. The ground level symbolized the secular and the lowest social hierarchy – the public; while the top level the sacred and the highest social hierarchy - the emperor. Different floor planes were, conceptually, *divided* instead of *connected* by steps. Visitors ascending from ground level to the top where the most important structures are located like a ceremony. Besides, the orientation of the Forbidden City also carried important symbolic meanings. The emperor's throne and the main palace located in the north of the City has halls, gates, dominant façade and steps looking down towards the south. During ceremonies and daily assembly, officials and noblemen entered the City's main gate from the south. They went through a massive open courtyard, which induced agoraphobia, a sense of inferior and smallness (an appropriate mental state before meeting the emperor), gates and halls looking up towards the north, then finally the royal compound. However, when the emperor performed celestial rituals such as on the day of winter solstice in the Altar of Heaven, his orientation of the worship was the opposite of that in the Forbidden City. He entered gates and approached the Altar from the south, where he performed the ceremony facing up towards the north. Along the central axis, after more gates and steps, there is a shrine that symbolized the house of Gods, located in the far north on top of platforms and facing down towards the south. According to traditional Chinese customs, when two parties meet, the superior side that was the head of a family, of a village, of an institute, of a country, of the universe sat in the north side and faced south; while the inferior side, which was the other group members sat in the south and faced north. Furthermore, walls were used historically to exclude and include people. The spaces of "inside" and "outside" are defined by extensive city walls and linked by relatively small arched portals. Traditionally, arched portals were only used in the entrances of city walls and tombs such as that of the Great Wall and Ming Tomb. There was little sense of transparency in these architectural forms because of the nature of seclusion of the feudal society. This entire ritual of experiencing spaces and other mentioned symbolic meanings are the most important content in traditional Chinese architecture, they are cultural leitmotifs.

Modern Chinese architecture as a contemporary national identity, may explore these cultural leitmotifs to establish its authenticity. Architects, for instance, may dissolve the hierarchical devices by increasing the sense of the transparency in their design schemes, and remove steps and multi-level floor planes in order to encourage public access. Alternatively, they may redefine and reinvent these hierarchical features to strengthen their meanings. The approach may be demonstrated in the Bank of China Tower (1988) in Hong Kong by Pei and the National Grand Theatre in Beijing proposed by Andreu in 2002. The Bank of China Tower was a combination of "a crystalline Euclidean vision in reflective glass and aluminum" (Rastorfer, 1985: 137) and traditional Chinese architectural features of geometrical purity, arched portal, lantern-shaped pillars and a broad promenade with triangular flanking water gardens, fish pool and stepped waterfalls. Its traditional approach but modern appearance showed an intelligent way of presenting a modern Chinese architecture. The cultural leitmotif of Andreu's project took the form of a single pavilion in the lake and bridges that provided ceremonial entry. The concept was expressed through simple spatial and figural arrangement, which invited literal understanding. Both designs were modern structures with great appreciation of the Chinese tradition. To develop a modern architectural style with national identity, Rowe and Seng (2002) suggested a pattern of imitation, selection/ rejection and incorporation. At the moment, rapid industrialization and modernization sent China into a state of frenzied construction fever. The architectural development of the country was still in a period of imitation. According to the pattern, the next stage shall be selective rejection and finally indigenization of foreign knowledge and technologies. Ideally, a broad theoretical alignment of the balance between "old" and "new", "East" and "West" may eventually be achieved. A modern architectural style that resonates with the people may finally prevail.

SHORTAGE IN LOCAL EXPERTISE

After being stifled for half a century by the massive socio-political changes, a more critically informed profession and public are needed in China. During the self-imposed isolated period from 1949 to 1977, local architects had no access to foreign publications and technologies apart from that of Russia. Architectural development was subjected to political proposition. Any architects with anti-revolutionary opinion or being considered "politically incorrect" could not have their works published and their designs approved (Dou, 1989: 68). Generally speaking, education in the period was emphasized on memorability and technical skills rather than critical studies and creativity. The situation was made worse by the political propaganda of the Cultural Revolution 1966-1976, which sent the whole country into turmoil and left many people emotionally traumatized. From cities to countryside, economic, cultural and educational activities were almost stopped for a decade. Architectural Dark Age started when architects were removed from their positions and sent to work in factories, farms and armies. No architect was professionally trained for ten years. The social turmoil of the past decades failed to provide both the quality and the quantity of expertise that are much needed by the economic growth since early 1980s. Gutheim (1981:85) urged for a restructuring in architectural education to accommodate the growth of cities and urbanization in China. Shortage of expertise in the construction field provides little time for new architects to gain enough experience before practicing independently. Sometimes architectural students are required to produce designs for real projects even before they graduate. Architects have to undertake the jobs of urban and road planners, landscape and interior designers. Although economic reforms and cultural exchanges in the last two decades exposed local architects to a massive pool of foreign references, they have little time to digest the information. Consequently, they tend to copy things without knowing how they work, because the majority has only seen the buildings in magazines. Besides, most construction works are carried out in fast, massive and cost effective manners. Most of the workers recruited to work on sites are untrained migrate farmers/ labors from other provinces. There is hardly any institute established to train building technicians and workers. Hence, the accident rate in construction sites stays high and the quality of work is difficult to control.

Rapid modernization created a gulf between the rich and the poor, between cities and countryside in China. The agricultural and rural sectors are becoming more industrialized. More farmers are replaced by machinery. Consequently, as many as 200 million workers and peasants (and their numbers are increasing) left their families and poor rural farms in search of jobs and better living standards in the booming coastal areas and major cities.

Thousands of migrate laborers gathered and stayed in front of the rail stations of every major city, waiting for jobs. They have no shelter, medical care, hardly any decent meals and dignity. Some of the labors were recruited to work in factories and construction sites. Nevertheless, gangster, prostitution, petty crime, homeless, poverty and social tension prevailed. The recent economic crisis in 1998 in the Far East only made matters worse. The drastic economic cycle overwhelmed the people with periods of negative inflation, followed by tighten credit and mass unemployment. In the construction industry, some developers went bankrupt before the project finished. The project was then either auctioned to sell to another developer, or put on halt. The recruited laborers were then discharged, sometimes unpaid. Currently, there is no regulated organization that protects the legal rights of these migrated laborers. These young healthy laborers who are ready to join the urban work force are an important resource for the country. As more international labels are setting up their production lines in China, the country is becoming the world's factory. Migrated laborers support the future growth of an industrialized China and therefore long term planning is vital to sustain their production activities.

The solution of the problem is to identify and to satisfy their immediate needs, and to supply them with the skills needed to generate income in the urban sector. Vocational training institutes may be set up for migrate labourers.[iii] They are long-term investment of the society. These institutes may be established at the fringe of major cities, where the land price is low. The institutes need sustainable cash flow to continue its mission. This possibly comes from government subsidies, funds raised from stock market, franchised or join-ventured with overseas institutes, undergoing public and commercial projects. Migrated laborers who join the institutes as apprentices may be offered a package deal – one-year training plus two-year work contract when the course finishes. Accommodation, food and medical insurance should be provided during the apprenticeship and contract period. Tuition fees for the training should be waived when the apprentice accepts the contract. The institutes could take on real construction projects to generate incomes to support the apprenticeships. Apprentices have the opportunities to participate in real projects and on-site trainings. Certificates and references are provided when the apprenticeship finishes. In a long run, the institutes bring benefits to all parties involved. The apprentices who accept the contract are guaranteed of consistent income immediately after the training. For the construction industry, fully trained skilled laborers with consistent quantity and quality are supplied. Instead of stretching the regional resources, migrated laborers provide taxable income for cities. The existing social tension between city dwellers and migrated laborers, and its associated social problems may be eased. The increase in the number of skilled laborers also provides the growing home market with sustainable work force, which may further attract foreign investment.

CONCLUSION
Despite the return of market economy, China is still very poor in many places and saddled with outmoded economic and institutional practices. The differentiation between upper and lower social strata persisted and sometimes magnified because of the sudden economic changes. Nevertheless, modernization and economic reforms encouraged multiculturalism.

In many provinces, modern cities emerge where foreign architectural accoutrements replete. These social circumstances formed the backdrop to and influenced contemporary architectural debate and production opportunities. Modern Chinese architecture is experiencing an unprecedented blooming period, which is both experimental and exhilarating. Nevertheless, rapid economic growth and immature governmental systems overwhelm the industry and create confusion. The resulted problems such as intellectual property, bureaucratic practice, the search for a national identity and the shortage in local expertise impose serious limitation to the healthy growth of the nation's economy. Long-term solutions and commitments from both the government and the construction industry are needed. Many suggestions above are far from ideal and subject to further feasibility studies. However, a thousand mile journey needs to start from the first step. It is no easy task and the problem will only multiply with time. There is no way out but to accept the challenge and put forward any possible solutions to the authorities.

NOTES

[i]Hundreds of thousands of litterateurs, professionals, scholars, industrialists, land owners and "people who entrenched" themselves in ideological and cultural positions" were denounced as "monsters and demons" by the newspaper People's Daily on the 1st of June 1966. All those ostensibly fit the description were hunted and presecuted by the Red Guards, the prosecution often included parents, relatives, frieds and even the Red Guards themselves.

[ii]See also the definition of Trilling's concept by Eduard Sekler, in Asia GSD Asian Pacific Design Conference, (March 2000).

[iii]The idea was proposed by the author to a local entrepreneur in China but was unfortunately turned down because of financial and political obstacles.

REFERENCES:

Apter, David and Tony Saich. (1994) Revolutionary Discourse in Mao's Republic. Cambridge: Harvard University Press.

Auden, Wystan Hugh. (1945) "Petition," The Collected Poetry of W. H. Auden. New York.

Chen, Bauzhen. (ed) (1992) Chinese Architecture in the Past Forty Years. Hong Kong: Euroasia.

Cong, Dachang. (1997) When Heroes Pass Away — The Invention of a Chinese Communist Pantheon. Lanham MD.: University Press of America.

Cradock, Percy. (ed) (1994) Experiences of China. London: Murray.

Dittmer, Lowell. (1974) Liu Shao-chi and the Chinese Cultural Revolution — The Politics of Mass Criticism. Berkeley: University of California Press.

Dou, Yide. (ed) (1989) An Outline of Modern Chinese Architectural History. Tianjin: Sunhua.

Esherick, Joseph W. (ed) (2000) Remaking the Chinese City: Modernity and National Identity, 1900-1950. Honolulu: University of Hawaii Press.

Geertz, Clifford. (1973) The Interpretation of Cultures. New York.

Gutheim, Frederick. (August 1981) "China Update: New Perspectives, New Directions, Whether Chinese Architecture?" Architectural Record. 81-87.

Li, Kwok-sing. (ed) (1995) A Glossary of Political Terms of the People's Republic of China. Hong Kong: The Chinese University Press.

MacFarquhar, Roderick. (1987) The Origins of the Cultural Revolution, Volume II: The Great Leap Forward, 1958-1960. Columbia University Press.

MacFarquhar, Roderick. (1999) The Origins of the Cultural Revolution, Volume III: The Coming of the Cataclysm. Columbia University Press.

Rastorfer, Darl. (September 1985), "The Logic of Eccentricity", Architectural Record. 136- 143.

Rowe, Peter G. and Seng Kuan (2002) Architectural Encounters With Essence and Form in Modern China. MIT.

Schoenhals, Michael. (ed) (1996) China's Cultural Revolution, 1966-1969 — Not A Dinner Party. Armonk NY: M.E Sharpe.

Teiwes, Frederick and Warren Sun (1998) China's Road to Disaster — Mao, Central Politicians, and Provincial Leaders in the Unfolding of the Great Leap Forward 1955-1959. Armonk: M.E. Sharpe.

Trilling, Lionel. (1974) Sincerity and Authenticity. Harcourt Brace Jovanovich.

Yan, Jiaqi and Gao Gao. (1996) Turbulent Decade — A History of the Cultural Revolution. Honolulu: University of Hawaii Press.

Zhang, Zaiyuan. (ed) (1989) Review and Prospect for China Architecture. Tianjin: Sunhua.

Notes on Contributors

Erik Bähre works at the Amsterdam institute for Metropolitan and Interntional Development Studies (AMIDSt), University of Amsterdam and is affiliated to the research school CERES. His current interest is on the effects of insurance policies on social capital and social security of the urban poor in South Africa. E-mail: e.bahre@uva.nl

Souymen Bandyopadhyay is a senior lecturer at the University of Liverpool. His research interest includes Culture, Society and Architecture, Traditional Settlement and Architecture of Oman, developed from initial field study of Bilad Manah, a central Omani settlement.E-mail: s.bandyopadhyay@liverpool.ac.uk

Michael Clark lecturers Geography and Environmental Management in the School of Natural Resources at the University of Central Lancashire. His research interests include the devolpoment of EIA, hazards and emergency planning, coastal planning and dockland redevelopment, and the relationship between urban form, regional planning and rapid changes in personal geographies and expectations. E-mail: mclark@uclan.ac.uk

Dania González Couret is a Professor and Vice Dean at Facultat de Arquitectura de La Habana, ISPJAE Cuba. She is currently a meber of the International Editorial Board for Global Built Environment Review (GBER). E-mail: dania@arquitectura.iaspjae.edu.cu

Arif Hasan, a Pakistani architect and planner, teacher, social researcher, and writer, studied architecture at the Oxford Polytechnic. He is renowned for his involvement with low-income settlement programmes, and is the architect of a large number of important residential, commercial, and educational facilities in Pakistan.
E-mail: ahasan@digicom.net.pk

Iain Jackson is researcher at School of Architecture at the University of Liverpool. His interests revolve around urbanity, the representations of space and the effects of colonialism on UK and Indian cities. He is currently researching the art and architecture of Chandigarh. E-mail: lowlife90@hotmail.com

Omar Khattab is an Associate Professor for the Architecture Department at College of Engineering and Petroleum, Kuwait University. His research interests lie in Environment and Behaviour Interface. E-mail: okhattab@kuc01.kuniv.edu.kw

Karen Leeming is a research fellow for the Centre for Local Policy Studies based at Edge Hill, she also lectures on urban policy, regeneration strategies, community inclusion/exclusion and the environment. Her current research strands are: sustainable regeneration; the sustainability of wintering wading bird flocks; knowledge transfer; and the practical application of theory utilising a local authority initiative involving young children. E-mail: leemingk@edgehill.ac.uk

Erica Liu is the award leader of BSc (Hons) Interior Design in the University of Glamorgan. Her research interest includes architecture, cities and interior design in relation to the socio-political aspects. E-mail: eliu@glam.ac.uk

Pedro Moctezuma-Barragan is a Director of the UAM Sierra Nevada Research Centre, an institution formed through University-Community partnerships in a region located under the Popocatepetl and Iztaccihuatl volcanoes in Mexico City's surroundings and is a doctoral candidate at the Department of Civic Design at The University of Liverpool. E-mail:Moctezum@liv.ac.uk

Noha Nasser is a lecturer in Architecture and Urban Design at the University of Central England in Birmingham. Her research focuses on the influence of Islam, as a culture, on the morphological change and regeneration of cities. Most recently, she has published on the changing cultural urban landscape of Britain by ethnic minorities, mainly South Asian communities. E-mail: noha.nasser@uce.ac.uk

Tasleem Shakur a one time architect/planner and a Fellow of the Royal Society of Arts (FRSA). Having taught at Oxford Brookes, University of Sheffield and SOAS (University of London) is currently the Co-ordinator/Senior Lecturer in Human Geography and Director of ICDES (International Centre for Development & Environmental Studies) at Edge Hill. He has published extensively on Development, Environment and South Asian Cultural Studies. He edits the e-journal on Architecture, Planning, Development and Environment (GBER: www.edgehill.ac.uk/gber). Recent major publications include *Picturing South Asian Culture in English: Textual and Visual Representations* edited with Karen D'Souza, published by Open House Press and *Unsustainable Environment and the Cities of the Developing world* co-authored with N. Dasgupta and D. Treloar, published simultaneously by Hegemon, City Press and Vrije Universiteit (Amsterdam). E-mail: shakurt@edgehill.ac.uk

Magda Sibley (nee Behloul) is an architect and teaches architecture at the University of Liverpool, UK. She is currently the Director of the BA Architecture course. Dr Sibley has been awarded various AHRB (Arts and Humanities Research Board- UK) grants to investigate the transformations of medieval Islamic cities with particular reference to courtyard housing and public baths. She has co-edited a book on courtyard housing: past present and future to be published by Spon Press in August 2005. E-mail: msibley@liverpool.ac.uk

Peer Smets is a research associate at ICDES and a lecturer at the department of social cultural sciences at the faculty of social studies, Vrije Universiteit, Amsterdam. His publications cover mainly financial self-help organisations, housing finance, housing, slum development, and the government bureaucracy in India. His current interest is on urban segregation, neighbourhood dynamics and the multicultural society in the western world. E-mail: pgsm.smets@fsw.vu.nl

Hülya Turgut is a Professor of Architecture at Istanbul Technical University. Her interests include Indigenous building and design traditions, Vernacular architecture, Traditional environment, Urban development, squatter settlements Architectural education and Environment Behaviour studies. Email: turguth1@itu.edu.tr

Index

Open House Press

Open House Press is a new publishing venture that has its primary remit the sharing of information on global issues by writers around the world.

Open House Press welcomes manuscripts from authors wishing to write on issues to promote and share knowledge and share knowledge and information about multicultural, social and political development in the non-western world.

Writers on post-colonial development or environment affairs are strongly encouraged to submit manuscripts for possible publication.

Open House Press is not a political publisher as such: it offers authors the opportunity to write from any contemporary or historical political perspective, as long as the views expressed do not cause offence to potential readers.

Open House Press publishes manuscripts written from strongly academic perspective by experts in their field, by people working in the third world, not necessarily first language speakers of English.

If you have a title that you would like us to consider for possible publication please contact: mail@openhousepress.co.uk

Previous and Forthcoming Publications:

Picturing South Asian Culture in English:
Textual and Visual Representations
Edited by Tasleem Shakur and Karen D'Souza (2003)

Language of Advertising in Bangladesh
A Salman Al-Azami (2006)